Debates in Monetary Macroeconomics

Steven Pressman · John Smithin
Editors

Debates in Monetary Macroeconomics

Tackling Some Unsettled Questions

palgrave
macmillan

Editors
Steven Pressman
Interlaken, NJ, USA

John Smithin
Aurora, ON, Canada

ISBN 978-3-031-11239-3 ISBN 978-3-031-11240-9 (eBook)
https://doi.org/10.1007/978-3-031-11240-9

This Palgrave Macmillan imprint is published by the registered company Springer Nature Switzerland AG
The registered company address is: Gewerbestrasse 11, 6330 Cham, Switzerland

For Ingrid Rima, who first brought us together.

Contents

Notes on Contributors

Barrows David has extensive global experience in public administration, education and training, business-government relations, and economic analysis. He was a senior executive in the government of the Province of Ontario with responsibility for industrial and trade policy. He retired as the Associate Director of the MPA program at the Schulich School of Business, York University, and is currently Capital Region Director (in Ottawa) of the Aurora Philosophy Institute (API). He has been nominated for and won numerous teaching awards. David has consulted for the Commonwealth of Nations, the OECD and the World Bank. He has taught in the UAE and Australia. He has trained senior public servants in China, Botswana, Vietnam, Thailand and Sri Lanka. David has publications and conference presentations in business, public sector administration, and economics.

Eichacker Nina is an Assistant Professor of Economics at the University of Rhode Island. She has work forthcoming in the *Journal of Economic Issues*, and has published in the *Review of Political Economy*, *Review of Keynesian Economics*, and *Challenge Magazine*. Her book *Financial Underpinnings of Europe's Financial Crisis* was published by Edward Elgar Press in 2018. Her work examines international finance, macroeconomic policy, and economic crisis through a Post-Keynesian lens.

Faudot Adrien is Assistant Professor of Economics at the University of Grenoble (France). He is a member of the CERAG (Centre d'Études et de Recherches Appliquées à la Gestion) and associate researcher of the CREG, two research laboratories based in Grenoble. His research focuses on international monetary economics, history of economic thought, and development economics.

Kam Eric is Associate Professor at Toronto Metropolitan University, an Associate of the Aurora Philosophy Institute (API), and a past Director of the Learning and Teaching Office at TMU. Dr. Kam has received many prestigious teaching awards including *Professor Who Made a Mark*, *Deans' Teaching Award* and a *President's Award for Teaching Excellence*. In addition to his teaching, Dr. Kam has published several articles in academic journals in the areas of monetary macroeconomics, the history of economic thought, and economic pedagogy.

Leclaire Joëlle is Professor of Economics and Finance at the State University of New York, Buffalo State. She also serves on the Editorial Board of the *Review of Political Economy* and on the Board of Directors of *Dollars and Sense*. Leclaire has published articles in the *Journal of Post Keynesian Economics*, the *International Journal of Political Economy*, and the *Review of Political Economy*, and several chapters to edited volumes. She authored the book *The Great Deficit Debacle (2008)* and edited *Heterodox Analysis and Financial Crisis and Reform (2011)*. She is also a contributor to local newspapers and appears frequently on local TV.

Nenovsky Nikolay is a professor at the University of Picardie, France, and associated researcher at the SU HSE and RUDN in Moscow. He has published widely in the areas of Currency Boards and Central banking, especially of post-communist countries. He has broad, practical experience as a researcher and later as a member of the Governing Council of the Bulgarian Central Bank.

Pantelopoulos George is a Ph.D. candidate at the University of Newcastle, NSW. His dissertation explores why global imbalances occur and persist within the international monetary system. George has published in a number of highly ranked journals and is currently collaborating with a senior member of the European Central Bank with a view towards publishing a book on payments and financial market infrastructures.

Pressman Steven is Emeritus Professor of Economics and Finance at Monmouth University, Part-Time Professor of Economics at the New School for Social Research, and Associate Editor of the *Review of Political Economy*. He has published nearly 200 articles in refereed journals and as book chapters, and has authored or edited 18 books, including *Understanding Piketty's Capital in the 21st Century* (Routledge, 2015), *A New Guide to Post Keynesian Economics* (Routledge, 2001), *Alternative Theories of the State* (Palgrave Macmillan, 2006), and *50 Major Economists,* 3rd edition (Routledge, 2013). He is also a frequent contributor to newspapers and popular periodicals such as *Challenge Magazine, The Washington Spectator* and *Dollars and Sense*.

Scarth William is Professor Emeritus of Economics at McMaster University. He has received both the President's Award for Excellence in Instruction and several McMaster Students Union Teaching Awards including the student union's highest honour—their Lifetime Achievement Award for Teaching. In addition to publishing many articles in academic journals (in the areas of macroeconomics, labour economics, international trade and public finance), Dr. Scarth has authored four textbooks, and he has been a Research Economist at the C.D. Howe Institute, Canada's leading non-profit policy institute, for 25 years. Some of his recent work concerns how globalization affects the ability of governments to provide support for those living on low incomes, and to deal with the tensions between young and old that have emerged with increased concern about the environment and our aging population.

Sinha Bhavya is a Ph.D. candidate in Economics at Colorado State University. She specializes in political economy and development economics. Bhavya earned her M.A. in Economics from Dr. B. R. Ambedkar University Delhi and her M.Phil. in Economics from the University of Hyderabad. Her research primarily focuses on accumulation and development in Global Production Networks and Special Economic Zones.

Small Sarah F. is an Assistant Professor in the Department of Economics at the University of Utah. Her research focuses on variety of topics in feminist economics including intra-household bargaining, entrepreneurship, the occupational crowding hypothesis, and feminist methodology. She was formerly a research fellow at Duke University's Center for the History of Political Economy and a postdoc at the Center for Women and Work at Rutgers University. Sarah holds a Ph.D. in economics from Colorado State University.

Smithin John is Executive Co-Director and a Fellow of the Aurora Philosophy Institute, and Professor Emeritus of Economics and Senior Scholar at York University, Toronto, Canada. He previously held teaching appointments at the University of Calgary and Lanchester Polytechnic at Coventry (now Coventry University), in England. In the academic year 1995–1996 he was elected Bye Fellow at Robinson College, Cambridge. He holds a Ph.D. and an M.A. from McMaster University, and a B.A. (Honours) from the City of London Polytechnic (now London Metropolitan University). His research interests are in the fields of macroeconomic policy, monetary theory, and the philosophy of money and finance. He is the author and/or editor of *Beyond Barter* (2022), *Rethinking the Theory of Money, Credit and Macroeconomics* (2018), *Essays in the Fundamental Theory of Monetary Economics and Macroeconomics* (2013), *Money, Enterprise, and Income Distribution* (2009), *Controversies in Monetary Economics* (2003, 1994), *What is Money?* (2000), *Macroeconomic Policy and the Future of Capitalism* (1996), *Macroeconomics after Thatcher and Reagan* (1990), and *Keynes and Public Policy After Fifty Years* (1988).

Watts Martin is an Emeritus Professor of Economics at the University of Newcastle, NSW, and Research Associate of the Centre of Full Employment and Equity (CofFEE). He has published over 60 peer-reviewed articles in leading international and domestic academic journals and co-authored 20 book chapters. In 2019, he co-authored a textbook entitled *Macroeconomics*. He has secured funding for Australia Research Council Discovery Projects with colleagues and also participated in an ARC Linkage grant. He holds a B.A. from Essex University, an M.A. from Manchester University and a Ph.D. from the University of British Columbia.

List of Tables

CHAPTER 1

Some Unsettled Questions in Monetary Macroeconomics

Steven Pressman and John Smithin

1 Introduction

This book attempts to stand on the shoulders of two previous notable works in economics—one by John Stuart Mill in the mid-nineteenth century and one by Robert Skidelsky in the early twenty-first century. Both works did something similar to what we are attempting to do here; that is, to address in a comprehensive way some of the key issues currently in dispute in monetary macroeconomics.

In the mid-nineteenth century, Mill (1844) published a book with the rather imposing title *Essays on Some Unsettled Questions of Political Economy.* The book was comprised of five essays on controversial topics in the field of economics, or 'political economy', as it was called then.

S. Pressman (✉)
Interlaken, NJ, USA
e-mail: pressman@monmouth.edu

J. Smithin
Aurora, ON, Canada
e-mail: jsmithin@yorku.ca

S. Pressman and J. Smithin (eds.), *Debates in Monetary Macroeconomics*,
https://doi.org/10.1007/978-3-031-11240-9_1

In order of their appearance in the book, these five controversies are (1) who gains from international trade, (2) the impact of consumption on production, (3) the difference between productive and unproductive labour, (4) the difference between interest and profits, and (5) the definition of 'political economy' and the correct method for investigating it. Mill had hoped to resolve these disputes, or at least contribute to a resolution of these 'unsettled questions', in the near future.

That did not happen, and our goal is not to critique or evaluate the answers that Mill set forth long ago. However, it is worth noting that in the 178 years since Mill's work was published, each of his five topics has experienced a rather different fate. Since the time of Keynes, 90 years after Mill, the issue of consumption and production has been resolved to a large extent. Economists today generally agree that additional consumer spending increases production, and that less consumer spending reduces production, all else being equal. Nonetheless, there are limits to what can be produced in any given year. Getting the right natural resources and parts is one good example of such a limitation. Perhaps one of the best examples of this today is a shortage of computer chips due to the small number of plants producing computer chips and the need for these chips in computers, cell phones, automobiles, and home appliances. A fire in a plant in Japan stopped production there for a while, and production is just starting to return as this book was going to print. At the same time, a drought in Taiwan limited water usage and chip manufacturing because the process requires a great deal of water. This problem still remains. As new plants cannot be built in a month or even a year, chip shortages remain. Furthermore, few firms will want to build new plants, as the problem is a temporary shortage of computer chips and not a long-term shortage that requires greater production capacity.

On the other hand, increased production does not mean that there will be increased consumption of these goods. Some of what is produced will go to profits and interest, and the wealthy individuals who receive most of this income may not spend it. Nor will savings necessarily be lent to individuals, who will then spend it, or to firms that will productively employ it. The result is overproduction or underconsumption, two sides of the same coin. As John Maynard Keynes (1936) pointed out, the consequence of this is that economies will experience bouts of high unemployment which (typically) will require some government remedy.

In contrast to the issue of consumption and production, the issue of international trade and how the supposed gains from trade are distributed between trading partners remains very much an unsettled question in economics. In fact, the question of trade, trade deficits, and their economic consequences is one of the five unsettled issues (not necessarily the same as Mill's list) covered in this volume. Chapter 8, for example, argues that nations should not seek to run trade surpluses and that when nations do seek to do this it has negative macroeconomic effects. Chapter 9, meanwhile, advances the case that some nations should seek to run trade deficits under some circumstances.

Mill's discussion of the nature of political economy, or its scientific status, and how we should study it, is something that has not been studied extensively. In the late twentieth century, there were several excellent contributions that addressed the question of the appropriate economic methodology, such as Blaug (1980), Caldwell (1982), McCloskey (1985), and Pheby (1988). However, when it comes to those who are actually doing economic analysis, this work on methodology is still generally ignored rather than turned to for insights about how to do economics better.

In his essay on the topic, Mill suggested that the science of political economy was something akin to geometry. It is a deductive science that begins with definitions of simple concepts. From these definitions, it builds theorems about relationships among the various defined terms. The theorems follow, by simple deductive logic, from the definitions of basic terms. This approach to economics is strange for two main reasons. First, Mill was that rare philosopher who has argued that mathematics is empirical in nature (Bloor, 1976). He contended that we learn things like 1 plus 2 equals 3 because of what we observe in the real world rather than a result of the logical properties of number systems, which is the standard view in the philosophy of mathematics (Barker, 1964). The approach is also strange because economists, old and new, have tended to view themselves as empirical scientists who work with data, and use that data to try to understand the world and devise policies that would let economies function better. This is true of the economic work of Adam Smith [1776] (1937), *The Wealth of Nations,* which is full of observations about how the economic world works and how people behave. And ironically it is also true of Mill's own *The Subjection of Women* (1869) which analyzed the impact of social forces on the individual and the economic consequences of this at both the microeconomic level and the macroeconomic level. It seems that economics is an empirical science. At the very least, it should be more empirical than mathematics. Mysteriously, Mill holds the opposite view.

The issue of productive and unproductive labour has a long history in economics. The Physiocrats in eighteenth-century France saw labour engaged in producing manufactured goods as unproductive, while labour employed growing food was productive. They argued for increasing the consumption, and thus the production, of agricultural goods to stimulate economic growth and development (Pressman, 1994). Adam Smith [1776] (1937) and many other economists have criticized the Physiocrats for this view, but they still tend to hold on to the Physiocratic distinction that some labour is productive and creates a surplus, while other labour is unproductive and does not. Following Smith, most classical economists held that labour engaged in manufacturing production was productive, but that labour engaged in services was unproductive, or less productive. This debate about the distinction between productive and unproductive labour, or the productiveness of labour in different economic sectors, however, disappeared with the rise of neoclassical economics. The standard view among economists was that all labour was productive and that the relative productivity of any worker could be measured by the wage received by that worker. The debate about productive and unproductive labour has thus developed into a debate about the relative productiveness of different types of labour, and whether wages (or wages plus benefits) are a good measure of how productive labour is and how productive different individuals are. More recently, Baumol et al. (2012) called attention to this fact, and argued that the limited ability to improve productivity in services is the reason that the cost of education and health care has been rising much more than the cost of manufactured goods in developed nations.

Finally, there is the question of the difference between profits and interest, which was the subject of the fourth, or penultimate, of Mill's five original essays. (The essay about methodology was the last.) The fourth essay dealt with the important issue of the ontological distinctions between interest and profit and their separate relationships to wages. Taken to its logic conclusion this would be bound to lead to some consideration of the necessarily monetary nature of interest, as opposed to the category of profit, and thereby to such questions as the old debate about the 'forced saving' effect (i.e., the effect of inflation on the rate of interest and on capital accumulation). This was, in fact, one of Mill's main concerns in 1844, but then dropped out of sight in Marxian economics and neoclassical economics, both of which had a basic two-class structure with 'labour', on the one hand, and 'capital', on the other, to explain income distribution. There was no room for Keynes's 'rentiers'. Nonetheless, this remains an important issue in macroeconomics and has been addressed in more recent times by such authors as Lavoie and Seccareccia (1988, 2016), Pasinetti (1980), and Smithin (2018).

Our other inspiration for this volume comes from the work of Lord Robert Skidelsky. In the mid-2010s Skidelsky was working on a book that he tentatively titled *Unsettled Questions in Macroeconomic Policy*. In the introduction to his *Rethinking the Theory of Money, Credit and Macroeconomics* (2018), John Smithin recounts a conversation with Professor Skidelsky at an academic conference in the mid-2010s which in many ways was ultimately the inspiration of the present volume. Skidelsky's book eventually appeared under a different title, *Money and Government* (Skidelsky, 2018), also in the year 2018. The book that was published mainly discusses the role of the government in the overall economy. As a biographer of Keynes (Skidelsky, 1983, 1992, 2000), it is not surprising that Skidelsky sought to revive the economics of Keynes. His book addresses two questions—one of which is why academic economics seemed, so dramatically, to have lost its usefulness in the late twentieth century, and how this malaise contributed to the real world 2008 economic/financial crisis and its aftermath. However, Skidelsky also takes his reader on a historical journey through past policy debates (for example, how *do* we control inflation) and returns to the philosophical question raised by Mill regarding how do we go about doing economics. For Skidelsky, many of our contemporary economic problems are the result of abandoning the master macroeconomist—Keynes—and instead adopting the questionable assumptions that individuals are always rational and that markets are always 'efficient'.

Our approach in this volume differs from those of Mill and Skidelsky in a number of ways. First, our focus is only on the unsettled questions in what we call monetary macroeconomics. There is no systematic attempt to answer some of the 'big picture' questions raised by Mill and Skidelsky, such as methodology, or how economists should go about doing economics or practicing their craft. Nor does this volume attempts to address things such as the difference between productive and unproductive labour, or more microeconomic questions such as the efficiency of markets. This is not to say that these issues do not arise from time to time in the various individual contributions. Nor does it say that these issues are not salient.

A more important way in which this volume differs from the similar works of Mill and Skidelsky is that rather than presenting just one perspective on each question, the book presents two different essays on each issue. Each essay defends a different point of view on the topic at hand. We leave it to our readers to decide the validity of the arguments and on which side the preponderance of evidence lies. This may perhaps give the volume less closure in the sense of definitively answering some important questions. But we hope that by adopting this approach we will give readers a sense of the current thinking in economics on each issue, as well as two sets of arguments for how we should resolve each unsettled question.

Third, this work focuses mainly on macroeconomic policy issues that remain a matter of some dispute among economists. We pay less attention to macroeconomic modelling *per se* or to the theoretical constructs devised by academic economists that may, or may not, have any basis in reality (things such as 'potential GDP', 'full employment', the 'NAIRU', or the 'natural rate of interest'). Furthermore, those theoretical concerns that do get debated, in the chapters that follow, all have clear policy implications. For example, when inflation rises and governments begin to think about policies to reduce the rate of price increases, should they employ tax hikes to achieve this end, or will raising taxes only throw fuel on the inflationary fires? Should monetary policy be conducted by setting strict rules that central banks must follow, or should central bankers be allowed discretion in terms of when and how much they change interest rates that are under their control?

The first four chapters in the book focus on the approach that should be taken when implementing domestic monetary policy and fiscal policy. The first two discuss whether central banks should follow strict monetary policy rules or be allowed discretion. This is followed by two papers that discuss whether governments should balance their budgets or not. The next two chapters examine the economic impact of taxes, as just discussed. This debate also has clear policy implications. If, for example, tax hikes create inflation, and were this policy then used to deal with inflation, it would worsen the problem. Finally, the last four chapters deal with two issues related to international economic relationships. One of these issues is something that Mill himself was concerned about—how the gains and losses are distributed when two nations trade with one another—and this too, has important policy implications. For example, the economic consequences of Brexit for the UK, and whether the USA is helped or hurt by trading with China and incurring a large trade deficit as a result. The other issue concerns what nations should do about managing the international value of their domestic currency. In particular, should exchange rates be fixed or should they be allowed to fluctuate? Again, the papers take different sides on each of these two policy questions.

2 What Are the Questions?

This was the title of a well-known paper published by Joan Robinson in the *Journal of Economic Literature* (Robinson, 1977), and it seems particularly apposite here. As already explained, the original premise in doing this volume was to ask, and to try to answer, what we think are the following five currently 'unsettled questions', in monetary macroeconomics. That we chose five, the same number as in Mill's book, is not entirely coincidental, but for the most part they are different questions. We list them in the order in which they now appear in the book, and also provide our own first thoughts (really our first instinctive reactions) about the correct answer to each of them.

1. *Rules versus discretion in monetary policy?*
   Pressman: DISCRETION — Smithin: RULES
2. *Should the central government always try to balance the budget?*
   Pressman: (qualified) YES — Smithin: NO
3. *Are tax increases inflationary or deflationary?*
   Pressman: DEFLATIONARY — Smithin: INFLATIONARY
4. *Should trade and financial policies always aim for a current account surplus?*
   Pressman: NO — Smithin: YES
5. *To fix or float exchange rates?*
   Pressman: FIXED (BUT 'ADJUSTABLE') — Smithin: FLOAT

Admittedly these questions were very blunt and straightforward, not leaving much room for nuance. But what surprised both of us was that in several of the cases at least our initial reactions were opposite. We thought that this was strange, because over the years (and it is getting to be very many years now since we were first introduced by our joint mentor, the late Professor Ingrid Rima), we have tended to have similar views on questions of macroeconomic theory and policy, typically of either a 'Keynesian' or 'Post Keynesian' orientation. So, here was something that certainly needed to be debated and discussed. What we eventually did, therefore, was to commission our contributors to write papers to give us their own views on these questions, for or against. As the reader can see, the contributors include several well-established scholars and Professors *Emeriti*, as well as several of the most promising younger scholars of the present generation. The results are the contributions to this volume. We hope that their collective efforts will assist readers to make up their own mind on these issues and thereby clarify their own views on public policy issues. What emerges (perhaps needless to say) from this long process of debate tends to be much more nuanced and balanced than the immediate reactions outlined above. That indeed is ultimately the purpose of the exercise. Consider, for example, the last question considered, the one about fixed *versus* floating exchange rates. As a practical matter, and on a fuller examination, the positions of Pressman and Smithin turn out to not so very different. Both authors agree that such things as a 'hard peg' for the exchange rate, metallic standards, or currency boards are undesirable. Similarly that currency unions across different political jurisdictions often do not turn out well. Pressman favours a 'fixed-but-adjustable' exchange rate similar to that advocated by Keynes at Bretton Woods, but accepts the position that a flexible exchange allows full monetary sovereignty. Smithin favours a floating exchange rate for the same reason but has also explicitly argued that a fixed-but-adjustable exchange allows for a degree of monetary sovereignty. Similarly, Smithin takes the view (which some have called 'radical Keynesian') that an increase in government spending as a percentage of GDP will always increase the economic growth rate and, in a similar manner to that of the school of modern monetary theory (MMT), to be discussed below, that taxes do not 'pay for' government spending. There is therefore no real downside to so-called deficit financing. Pressman, on the other hand, accepts the Keynesian view in a recession or downturn, but also takes the view that the budget should be balanced over the cycle for distributional reasons. Therefore, every time that one digs a little deeper into each of the original five questions, more and more areas of overlap and agreement emerge.

The next three sections of this introductory chapter provide brief summaries of the papers presented in the chapters that follow. We end with an overview of these macroeconomic policy debates, and how they may be resolved.

3 Domestic Economic Policy: Monetary Policy Rules and Budget Deficits

One important contemporary macroeconomic issue concerns whether policymakers should always follow some sort of rule, or whether they should be given discretion to make policy changes. The issue arises for both monetary and fiscal policy. For fiscal policy, as just discussed, the debate has been over whether government should be required to balance their budget. For monetary policy, the debate has been over whether there should be rules for central bankers to follow regarding either increases in the money supply or, more importantly in the current economic environment, rules regarding the setting of interest rates that the central bank controls.

In Chapter 2, Martin Watts and George Pantelopoulos argue for employing monetary policy rules, specifically an interest rate rule.

They begin by making a historical point. Since the monetarist revolution of the late 1960s, monetary policy has been the main instrument of macroeconomic policy. Fiscal policy has taken a backseat. Empirically, the macroeconomic performance of most advanced countries has been inferior during this time when compared to the several decades following World War II. For example, except for a brief period of fiscal stimulus in the USA and UK at the beginning of the global financial crisis (GFC) and 'Great Recession', these countries employed a tight fiscal policy and a loose monetary policy. Yet their economic recoveries were the weakest since the Great Depression. Moreover, interest rates remained so low in many high-income nations that there was very limited scope for monetary policy in response to the economic damage wrought by the Covid-19 pandemic, without resorting to negative interest rates. As a result, countries have resorted to significant fiscal stimulus measures, which have stronger and more predictable short-term effects.

Watts and Pantelopoulos argue that rather than allowing central bankers to change interest rates based on economic circumstances, interest rates should be subject to rules, such as the imposition of a fixed target rate, rather than remaining at the discretion of central bankers. This means that monetary policy no longer takes the lead in economic policy making. Instead, fiscal policy becomes the main policy instrument and monetary policy occupies the backseat. The authors argue that introducing a job guarantee, in conjunction with infrastructure spending, would remedy the challenges associated with attempting to maintain both full employment and price stability in the absence of discretionary monetary policy.

After a brief overview of the history of the rules *versus* discretion debate, in Chapter 3 Sarah Small and Bhavya Sinha take the opposite position and come down in favour of discretion in monetary policy. They criticize five well-known monetary policy rules—the Friedman Rule, the Taylor Rule, the Kansas City Rule, the Pasinetti Rule, and the Smithin Rule. One conclusion arising from their summary is that the position economists have taken in this debate over rules (especially the sort of rules suggested) depends on whether they place a greater value on price stability or on economic growth. Some advocates of rules (especially Friedman and Taylor) designed their rules to ensure greater price stability. Opponents of such policy rules generally argue that these rules hinder economic growth. The other three rules, at the other end of the spectrum, push for greater economic growth. In this group are more activist rules, which allow for some discretion based on economic circumstances such as recessions and depressions, and 'Park-it' rules (such as the Kansas City rule or the Smithin rule) that tie the hands of central bankers, and therefore require fiscal policy to achieve economic growth and macroeconomic stability.

Small and Sinha criticize monetary policy rules in general because policymakers cannot observe or measure output gaps or potential GDP, as required by say the Taylor rule. In addition, attempts to follow a similar rule in the 1970s led to inflation. They also note that the Friedman rule would have worked poorly during the Great Recession, when it would have required a decrease in monetary growth that would have increased interest rates and made the economic crisis even worse.

Rules also have distributional effects as is clear in the Kansas City, Pasinetti and Smithin rules. High interest rates benefit rentiers or finance but squeeze workers and firms, as well as debtors. By keeping rates low, the Kansas City, Pasinetti and Smithin rules all seek to help debtors, workers, and firms at the expense of rentiers. The latest incarnation of the Smithin rule (Smithin, 2018, 2021, 2022) makes the distributional aspect explicit. This is the 'zero *real* policy rate' (ZRPR) which argues that the real rate of return on holdings of base money should be exactly zero, neither positive nor negative, implying that the policy rate of the central bank should always be adjusted one-for-one with the inflation rate.

In any event, Small and Sinha come out *against* rules and for discretionary monetary policy. They argue that while rules can be a useful guide for central bankers and others to think about monetary policy, they don't provide 'infallible answers', as Keynes (1936, p. 297) noted. A large part of the reason for this is that macroeconomic performance is driven by expectations, uncertainty, and particular socio-economic circumstances. Central banks must pay attention to these rather than blindly following some monetary policy rule.

The economic consequences of government budget deficits have similarly been a perennial economic issue. In practice, governments often tend to resort to borrowing rather than taxation to support needed or desired spending. In theory, however, many economists worry about the economic consequences of large government deficits and think that budget deficits matter a great deal.

Chapter 4, by Steven Pressman, begins by presenting several differing views regarding government debt. It then makes a case for running balanced government budgets most of the time—in large part because of the potential impact of government debt on wealth and income inequality. This case rests on the work of Keynes and Thomas Piketty.

The debate about budget deficits was first given prominence long ago by the work of David Ricardo. Ricardo opposed deficit financing, believing that it would crowd out other types of spending, mainly the investment spending that was necessary to put off the day of reckoning when economies would reach a stationary state. More recently, Robert Barro (1979) has updated Ricardo. He argues that government deficits have no impact on economic growth because they crowd out other categories of expenditure. Like Ricardo, Barro believes that governments should always balance their budgets. On the other hand, Abba Lerner developed the doctrine of functional finance (FF) to get around the 'crowding out' argument. Lerner contended that as long as people are willing to lend money to the government there should be no crowding out. This opens the door for expansionary fiscal policy to improve economic outcomes and generate economic growth. The work of Lerner inspired modern monetary theory (MMT) which takes Lerner one step further and contends that the central government of an economy with its own sovereign currency, and either a floating exchange rate or a fixed-but-adjustable exchange rate, faces no binding financial constraint.

One middle position comes from Keynes. While he is generally thought to have favoured government deficits, and argued that theoretical case in the *General Theory*, in later policy work Keynes actually held that governments should balance their budget over the business cycle—running surpluses in good economic times and deficits to stimulate the economy during recessions and depressions. *Capital in the 21st Century* presents yet another perspective on government deficits and national debt. In this book, Piketty (2014, Ch. 16) opposes government budget deficits because of their distributional consequences. Going even further, Piketty (2014, p. 567) contends that existing government debt should be reduced as quickly as possible. His argument is that bond financing of government spending gives the wealthy an asset that earns them interest. This maintains the rate of return on wealth and contributes to rising income and wealth inequality (due to the rate of return on wealth being greater than the economic growth rate, $r > g$). Rather than borrowing to finance spending, Piketty prefers taxing the rich. Piketty does allow for a Keynesian exception, however, when economies are in recession and need some economic stimulus. Pressman argues that countries should maintain a balanced budget over the business cycle, running surpluses during good economic times and deficits during recessionary times. This is needed both to mitigate income inequality and also to ensure the full employment of labour.

In Chapter 5, David Barrows argues that the debate about public debt has two sides. One is scientific, the other is emotional. The emotional component is based upon perceptions with respect to the role of the state. On the one hand, the state is seen as similar to the family or community. It is regarded as friendly and helpful. The alternative viewpoint portrays the state as distant and as having dominating and dictatorial tendencies. The ancient condemnation of usury, from the criticisms of Aristotle to the censures of medieval church councils, Judaism, and Islam arose from exploitation of the poor—forcing them to borrow to survive a crisis beyond their control. Aquinas provided a qualified defence of lending, which coincided with the origin and growth of modern private banking and lending. With the Protestant reformation came a defence of usury by Martin Luther. The industrial revolution led to further defences of usury by Bentham, Smith, Ricardo, Say, and (once again) Mill.

MMT argues that a county's currency is a public monopoly and can be viewed as a version of Lerner's functional finance. FF is based on the principle of effective demand. Government can finance itself to meet explicit goals such as achieving full employment, ensuring growth, and low inflation. Balancing tax revenue and government spending is of secondary importance. Prosperity is the primary goal. In this view, taxation should be used to impact the economy, in particular, to reduce inflation, rather than to raise revenue and finance spending. Growth and development are unequal among countries. The paper classifies countries as (1) high-income, with robust institutions and dominant currency, (2) high-income, with efficient government, (3) middle-income, (4) weak-state trap countries, and (5) transition/failed states. The amounts and composition of national debt are contingent upon the competitiveness of the nation. China, the European Union (as a whole), and the USA are best equipped to practice FF and MMT. For these entities national debt is irrelevant. Other developed countries can practice some form of FF and MMT but must deal with a number of constraints, such as externally held debt, supply limitations, and asset-price inflation. Middle-income, weak and failed states are incapable of utilizing FF and MMT. They must treat national debt as an important public policy variable. Overall, FF and MMT provide an important framework for the analysis of national debt. Whether or not FF and MMT can be used effectively depends upon the competitive structure of the economy.

4 Do Higher Taxes Cause Inflation?

No one likes having to pay taxes. But as former US Supreme Court Justice Oliver Wendell Holmes famously said: 'taxes are what we pay for a civilized society'.[1] While this may provide a nice general principle regarding taxation, it doesn't tell us anything about what to tax, how to tax it, or how large a tax should be imposed. It also doesn't tell us anything about the economic consequences of taxation on individual behaviour or firm behaviour, something much discussed and debated by economists over the past century (see Zorn & Pressman, 2020). Taxes also have macroeconomic consequences.

Just as no one likes paying taxes, no one likes high inflation. Weimar Germany, where people loaded wheelbarrows with cash to purchase a loaf of bread, and Zimbabwe, which printed up currency notes worth $1 trillion, are the two examples always wheeled out whenever inflation starts to rise. A little inflation, it is thought, can easily balloon into hyperinflation, and so we must be vigilant against inflation. To be sure, there are many losers as a result of inflation. Lenders, such as banks, get repaid with dollars that are worth less than the value of the dollars that they lent out. This runs the risk of bank failures, and more serious economic consequences, such as another Great Recession or Great Depression. Workers also lose, as their hard-earned and deserved pay increases get taken away from them because prices have gone up. A feeling that this is unfair may lead workers to work less hard. The main gainers from inflation are people in debt, who repay their loans with money that has fallen in value. But, as surveys have shown, even people in debt, who stand to gain from inflation, do not like inflation.

Two chapters in the book address the question of whether tax increases can be used as a means of reducing inflation or, instead, if tax hikes actually contribute to inflationary pressures.

In Chapter 6, John Smithin makes the case that taxes are inflationary, specifically that an increase in the average tax rate (the ratio of total collections to GDP) will lead to inflation. As an increase in the average tax rate will also reduce the rate of economic growth, the end result is 'stagflation', an increase in both the inflation rate and unemployment. Furthermore, a 'balanced budget' increase in government spending as percentage of GDP (that is, an increase in spending financed by an equal increase in taxes) will have the same effect. This cuts across the conventional wisdom according to Paul Samuelson (1964) who, in an early edition of his influential textbook, argued that the balanced-budget multiplier is positive. An important implication is that so-called 'tax and spend' policies, as opposed to Keynes's original recommendation of 'loan expenditure' (borrowing), are unlikely to have positive effects. In fact, they will cause stagflation.

In Chapter 7, Joëlle Leclaire makes the opposite case—that tax hikes can help rid the economy of inflationary forces. During the 1970s, in the aftermath of the oil price shocks in the USA, inflation fighting took the form of increases in interest rates. Using interest rates to control inflation can work, but interest rates were increased by so much that firms were unable to handle the higher rates and many went bankrupt. This brought about a recession, which meant less production, fewer jobs, as well as the desired outcome, which was lower levels of inflation. But it was not necessary to reduce production, and hence jobs, in order to achieve the lower inflation target. This, she argues, could have been done by raising taxes instead of interest rates. Leclaire identifies the three types of inflation (asset-price inflation, consumer-price inflation, and true inflation) and discusses the best ways to handle each type of inflation when it occurs. Her paper contends that the best way to handle inflation is by increasing taxes.

Her paper identifies the many different sorts of taxes imposed by governments, and their impact on both spending and prices. Corporate income taxes, individual income taxes, and social insurance taxes decrease disposable income and reduce spending. Since they do not increase the costs of production, they should not increase prices. Leclaire contends that excise taxes, and sales or value-added taxes, exert both deflationary and inflationary forces on the economy. However, she notes that most Federal taxes in the USA are of the former variety; they fall on incomes rather than sales. In the US, corporate income, individual income, and social insurance taxes combined are 30 times greater than all other sources of Federal government revenue. As a result, tax hikes that (usually) involve raising corporate and individual income taxes, reduce spending and demand, and put downward pressure on prices.

5 International Issues: Trade Balances and Exchange Rates

Whether nations should seek to run current account surpluses, or export more than they import, has a long history in economics. The mercantilists argued that nations should pursue trade surpluses as a means to spur economic growth and development. Since international trade was carried out primarily using gold, the mercantilists argued that a trade surplus would increase the national stock of gold. Since the mercantilists believed that gold was wealth, trade surpluses would increase the wealth of nations. Adam Smith and David Ricardo both criticized mercantilism. Instead, these economists supported free international trade in order to increase global efficiency and output. This view has become the dominant view in economics. However, there are still sceptics and doubters. In particular, many Keynesian and Post-Keynesian economists stress the importance of effective demand in generating economic growth. As such, a trade surplus would promote growth in each nation. One way to achieve this end is to push for economies to promote their exports, seeking to develop trade surpluses through a policy of export-led growth. Another avenue toward this end is to limit imports through quotas, tariffs, and other trade restrictions.

In Chapter 8, Nina Eichacker argues that while trade surpluses should have positive implications for GDP (all else being equal), the practice of governments prioritizing trade surpluses as a policy tool and the economic consequences of seeking to maintain a trade surplus are likely to have negative costs for an economy as a whole. Building on the work of John Maynard Keynes and Joan Robinson (1977), who both worried about 'beggar-thy-neighbour' trade policy, Eichacker explains how competition among trading partners to run a trade surplus may generate a sort of paradox of thrift, with nations seeking to reduce their spending of foreign-made goods in order to achieve their end of a trade surplus. This lack of spending will depress growth in both nations. When such neo-mercantilist policies are adopted in many nations, the result will be slow economic growth throughout the world, or even worse negative growth rates. As such, the costs of attempting to prevent trade deficits and run trade surpluses may be greater than the benefits of the strategy of nations seeking to run trade surpluses.

Building upon the work of Tony Thirlwall (1980) and his notion of balance-of-payments constrained growth, this chapter contends that it may be rational for developing economies to target trade surpluses, if their access to foreign exchange reserves constrains domestic production. However, Eichacker notes that this is not the case for large economies that are not vulnerable to balance-of-payment constraints. There is no advantage for these countries to target a trade surplus over domestic demand. However, when large economies pursue trade surpluses this can negatively affect the economic prospects of smaller economies that are vulnerable to balance-of-payment constraints. Building on the work of Robert Blecker (2016), she argues that to compete with lower-priced goods coming from countries seeking to run a trade surplus, domestic firms are likely to reduce their markup and prices, which will lower profits, lower wages, or both. This, in turn, will reduce demand.

In addition, there is no escape from the simple math of trade balances—one nation's trade surplus must be another nation's trade deficit. So, at the international level, policies of export-led growth cannot increase demand. But if countries that run trade deficits seek to employ policies that create trade surpluses, and countries whose trade surpluses have been turned into trade deficits engage in policies seeking to return to their previous position of a trade surplus, the result may economic volatility, which can reduce spending, especially investment spending, and slow global economic growth.

Finally, in the present era which is very much concerned with the problem of climate change, Eichacker notes that targeting trade surpluses might generate negative externalities that have both domestic and global implications. She argues that domestic policies that reduce incentives for transiting away from fossil fuels to mitigate environmental damage are shortsighted, for both large and small economies. If mitigating environmental degradation raises trade deficits, those priorities should prevail over any desire for surpluses.

In Chapter 9, William Scarth begins by noting that many people are opposed to trade deficits. They focus on the short-run performance of the economy, particularly the level of employment and the unemployment rate. Since exports create domestic jobs, while imports create foreign jobs, exports are regarded as 'good' while imports are taken to be 'bad'. This short-run focus leads to the verdict that a current account deficit is 'bad'. But this does not mean that policymakers should always aim for a current account surplus. There are several different policy objectives, and the desirability of a surplus depends on which of these objectives is deemed the most important. If monetary and fiscal policy can maintain reasonably full employment, then we can focus on long-run issues, and use variations in the current account to smooth domestic material living standards over time.

Economists also look at trade deficits and current account deficits themselves from a long-run perspective. When imports exceed exports in one country, economists hold that people are 'living beyond their means', i.e., the nation is financing its current overspending by increasing its indebtedness to the rest of the world. If this debt becomes large relative to GDP, or the inability to repay that debt becomes too great, future generations (who must pay the interest on that debt) will need to transfer a significant fraction of each year's output to foreigners. As such, trade deficits and current account deficits involve a transfer in material welfare from future generations to current generations.

According to Scarth, whether a surplus or deficit is appropriate depends on which individuals we think are more deserving. The more we value future generations compared to those living now, and the less we care about income inequality within each generation, the more likely it is that standard economic analysis will support a current account surplus. But it is not up to economic analysts to decide which groups within society should be valued more than others. Further, we cannot always focus on the long run, since full employment is not always easily achieved. As a result, some countries—especially developing ones—can benefit from having a contingency fund of foreign exchange reserves to help the economy cope with short-run instabilities. Current account surpluses contribute to building up such a fund.

Scarth argues that economists should not decree, or determine, whether a transfer across generations is desirable or not. And he argues that such an inter-generational transfer could be defended. For example, if the current generation is fighting a pandemic, and it is thought to be 'fair' to transfer some of that burden to future generations who are not expected to face such hardship, then there is nothing wrong with a nation seeking a trade or current account deficit to aid the current generation. A current account or trade deficit could also be defended if current overspending involves investing in infrastructure that will benefit future generations by more than the lost interest-payment obligations. Scarth admits that foreigners will be less willing to lend to a country that is highly indebted, but contends that avoiding this possible problem by *always* pursuing a current account surplus represents an inordinate pursuit of prudence.

A second international economic issue concerns whether economies should adopt fixed exchange rates with their trading partners or whether they should allow the exchange rate to fluctuate based on the supply of, and demand for, the two currencies. Each policy has advantages and disadvantages. In fact, the advantages of each policy are the disadvantages of the alternative policy. Fixed exchange rates enable firms to plan production better, as they can be more certain of foreign demand if the price faced by foreign buyers does not change much due to changes in exchange rates. This can even spur additional domestic investment. On the other hand, there is a downside to fixed exchange rates. To maintain a fixed exchange rate, monetary policy needs to be used to keep the rate fixed. Domestic interest rates must be raised when the domestic currency needs to be supported and cut when the value of the domestic currency needs to drop. The advantages and disadvantages of flexible exchange rates are just the reverse of these. On the plus side, flexible exchange rates free up monetary policy to have an impact on employment and the growth rate of the domestic economy. On the downside, flexible rates can be volatile, which reduce investment and economic growth.

In Chapter 10, Adrien Faudot and Nikolay Nenovsky make the case for fixed exchange rate regimes. They provide several arguments in favour of fixed exchange rates. First, they argue that any firm doing business abroad needs a stable and orderly exchange rate system, which is supported by the fact that most internationalized corporations have chosen the US dollar as a functional currency out of necessity, including countries whose local currency floats vis-à-vis the US dollar. Second, although fixed regimes have been accused of hindering domestic currency sovereignty through monetary policy alienation, the paper argues that floating regimes do not guarantee currency sovereignty. Whether floating or fixed, the balance-of-payments constraint continues to apply to economic policies. Third, an exchange rate peg is a commitment to maintaining a stable relationship with the trade partner. Although history is replete with examples of 'bad' exchange rate fixing, fostering disequilibria and crises, fixed rates can pave the way for greater international monetary coordination, which is impossible if so-called independent monetary policies lead to currency devaluations and beggar-thy-neighbour measures. However, fixed exchange rates are hardly sustainable without the implementation of an appropriate policy framework.

The paper considers two different proposals, a hard peg (currency boards and dollarization) and short-term capital controls. Ultimately, the paper outlines the principles of a more ambitious, albeit necessary, reform of the international payments system in the spirit of Keynes's international clearing union (ICU).

In Chapter 11, Eric Kam presents a contrary argument for flexible exchange rates. He supports flexible exchange rates for small open economies. His paper notes that it is important to distinguish between nominal and real exchange rates. Following Smithin (2018), he notes that various hard pegs for a nation's exchange rate (such as the gold standard and irrevocably fixed exchange rates) have failed. The result has been macroeconomic instability.

Kam's argument is that for a capitalist economy operating in the real world of financial and monetary markets, the only stable and viable exchange rate regimes are either ones with floating exchange rates or, at a minimum, fixed-but-adjustable exchange rates. Kam also asks the leading question, 'why then are so many theorists in favour of such things as hard pegs or currency unions'? The answer is that each of these systems only performs well in abstract theoretical terms, which fail to translate into the real world. In reality, such systems are fundamentally unstable.

The crux of the argument lies in the failure of many neoclassical theorists to properly model the macroeconomy. Contrary to neoclassical theories of the open economy, there has never been any such thing as an exogenously fixed 'natural rate' of interest, still less a 'world' interest rate, in real capitalist economies. These concepts are relevant only to a hypothetical barter or 'real exchange' economy. These are popular in the literature only because they are convenient mathematical simplifications to create closed-form solutions. But at the same time they induce a bias in favour of fixed exchange rates—in defiance of many of the realities on the ground.

6 Conclusion

While we make no pretense that the essays that follow in this volume will solve any contemporary macroeconomic problems, we do hope that they will lead to a dialogue concerning these important issues.

In trying to answer the original questions (which were very starkly posed) there has certainly been some progress toward the middle on several of the policy questions and, at the very least, a better understanding of the different points of view and the reasoning behind them. We have given several examples in the discussion above. But, equally, a number of differences remain. Resolving the remaining disputes will involve careful analysis, both at the theoretical and empirical levels. This is the way forward in monetary macroeconomics, and indeed the way forward for any discipline seeking to understand how the world works in an attempt to improve economic performance and people's lives.

Note

1. Even the MMT group would likely agree with this general statement. They do not believe that taxes 'pay for' government expenditure but they do believe that 'taxes drive money'. That is, some form of taxation is a prerequisite for the development of money and banking and hence for the commercial society itself to come into being.

References

Barker, S. (1964). *Philosophy of mathematics*. Prentice-Hall.

Barro, R. (1979). On the determinants of the public debt. *Journal of Political Economy, 87*, 940–971.

Baumol, W., et al. (2012). *The cost disease: Why computers get cheaper and health care doesn't*. Yale University Press.

Blaug, M. (1980). *The methodology of economics*. Cambridge University Press.

Blecker, R. (2016). The debate over 'Thirlwall's Law': Balance-of-payments constrained growth reconsidered. *European Journal of Economics and Economic Policies: Intervention, 13*(3), 275–290.

Bloor, D. (1976). *Knowledge and social imagery*. Routledge and Kegan Paul.

Caldwell, B. (1982). *Beyond positivism: Economic methodology in the twentieth century*. George Allen & Unwin.
Keynes, J. M. (1936). *The general theory of employment interest and money*. Macmillan.
Lavoie, M., & Seccareccia, M. (1988). Money, interest and rentiers: The twilight of rentier capitalism in Keynes's *general theory*. In O. F. Hamouda, & J. Smithin (Eds.), *Keynes and public policy after fifty years, vol. II: Theories and method* (pp. 145–158). Edward Elgar.
Lavoie, M., & Seccareccia, M. (2016). Income distribution, rentiers, and their role in a capitalist economy. *International Journal of Political Economy, 45*, 200–223.
McCloskey, D. (1985). *The rhetoric of economics*. University of Wisconsin Press.
Mill, J. S. (1844). *Essays on some unsettled questions of political economy*. John W. Parker.
Mill, J. S. (1869). *The subjection of women*. Longmans, Green, Reader & Dyer.
Pasinetti, L. (1980/81). The rate of interest and the distribution of income in a pure labor economy. *Journal of Post Keynesian Economics, 3*, 170–182.
Pheby, J. (1988). *Methodology and economics: A critical introduction*. M.E. Sharpe.
Piketty, T. (2014). *Capital in the twenty-first century*. Harvard University Press.
Pressman, S. (1994). *Quesnay's Tableau Économique: A critique and reconstruction*. Augustus Kelley.
Pressman, S. (2016). *Understanding Piketty's capital in the twenty-first century*. Routledge.
Robinson, J. (1977). What are the questions? *Journal of Economic Literature, 15*, 1318–1339.
Samuelson, P. (1964). *Economics: An introductory analysis* (6th ed.). McGraw-Hill.
Skidelsky, R. (1983). *John Maynard Keynes: Hopes betrayed, 1883–1920*. Viking.
Skidelsky, R. (1992). *John Maynard Keynes: The economist as saviour, 1920–1937*. Viking.
Skidelsky, R. (2000). *John Maynard Keynes: Fighting for freedom, 1937–1946*. Viking.
Skidelsky, R. (2018). *Money and government: The past and future of economics*. Yale University Press.
Smith, A. [1776] (1937). *The wealth of nations*. Modern Library.
Smithin, J. (2018). *Rethinking the theory of money, credit and macroeconomics: A new statement for the twenty-first century*. Lexington Books.
Smithin, J. (2021). The methodology for assessing interest rate rules: A reply. *European Journal of Economics and Economic Policies: Intervention, 18*(3), 286–292.

Smithin, J. (2022). *Beyond barter: Lectures in monetary macroeconomics after 'rethinking.'* World Scientific Publishing.

Thirlwall, A. P. (1980). Regional problems are 'balance-of-payments' problems. *Regional Studies, 14*, 419–425.

Zorn, N., & Pressman, S. (2020). A consensus on taxing the rich? Comparing mainstream economics, Piketty, and Post-Keynesian economics. *International Review of Political Economy, 49*, 43–61.

CHAPTER 2

Should the Implementation of Monetary Policy Be Subject to Rules?

Martin Watts and George Pantelopoulos

1 Introduction

Since the monetarist revolution of the late 1960s, monetary policy has been the main instrument of macroeconomic policy in developed economies. This is despite their economic performance being inferior in subsequent years, as compared to the post-war period. The subordination of fiscal policy persisted in the aftermath of the 'Global Financial Crisis' (GFC), despite a short period of effective fiscal stimulus measures in countries including the UK, the USA and Australia in the years 2009–2011. The IMF and the OECD then reaffirmed the principles of fiscal consolidation in view of the higher debt-to-GDP ratios, which led to the cessation of these measures (Sharpe & Watts, 2012). However, among others, the

M. Watts (✉) · G. Pantelopoulos
Newcastle Business School, The University of Newcastle, Newcastle, NSW, Australia
e-mail: martin.watts@newcastle.edu.au

G. Pantelopoulos
e-mail: George.Pantelopoulos@newcastle.edu.au

S. Pressman and J. Smithin (eds.), *Debates in Monetary Macroeconomics*,
https://doi.org/10.1007/978-3-031-11240-9_2

USA and the UK had the slowest economic recoveries following the GFC since the 'Great Depression' of the 1930s.

Confronted by the constraint on active monetary policy imposed by the zero-lower band (ZLB) on the policy rate, unconventional monetary policy in the form of quantitative easing (QE) was adopted in Japan, the USA, the UK and the Eurozone. Later countries including Sweden, Denmark, Japan and the Eurozone, adopted modest negative policy rates which have had limited economic impact (IMF, 2021a; Pressman, 2019). Arguments about the efficacy of monetary policy were buttressed by the claim that central banks, which are typically construed as politically independent, would implement superior policies. However, many developed economies are mired in low growth, stagnant wages, rising inequality but rising inflation, in part due to disruptions to supply chains.

Notwithstanding this evidence, Assenmacher and Krogstrup (2018), Agarwal and Kimball (2019) and Lilley and Rogoff (2019) investigated the implementation of deep negative interest rates. At the other end of the policy spectrum, monetary management could assume a more passive role by adopting a zero nominal interest rate policy (ZIRP), or target a real policy rate, or market rate, of interest with fiscal policy playing a more proactive role (Asensio & Hayes, 2009; Aspromourgos, 2011; Forstater & Mosler, 2005; Lavoie & Seccareccia, 2019; Mitchell, 2009a, 2009b; Pasinetti, 1981; Rochon & Setterfield, 2007, 2012; Smithin, 2007, 2016a, 2016b, 2018, 2020; Wray, 2007).

The objective of this chapter is to use the lens of 'modern monetary theory' (MMT)[1] to ask the question as to whether monetary policy should be subject to rules, rather than the current use of discretion in most developed economies. We argue that the current macroeconomic policy malaise should be addressed by the imposition of an interest rate rule which would provide a more certain interest rate environment within which the private sector could function. The distributional implications of the different rules in the context of the prevailing transfer system (in particular, the pension system) should be a major consideration in the choice of rule. However, it is imperative that a counter-inflation mechanism is embedded in the conduct of fiscal policy. Towards this end, the chapter outlines the merits of a 'job guarantee' (JG) as a means to achieve both full employment and price stability.

In Sect. 2, we assess the competing arguments for the continued adherence to the primacy of monetary policy through the discretionary setting of interest rates. Different forms of fixed interest rate policy which have been developed by some of the aforementioned authors are then evaluated (in Sect. 3). In Sect. 4, we conclude that the adoption of an interest rate rule is a superior option but argue that the conduct of fiscal policy must fundamentally change under a passive monetary policy to achieve sustained high levels of economic activity. Concluding comments complete the paper, with some words of caution about using incomplete models to contrast the macroeconomic outcomes from different policy options.

2 Monetary Policy Dominance

In this section, we first examine the arguments for and against discretionary interest rate setting including the adoption of deep negative policy rates. We then outline and assess some different fixed interest rate policies in Sect. 3.

Conventional Monetary Policy

The reliance on discretionary monetary policy as the main macroeconomic policy tool is undesirable for the following reasons.

First, Mosler and Armstrong (2019, 16) argue that central bankers believe higher rates of interest reduce aggregate demand and hence inflationary pressures because income is shifted from private sector borrowers with a high spending propensity to lenders with a lower propensity to spend. Even if this claim is correct, the state is a net payer of interest, so that higher rates increase interest income for bondholders. With debt to GDP ratios of about 100 per cent in some countries, the rise in spending out of interest income is likely to dwarf the effect of the differing consumption propensities (Wray, 2007), but will only occur following the purchase of bonds.[2] On the other hand, current bondholders suffer paper capital losses from higher rates, but wealth effects are only generated by selling these bonds (Palley, 2016, 11).

Second, Keynes argued that expected returns, reflecting 'animal spirits', were more important than interest rates in terms of investment decisions. Third, the presence of excess capacity would inhibit new investment, irrespective of the level of interest rates. Fourth, discretionary monetary policy which is designed to reduce inflation arbitrarily imposes the burden of adjustment on those with a net debt position (Aspromourgos, 2011, 639). According to the Bank of England (1999) and Batini and Nelson (2002), a systematic relationship between interest rates and economic activity is questionable because the relationship tends to be long, variable, and uncertain. Fifth, before the introduction of forward guidance in some countries including the USA,[3] a change in the policy rate could lead to immediate and disruptive effects on asset prices and promote financial innovations that increase fragility, because of the disincentive to hold asset positions that are interest-sensitive (Tymoigne, 2009) or promote the use of derivatives to hedge risks or gamble on the future path of the federal funds rate (Dantas, 2016, 32–33; Wray, 2007). Thus, there is a trade-off between efficacy and transparency. However, via forward guidance, a central bank can commit to raise rates only when particular economic conditions were satisfied, but is then committed to follow its 'rule', even when other macroeconomic changes have occurred which may undermine its rule.

The post-GFC economic recovery was initially weak and inflation rates were low across both sovereign economies, such as the UK and the USA, and non-sovereign economies, including many Eurozone nations (*e.g.* Greece and Spain), despite their respective policy rates falling to their lowest levels ever. Given the apparent constraint on the policy rate imposed by the zero-lower-bound (ZLB), there was subsequent reliance on unconventional monetary policy, specifically QE in some sovereign economies and latterly in the Eurozone. These outcomes attest to the inability of monetary policy, in general, to affect real macroeconomic variables in a timely manner, particularly after a major negative demand shock (Borio & Hofmann, 2017; Mosler & Armstrong, 2019, 16).[4,5]

(Deep) Negative Interest Rates

Negative interest rate policy (NIRP) is alleged to allow policymakers to sidestep the constraints imposed by the ZLB, thereby reducing the need for complementary fiscal policy. In 2012 Denmark (2012) introduced a NIRP to stimulate its economy and achieve its inflation rate target and its exchange rate target with the euro. Given the interdependence of their respective economies, Switzerland and Sweden followed suit in 2015 after the European Central Bank (ECB) had imposed negative rates in 2014 (Graham, 2019). Negative rates were also adopted in Japan in 2016 which were expected to lower 'interest rates across the entire yield curve' and to promptly 'achieve the price stability target of 2 per cent' but this policy had limited success (Kuroda, 2016, 7).

The usual means for implementing a negative policy rate is for the central bank to charge a nominal interest rate on commercial bank deposits, which may be passed on to their depositors via lower rates (Palley, 2016, 10). Yet banks may choose to (i) absorb these charges but reduce more risky lending, (ii) impose fees and charges on depositors which are less easy to compare across banks, or (iii) pass the central bank's charges on to borrowers via higher loan rates, which would negate the intent of NIRP.

The impact of lower deposit rates on saving is uncertain, but is likely to be small, since saving is treated as a residual (Keynes, 1936, 166). Lower deposit rates lower the interest income of depositors, which may decrease their consumption spending. Households have an incentive to economize on holdings of deposits and bonds and increase holdings of risky assets. This disintermediation of banks will reduce their funding.

Rather than investing in negative return projects (which could still earn a positive return over the borrowing costs) firms would choose to acquire non-produced assets 'such as land, commodities like gold, patents and copyrights, and technical know-how and organizational capital embodied in existing firms acquired through mergers' which have a positive return (Palley, 2016, 11). In addition, firms would tend to switch from equity finance to loan finance, via debt-financed share buybacks, due to the lower cost of loan finance. This has occurred since the 2008 recession and has led to higher corporate indebtedness. The resulting inflation of asset prices, which may promote higher consumption via wealth effects, is then reversed when interest rates are later raised. This further highlights the ambiguous role of discretionary monetary policy in targeting inflation.

Moreover, Palley points to undesirable 'beggar-thy–neighbour' currency wars that can arise when a country lowers its interest rates, which occurred among European countries as, mentioned above. Also, agents could borrow at a negative interest rate, then enter the FX market to convert their currency into (say) $US, which would lead to a depreciation of their currency. They would then purchase higher yielding $US denominated financial assets.

These competitive devaluations are unlikely to represent a zero-sum game in terms of net exports, due to volatile exchange rates. Also, a commitment to low or negative interest rates for a long time reinforces trends in income and wealth inequality with holders of risky assets enjoying capital gains.

Aspromourgos (2011, 649–650) rejects the claim that a zero riskless component of the interest rate under ZIRP leads to more risk-taking behaviour.[6] However, both insurance companies and pension funds are vulnerable to low (and negative) interest rates because they rely on investment income to meet long-standing financial obligations. This can cause financial disruption by undermining their business models. Insurance companies could raise premiums, which may reduce aggregate demand. These organizations can also shift the composition of their portfolios towards riskier assets (Palley, 2016, 11–12).

Generally, banks have been reluctant to impose negative interest rates on customers,[7] although there are quite significant transaction costs of holding cash, should customers close deposit accounts to avoid being subject to negative returns. Pressman (2019, 145) concludes that negative rates had a small effect on spending and economic growth and bank profitability was little affected (see also, IMF, 2021a, 2021b).

Pressman (2019) argues that there is an effective interest rate lower bound of about minus 0.7 per cent on deposits, so the expectation of ongoing (deep) negative rates, would lead customers to increase their use of cash and credit cards and seek other stores of value and means of exchange, and even close bank accounts.[8,9] They would also make long-term arrangements for the security of their cash. Increased tax evasion and a larger underground economy are likely. Advocates of deep negative interest rates would like a transition to a cashless economy (see Rogoff, 2017), but they recognize that this is currently infeasible.

Assenmacher and Krogstrup (2018) and Agarwal and Kimball (2019) consider the logistical challenges to central banks of imposing a negative interest rate on cash to deter the increased holding of cash, which would then enable the imposition of 'deep negative interest rates to fight recessions'. Lilley and Rogoff (2019, 24) were also enthusiastic '[A]n elegant and effective tool to restore MP effectiveness at the zero bound'. This is a typical orthodox response to a failed policy. Evidently, the interest rate on cash would have to be linked to the prevailing negative interest rate on deposits, which would create considerable logistical complexity and in turn uncertainty within the financial sector. The impact of this policy on the real market interest rate, of course, would depend on the 'pass-through' from the policy rate to the market rate and the prevailing rate of price inflation.

3 Fixed Interest Rates

A fixed interest rate policy is referred to euphemistically as 'parking it' and represents a departure from the use of discretion. Rochon and Setterfield (2007, 23) note the emerging Post-Keynesian consensus that the interest rate affects the distribution of income (Lavoie, 2014; Rogers, 1989) rather than being an appropriate policy tool for fine-tuning the macroeconomy (Davidson, 2006; Wray, 2007).

On one hand, MMT advocates, including Forstater and Mosler (2005), Mitchell (2009a), and Wray (2007) have argued for the adoption of a ZIRP, which may lead to a negative real policy rate. In the past, Smithin (2007, 2013) has supported a constant, near zero, real market rate of interest, but now advocates a zero real policy rate of interest (Smithin, 2020, 2021). Finally, among others, Lavoie and Seccareccia (2019) support the introduction of a 'fair' interest rate which was first devised by Pasinetti (1981). On this topic, see also Gnos and Rochon (2007).

Rochon and Setterfield (2007, 2012) explore the impact of different interest rate rules by analysing an inflation model based on a conflict over income shares, complemented by a neo-Kaleckian model of the real economy. Smithin (2020, 382) outlines a difference equation model in which price inflation is a negative function of the change in the real interest rate which he uses to assess different interest rate rules. He assumes a symmetric 'pass-through' relationship between the nominal policy rate and a nominal market interest rate.

Below, we review the arguments for these different fixed rate policies and also briefly report the results of modelling these policies by these authors.

A Zero (Nominal) Interest Rate Policy (ZIRP)

The principle of cheap money has its origins in the work of Keynes (1936) who famously recommended the euthanasia of the rentier. This was justified by the inequitable distribution of wealth and incomes and persistent unemployment. The imposition of a ZIRP has been justified because the nominal (riskless) short-term policy rate is claimed to be its 'natural' level, given the operation of the payments system and policies designed to achieve full employment, including fiscal policy (Forstater & Mosler, 2005; Mitchell, 2009a).

A ZIRP is consistent with low positive deposit rates due to competition among banks for retail funding, and, more generally, a positively sloped yield curve for financial assets. Investment, output and employment would be stimulated under conditions of robust business and consumer confidence given the persistence of low nominal rates (Aspromourgos, 2011; Forstater & Mosler, 2005; Mitchell, 2009a).[10] A permanent ZIRP can improve the stability of the financial system (Tymoigne, 2009; Wray, 2007) as 'it eliminates one element of uncertainty' (Dantas, 2016, 33), namely unstable interest rates which is conducive to better-informed borrowing decisions by both households and firms. Wray (2007) acknowledges that the operation of ZIRP is based on a floating exchange rate regime.

The implementation of a ZIRP means that income from the mere ownership of capital assets is reduced and could be negative in real terms, as opposed to returns for risk-bearing, illiquidity and so on. Also, low borrowing rates can encourage innovation.

A fixed interest rate policy is not an inflation-targeting instrument. Also, the risk of policy mistakes is removed (Aspromourgos, 2011, 638–39). In particular, preemptive increases in rates can cause major contractions.

Palley's concerns about financial instability in respect of NIRP equally apply to ZIRP and other low interest rate policies, but there are remedies other than the discretionary use of monetary policy. Monitoring asset markets and avoiding 'bubbles', should be addressed by tax policy (*e.g.* capital gains taxes) and financial regulation to limit lending for speculation in asset markets (Aspromourgos, 2011, 650). According to Mitchell (2009b), '[A]n appropriately designed taxation system with targeted policies to stop housing speculation would be far more efficient at controlling asset price bubbles than using the blunt end of monetary policy'. See also Mitchell (2015), Wray (2007), and Wright (2021). However, 'the reality is that in the absence of appropriate proactive regulation, supervision, and oversight by central banks and other government bodies, the plasticity of the financial system will recreate fragility, regardless of the level of overnight rates or the monetary policy stance' (Dantas, 2016, 33). See also Posen (2006, 3).

Palley (2015b, 55) claims that a zero nominal interest rate policy is inconsistent with covered interest rate parity (CIP). Both Mason (2014) and Smithin (2016a) argue that Palley has confused CIP, a well-established empirical regularity,[11] with uncovered interest parity (UIP) which, at best, has mixed support in the literature.[12] Also, if open financial markets rule out a ZIRP, interest rates cannot then be used as a tool for demand management policy either (Mason, 2014). Palley's claims are flawed, at least in respect of those sovereign developed economies with international currencies, including the USA, Japan, UK, Canada and Australia.

A Constant Low Real Rate of Interest

Smithin (2007, 2013) advocates a constant (near zero) real market rate which is difficult to implement, since it relies on both the inflationary expectations of the central bank and the 'pass-through' relationship between the policy rate and market rate(s) which might differ according to whether the policy rate is being increased or decreased. A constant, low or zero, real policy rate is easier to implement but is again reliant on the central bank incorporating accurate inflationary expectations, which may be affected by prevailing interest rates. Wray (2007, 129–130) notes that portfolio choice is unaffected by whether real rates or nominal rates are considered since a common inflation rate converts each nominal rate to a real return. However, economies do operate differently according to the rate of inflation, even in the presence of the same real rate of interest.

While at face value discretionary interest rate policy has been discarded under a constant (zero) real policy rate target, the nominal policy rate is being adjusted *pari passu* with changing expectations of the inflation rate, so, *de facto*, nominal policy rates are still being used as a counter-inflation device.[13] If a constant positive rate of inflation is effectively targeted, through agile fiscal policy, then a fixed real interest rate policy is effectively a fixed positive nominal interest rate policy.

Pasinetti's 'Fair' Interest Rate[14]

The fair rate rule, outlined by Aspromourgos (2011) and Lavoie and Seccareccia (2019), among others, has its origins in the work of Pasinetti (1981, 156–175) who views the rentier as a permanent feature of capitalism.

In a pure labour economy 'income is to be distributed in proportion to labour contributed to the production process' (Pasinetti, 1981, 177). In an economy with capital goods and vertically integrated sectors, prices will remain proportional to the quantities of direct and (hyper-indirect) labour

(Lavoie & Seccareccia, 2019, 147–149). Pasinetti frames his rule in terms of the annual rate of labour productivity growth because the wage share of national income remains constant if real wage growth equals labour productivity growth.

Lavoie and Seccareccia (2019, 148) explain that the fair rate of interest is such that the amount of labour time equivalent to a loan can still be purchased say 12 months later when the loan is repaid. Then the fair nominal rate of interest would equal the annual rate of growth in the money wage. However, in many developed economies, including the USA, UK and Australia, the growth of money wages has been insufficient to maintain a constant wage share, so that the labour productivity growth has exceeded real wage growth.

Lavoie and Seccareccia (2019, 152) argue that the rule should be amended so that the real rate of interest equals the growth of real wages. They conclude that the appropriate interest rate to target is the long-term government bond rate.[15] At face value, the difficulties of achieving a target real interest rate which were highlighted in the discussion of Smithin's near-zero real rate of interest rule reappear, but the nominal rate of interest can be set equal to the projected increase in money wages. However, the fair policy rate will effectively operate as a counter-inflation instrument in the event of an inflationary (cost-push) episode. If real wages continue to grow more slowly than labour productivity then the profit share would continue to rise at the expense of both the rentier and wage shares of national income, if the amended fair interest rate rule is followed.[16] This points to the need to adopt labour market policies to promote higher money wage growth.

A Comparison of Fixed Interest Rate Policies

Rochon and Setterfield (2012) consider the three interest rate policies outlined above, namely ZIRP, the 'Smithin rule' (*i.e.* a low real market rate of interest), and Pasinetti's *fair* interest rate. ZIRP yields the highest rate of output growth due to the impact of the lowest real interest rate and is also associated with the lowest rate of inflation, due to the incorporation of a Verdoorn effect and the invariance of their wage share dynamics to the level of economic activity. Even if workers' target wage share is endogenous, the superiority of ZIRP persists, because the nominal interest rate is not adjusted in the light of the inflationary outcome.

Smithin (2020) rejects ZIRP due to alleged instability issues and advocates a zero real policy rate. Watts (2021a) is critical of Smithin's specification of his inflation model and his treatment of inflationary expectations. With the incorporation of adaptive expectations, and the definition of the real rate of interest in terms of the nominal interest rate and the contemporaneous inflation rate, the rate of inflation stabilizes for both target real and nominal policy rates as well as for a target real market rate. Rochon and Setterfield (2007, 2012) adopted a more complete macroeconomic model than does Smithin (2020) but both rely on a systematic, negative relationship between interest rates and economic activity. Also, a meaningful evaluation of interest rate policies is impossible in either case if their respective impacts on real activity, the distribution of income and inflationary dynamics are finessed.

Final Remarks on Fixed Interest Rates

The euthanasia of the rentier, which characterizes ZIRP, may have some appeal, but with an increasing number of national superannuation (pension) systems being privatized, the preservation of real accumulated savings is important, particularly for wage earners, who may also need or wish to engage in discretionary saving. Thus, a low or zero real policy rate target may be the most appropriate fixed rate target and avoids the need for policymakers to anticipate the nature of the pass-through relationship over time. As noted above, the competition for retail funding will drive the real market rate higher than the real policy rate, so that real values of financial assets would be sustained in the presence of a positive inflation rate, in contrast to ZIRP.

The commitment to persistently low policy or market interest rates may lead to financial speculation at least in the short-term in the pursuit of higher yields, particularly by financial institutions with long-dated liabilities, such as superannuation and pension funds. These observations point to the importance of financial re-regulation to direct credit creation towards supporting new investment spending and deterring unproductive speculation associated with transactions in existing financial and physical assets (*e.g.* housing).

Although many heterodox economists support a 'park-it' policy of interest rate setting, the merits of such a policy can only be rigorously evaluated if supporters can explain how sustained full employment and moderate inflation would be achieved via an agile fiscal policy, such that the redesign of policy instruments actually improves broad macroeconomic outcomes, rather than just the income distribution.[17] We now address this issue.

4 Full Employment

We define full employment as every individual of working age wishing to work at prevailing wages being able to secure employment, and the hours of work which they choose, up to a maximum.[18] Thus, fiscal policy should be informed by public purpose, rather than the imposition of fiscal rules (*cf.* Wren-Lewis, 2020).

Even before the pandemic, central bank governors, including Carney (UK) and Lowe (Australia), were advocating complementary fiscal stimulus measures, given the very limited scope for looser monetary policy in these countries within the constraints of the ZLB. Most heterodox economists would agree that fiscal policy is superior to monetary policy in terms of its capacity to influence aggregate demand in a timely manner. Implementation lags would be shorter for tax instruments as compared to government spending.

Godley and Lavoie (2007, 96–97) claim that 'fiscal policy is, in theory, capable of achieving full employment at some target inflation rate'. Aspromourgos (2011) expresses concern about active fiscal policy since, in the absence of other counter-inflation instruments, such as incomes policy, pump priming would need to target both full employment and moderate inflation, which is ambitious. Indeed, a casual examination of labour market data for any country would reveal the persistence of higher rates of unemployment among disadvantaged groups and in particular areas, because stimulatory measures have been discontinued before genuine full employment has been achieved.

MMT advocates support a Job Guarantee (JG) which is a full employment, macroeconomic stabilization policy (Juniper et al., 2014; Mitchell, 1998; Tcherneva, 2020; Tymoigne & Wray, 2015). Tymoigne and Wray (2015, 40) emphasize that employment *per se* is targeted, rather than a level of aggregate demand which is believed to be consistent with full employment (as in pump priming). The JG buffer stock provides a minimum wage job to all workers who desire one, and incorporates counter-inflation mechanisms. Also, the JG can be complemented by incomes policy.

Policymakers would wish to minimise the size of the employment buffer stock to minimise the number of additional workers earning minimum wages. However, the buffer stock must be large enough to accommodate the fluctuations in non-Government employment, since it is designed to operate as an automatic (full employment) stabilizer within a capitalist economy, rather than policymakers relying on fine-tuning (*cf.* Palley, 2015b, 53). These fluctuations would tend to be smaller once the economy had achieved sustained full employment, due to the greater stability of both investment and consumption spending. There is also a role for infrastructure spending by the government and the provision of more resources to enhance the provision of government services including health, which has been put under pressure in many countries during the Covid-19 pandemic.

The JG program has two features that address inflationary pressures. First, employment buffer stocks are exploited which addresses the hysteretic inertia that is characteristic of unemployment buffer stocks, by reducing 'recruiting and hiring costs as employers would have an employed pool of workers demonstrating work readiness' (Tymoigne & Wray, 2015, 41). Second, by cutting government spending or raising tax rates, the proportion of workers in JG jobs is increased, but full employment is maintained. Some highly trained workers may choose to wait for unemployment. There is no longer a trade-off between inflation and unemployment, but rather between the inflation rate and the Buffer Employment Ratio (BER), that is, the share of total employment located in the JG sector. Hence the implementation of a JG brings about a regime shift. Given the segmented nature of the labour market, the promise of job security for workers earning the minimum wage is unlikely to have a significant impact on wage bargaining, in general.

Among Post-Keynesians, Palley (2015a, 2015b) is hostile to a JG but does not outline a set of macroeconomic policies which will achieve sustained full employment and stable inflation (Juniper et al., 2014). Sawyer (2003) refers to the implementation of incomes policy in conjunction with pump priming, but operational details are scarce. A well-publicized JG would strengthen the wage floor, thereby eliminating wage theft which continues to be prevalent in some countries, including Australia, given significant rates of labour underutilization.[19] If there is a continuing reliance on a contributory superannuation scheme, then a robust wage floor and plentiful job opportunities are essential. In addition, regular increases in the minimum wage should provide the impetus for general money wage growth which could be consistent with maintaining the wage share.[20]

Most developed economies already operate an (un)employment services department that maintains detailed data on the spatial distribution of public and private sector job vacancies and the skills and residential locations of the unemployed. Databases of JG employment opportunities by location and jobs currently being undertaken can be added.

Few, if any, developed economies have achieved sustained full employment even prior to the GFC, and none with a stabilization scheme resembling a JG, so there is limited scope for rigorous empirical work.[21] At best, meaningful insights about the macroeconomic implications of a JG can only be generated at a theoretical level, which can be problematic if contentious assumptions are made.[22]

5 Conclusion

This chapter has explored the debates about the appropriate conduct of monetary policy in a modern monetary economy. While most heterodox economists reject discretionary interest rate adjustment, disagreement persists as to whether a fixed target policy or market interest rate should be expressed in nominal or real terms, given that the latter necessitates the accurate and timely generation of inflation rate expectations. The distributional implications of the different interest rate rules in the context of the prevailing transfer and superannuation systems should be a major consideration in the choice of rule. If discretionary monetary policy is discontinued and replaced by an interest rate rule then the policy objectives of central banks should be confined to monetary and financial stability, as is the case for the Bank of England.[23,24] The responsibility for inflation management should be transferred to fiscal policy through the operation of a JG.

In our view, the models developed by Smithin (2020) and Rochon and Setterfield (2007, 2012) are incomplete in terms of exploring the capacity of the different interest rate regimes to achieve sustained full employment and price stability in conjunction with fiscal policy. (For further discussion see Watts, 2021a, and a reply by Smithin, 2021) Rigorous models incorporating transparent assumptions do have an important role to play in macroeconomics, but not to the exclusion of 'ordinary discourse' to convey economic concepts and theories. There is the danger that by manipulating deterministic models, the practical difficulties of achieving policy outcomes can be underestimated. A cautionary quote from Keynes (1936, 297) is apposite here:

> It is a great fault of symbolic pseudo-mathematical methods of formalizing a system of economic analysis ... that they expressly assume strict independence between the factors involved and lose their cogency and authority if this hypothesis is disallowed; whereas, in ordinary discourse, where we are not blindly manipulating and know all the time what we are doing and what the words mean, we can keep 'at the back of our heads' the necessary reserves and qualifications and the adjustments which we shall have to make later on, in a way in which we cannot keep complicated partial differentials 'at the back' of several pages of algebra which assume they all vanish. Too large a proportion of recent 'mathematical' economics are merely concoctions, as imprecise as the initial assumptions they rest on, which allow the author to lose sight of the complexities and interdependencies of the real world in a maze of pretentious and unhelpful symbols.

Notes

1. In short, MMT combines the principles of chartalism (Knapp, 1924; Minsky, 1986; Wray, 1998) and functional finance (Lerner, 1944; Forstater, 1999) and is grounded in institutional practice, that is, how the key macroeconomic institutions, such as the central bank, treasury and the commercial banks, actually operate. Chartalism is based on the premise that money has its origins in the desire of states to affect economic activity. A fiat currency issued by the state is a unit of account which has value because the state can levy taxes that are payable in that currency. Functional finance is based on the argument that fiscal policy should be adopted to counteract economic fluctuations and secure full employment and price stability, without consideration of the impact on fiscal deficits or the accumulated debt (Lerner, 1944). For further discussions, see *inter alia* Wray (1998), Mitchell and Muysken (2008), Juniper et al. (2021) and Pantelopoulos and Watts (2021).
2. However, a series of interest rate increases could have a profound effect on firm's expectations and preparedness to borrow. In addition, the spending capacity of mortgagees would fall and hence aggregate private sector spending could soften leading to both a major slowdown in economic activity and a fall in inflation. This occurred in Australia in 1991, in what the then Treasurer Paul Keating famously described as 'the recession we had to have'.

3. Under forward guidance, the central bank both sets an overnight policy rate target but also generates projections about the path of future policy to enhance the public's understanding of the Central Bank's reaction function (Coenen et al., 2017).
4. The UK bank rate was set at 0.5 per cent in March 2009 when QE was introduced. The UK economy surpassed its pre-downturn GDP peak, 21 quarters later in 2013 Q_2. This represented the sharpest downturn and slowest recovery on record. After the bank rate fell to 0.25 per cent in August 2016, UK investment still remained below to its pre-GFC share of GDP in 2017 (Mitchell, 2017a).
5. The Federal Reserve Bank of Minneapolis shows that post-GFC, US employment took longer to recover to its previous peak (77 months) than during any other of the 10 recessions since 1948.
6. The Bank of England (2015, 3) is clear: 'Implementing monetary policy, the Bank normally seeks to affect only the risk-free element of market rates and seeks to avoid distorting the credit and other spreads established in the market'. See also, Bank of Japan (2016).
7. In 2019 Swiss banks started passing on negative rates to savers with high net worth. Denmark too has imposed a rate of –0.6 per cent on retail deposits above a threshold of 100,000 kroner ($16,000 US).
8. Indeed, there have been sizeable shifts of deposits into banknotes in some economies during financial crises, despite banknotes attracting a zero-interest rate (IMF, 2018).
9. Cliffe (2016) reports the results of a survey which suggests that a high percentage (77 per cent) of savers would withdraw their funds from their savings accounts when an interest rate cut caused an outright income loss (*i.e.*, a negative rate) as opposed to a smaller gain. Thus, savers are perhaps more proactive than is anticipated by Pressman (2019). However, only 12 per cent would spend more, with most either hoarding cash or switching to riskier investments.
10. Aspromourgos (2011, 638) claims that cheap money eases the financing constraints on a government's capacity to undertake expansionary fiscal policy (see also Palley, 2016, 11). Setterfield (2009, 288) refers to the fiscal dividend associated with incomes policy complementing fiscal policy. However, currency sovereign governments face no financing constraints on their domestic spending (Greenspan, 1997; Mitchell, 2009b).
11. However, in the aftermath of a financial crisis, even CIP may not hold. Since 2007, there have been persistent CIP deviations, which can be attributed to expansionary monetary policies pursued by the ECB and BOJ, which has affected the relative demand for US dollar assets (Jauregui & Natraj, 2017). The authors conclude that convergent monetary policies would reduce CIP deviations, 'by eliminating the excess 'carry

trade' of banks borrowing in low interest rate currencies and investing in high interest rate currencies' (see also Borio et al., 2016; IMF, 2021b).

12. CIP only states that there is no arbitrage possible between the spot and forward markets for a given exchange rate (Keynes, 1923). UIP is consistent with interest rate arbitrage in the form of the carry trade, since the forward rate differs from the future expected spot rate (Smithin, 2016a). If UIP held, an ongoing zero interest policy in one economy would require that its currency persistently appreciated, but Japan has sustained near-zero interest rates for 15 years without offsetting exchange rate movements (Mason, 2014). For a survey on UIP, CIP and exchange rate fundamentals, see Harvey (2009) and Lavoie (2014, 477–494).
13. In Australia, the policy rate is typically adjusted by 25 basis points at a time, so it would be expected that small (forecast) changes in the inflation would not lead to a change in interest rates.
14. Pasinetti refers to the 'natural' rate of interest, with its Wicksellian overtones. Lavoie and Seccareccia (2019, 147)—and in their earlier articles—recommend the use of the term 'fair'.
15. Under the widely adopted auction system, bond buyers will determine the 10-year bond rate in the primary market, so that authorities would need to anticipate the pass-through relationship between the overnight policy rate and the bond rate, in order to set the appropriate policy rate. On the other hand, under the tap system, rates are set by the agency overseeing the primary market transactions and the quantities of bonds of different maturities that are purchased are determined by the buyers.
16. Additional bank credit creation and other forms of lending can be directed to enhancing the real economy through the facilitation of new investment. However, in the absence of stronger financial regulation, the increase in lending may be directed to the purchase of existing assets, such as property, which will further shift the distribution of income towards rentiers and be counterproductive for the real economy.
17. For example, among many others, neither Smithin (2020) nor Asensio and Hayes (2009) consider the overall macroeconomic policy framework when assessing different monetary policy options.
18. There would be frictional unemployment, but no hidden unemployment and under-employment.
19. The rate of labour underutilization is the levels of unemployment plus underemployment plus discouraged unemployment expressed as a percentage of the labour force plus discouraged unemployment. Ideally its components are measured in (desired) hours worked.
20. Watts (2010) argues that the minimum wage case deliberations in Australia should be scrapped and replaced by a simple rule of increasing the minimum wage annually by the rate of labour productivity increase plus

the rate of inflation. If all wages increased by this magnitude the wage share would remain constant.

21. While countries have experimented with forms of JG, such as Argentina (Jefes scheme for poor heads of households), India (rural poor) and European Commission (youth), (Mitchell, 2017b), an ongoing JG covering all workers has not been implemented.
22. That being said, Fullwiler (2013) does model and simulate the operation of a JG using the Fair model.
23. The mandate for the RBA includes the stability of the currency and the maintenance of full employment, which is similar to the Fed's mandate in the USA.
24. MMT advocates note the accommodating role played by central banks in most developed economies to ensure the smooth functioning of the payments system.

References

Agarwal, R., & Kimball, M. S. (2019). Enabling deep negative rates to fight recessions: A guide. WP/19/84. International Monetary Fund.

Asensio, A., & Hayes, M. (2009). The post Keynesian alternative to inflation targeting. *European Journal of Economics and Economic Policies: Intervention, 6*(1), 65–79.

Aspromourgos, T. (2011). Can and should monetary policy pursue a zero real interest rate, permanently? *Metroeconomica, 62*, 635–655.

Assenmacher, K., & Krogstrup, S. (2018). *Monetary policy with negative interest rates: Decoupling cash from electronic money*, WP/18/191. International Monetary Fund.

Bank of England. (1999). The transmission mechanism of monetary policy. *Bank of England*. http://www.bankofengland.co.uk/publications/Documents/other/monetary/montrans.pdf

Bank of England. (2015). The Bank of England's sterling monetary framework. *Bank of England*. www.bankofengland.co.uk/markets/Pages/sterlingoperations/redbook.aspx

Batini, N., & Nelson, E. (2002). The lag from monetary policy actions to inflation: Friedman revisited. Discussion Paper No. 6, External MPC Unit, Bank of England.

Borio, C., & Hofmann, B. (2017). Is monetary policy less effective when interest rates are persistently low? Monetary and Economics Department, BIS Working Papers No. 628, April.

Borio, C. E., McCauley, R. N., McGuire, P., & Sushko, V. (2016, September). Covered interest parity lost: Understanding the cross-currency basis. *BIS Quarterly Review*.

Cliffe, M. (2016, 26 February). Negative rates, negative reactions. *VoxEU.org*. https://voxeu.org/article/negative-rates-negative-reactions

Coenen, G., Ehrmann, M., Gaballo, G., Hoffmann, P., Nakov, A., Nardelli, S., Persson, E., & Strasser, G. (2017). Communication of monetary policy in unconventional times. *ECB Working Paper Series,* No. 2080.

Dantas, F. (2016, October). Normalizing the fed funds rate: The fed's unjustified rationale. *Levy Institute Working Paper No. 876.*

Davidson, P. (2006). Can, or should, a central bank inflation target? *Journal of Post Keynesian Economics, 28*(4), 689–703.

Federal Reserve Bank of Minneapolis. (no date). The recession and recovery in perspective, Special Studies. https://www.minneapolisfed.org/publications/special-studies/recession-in-perspective

Forstater, M. (1999). Flexible full employment: Structural implications of discretionary public sector employment. *Journal of Economic Issues, 32*(2), 557–563.

Forstater, M., & Mosler, W. (2005). The natural rate of interest is zero. *Journal of Economic Issues, 39*(2), 535–542.

Friedman, M. (1961). The lag in effects of monetary policy. *Journal of Political Economy, 69*, 447–466.

Fullwiler, S. (2013). The costs and benefits of a job guarantee: Estimates from a multi-country econometric model. In M. J. Murray, & M. Forstater (Eds.), *The job guarantee program: Toward true full employment.* Palgrave Macmillan.

Gnos, C., & Rochon, L.-P. (2007). The new consensus and Post-Keynesian interest rate policy. *Review of Political Economy, 17*(3), 369–386.

Godley, W., & Lavoie, M. (2007). Fiscal policy in a stock-flow consistent (SFC) model. *Journal of Post Keynesian Economics, 30*(1), 79–100.

Graham, A. (2019). Analyzing the effects of negative interest rates across five economies. https://www.toptal.com/finance/market-research-analysts/effects-of-negative-interest-rates

Greenspan, A. (1997, August). *Maintaining financial stability in a global economy.* Remarks from the Annual Economic Symposium sponsored by FRB Kansas City, Jackson Hole WY. http://www.minneapolisfed.org/publications_papers/pub_display.cfm?id=3629

Harvey, J. (2009). *Currencies, capital flows and crises: A post Keynesian analysis of exchange rate determination.* Routledge.

International Monetary Fund. (2018). *Casting light on central bank digital currency.* International Monetary Fund Staff Discussion Report No. 18/08. International Monetary Fund.

International Monetary Fund. (2021a, 3 March). The evidence is in on negative interest rate policies. *IMF Blog.* https://blogs.imf.org/2021a/03/03/the-evidence-is-in-on-negative-interest-rate-policies/

International Monetary Fund (IMF). (2021b, 5 May). US dollar share of global foreign exchange reserves drops to 25-year low. *IMF Blog*. exchange-reserves-drops-to-25-year-low/?utm_medium=email&utm_source=g

Jauregui, C., & Natraj, G. V. (2017, 13–15 December). The puzzle of persistent covered interest rate parity deviations: Does monetary policy matter? *Mimeo*, RBA Workshop, Quantitative Macroeconomics. https://www.rba.gov.au/publications/workshops/research/2017/pdf/rba-workshop-2017-ganesh-viswan.pdf

Juniper, J., Sharpe, T. P., & Watts, M. J. (2014–15). Modern monetary theory: Contributions and critics. *Journal of Post Keynesian Economics, 37*(2), 281–307.

Juniper, J., Nadolny, A., Pantelopoulos, G. & Watts, M. J. (2021, June). Orthodox macroeconomic textbooks: A critical evaluation using institutional practice as a benchmark. *International Review of Economics Education, 37*, 1–11.

Keynes, J. M. (1923). *A tract on monetary reform*. Macmillan.

Keynes, J. M. (1936). *The general theory of employment interest and money*. Macmillan.

Knapp, G. F. (1924). *The state theory of money*. Reprinted by Augustus M. Kelley, Clifton, NJ: 1973.

Kuroda, H. (2016, 3 February). Introduction to 'Quantitative and qualitative monetary easing with a negative interest rate'. Speech given by the Governor of the Bank of Japan at the Kisaragi-kai Meeting in Tokyo. https://www.boj.or.jp/en/announcements/press/koen_2016/data/ko160203a1.pdf

Lavoie, M. (2014). *Post-Keynesian economics: New foundations*. Edward Elgar.

Lavoie, M., & Seccareccia, M. (2019). Some reflections on Pasinetti's fair rate of interest. *Bulletin of Political Economy, 13*(2), 85–111.

Lerner, A. (1944). *The economics of control: Principles of welfare economics*. Macmillan.

Lilley, A., & Rogoff, K. (2019). *The case for implementing effective negative interest rate policy, strategies for monetary policy*. Hoover Institution Press.

Mason, J. W. (2014, 17 February). A response to Tom Palley. http://jwmason.org/slackwire/a-response-to-tom-palley/

Minsky, H. P. (1986). *Stabilizing an unstable economy*. Yale University Press.

Mitchell, W. F. (1998). The buffer stock employment model—full employment without a NAIRU. *Journal of Economic Issues, 32*(2), 547–555.

Mitchell, W. F. (2009a, 30 August). The natural rate of interest is zero. *Billy Blog*. http://bilbo.economicoutlook.net/blog/?p=4656

Mitchell, W. F. (2009b, 20 September). Operational design arising from modern monetary theory. *Billy Blog*. http://bilbo.economicoutlook.net/blog/?p=5098

Mitchell, W. F. (2015, 6 May). Iceland's sovereign money proposal—part 2. *Billy Blog*. http://bilbo.economicoutlook.net/blog/?p=30833

Mitchell, W. F. (2017a, 18 October). British productivity slump—all down to George Osborne's austerity obsession. *Billy Blog*. http://bilbo.economicoutlook.net/blog/?p=37118

Mitchell, W. F. (2017b, 25 May). 4 Years later—the European youth guarantee is an under-funded failure. *Billy Blog*. http://bilbo.economicoutlook.net/blog/?p=36078

Mitchell, W. F., & Muysken, J. (2008). *Full employment abandoned: Shifting sands and policy failures*. Edward Elgar.

Mitchell, W. F. & Watts, M. J. (2013, November). Capacity constraints and the job guarantee. Centre of Full Employment and Equity (CofFEE) Working Paper No. 04–13.

Moler, W., & Armstrong, P. (2019). A discussion of central bank operations and interest rate policy. https://gimms.org.uk/2019/02/24/central-bank-operations-interest-rate-policy/

Palley, T. I. (2015a). Money, fiscal policy, and interest rates: A critique of modern monetary theory. *Review of Political Economy, 27*(1), 1–23.

Palley, T. I. (2015b). The critics of modern money theory (MMT) are right. *Review of Political Economy, 27*(1), 45–61.

Palley, T. I. (2016). Why negative interest rate policy (NIRP) is ineffective and dangerous. *Real World Economics Review, 76*(1), 5–15.

Pantelopoulos, G., & Watts, M. J. (2021). Voluntary and involuntary constraints on the conduct of macroeconomic policy: An application to the UK. *Journal of Economic Issues, 55*(1), 225–245.

Pasinetti, L. L. (1981). *Structural change and economic growth: A theoretical essay on the dynamics of the wealth of nations*. Cambridge University Press.

Posen, A. (2006). Why central banks should not burst bubbles. *International Finance, 9*(1), 109–124.

Pressman, S. (2019). How low can we go? The limits of monetary policy. *Review of Keynesian Economics, 7*(2), 137–150.

Rochon, L.-P., & Setterfield, M. (2007). Interest rates, income distribution and monetary policy dominance: Post-Keynesians and the 'fair rate' of interest. *Journal of Post Keynesian Economics, 30*(1), 13–41.

Rochon, L.-P., & Setterfield, M. (2012). A Kaleckian model of growth and distribution with conflict inflation and Post Keynesian nominal interest rate rules. *Journal of Post Keynesian Economics, 34*(3), 497–520.

Rogers, C. (1989). *Money, interest and capital: A study in the foundations of monetary theory*. Cambridge University Press.

Rogoff, K. (2017). *The curse of cash*. Princeton University Press.

Sawyer, M. (2003). Employer of last resort: Could it deliver full employment and price stability? *Journal of Economic Issues, 37*(4), 881–907.

Setterfield, M. (2009). Macroeconomics without the LM curve: An alternative view. *Cambridge Journal of Economics, 33*(1), 273–293.

Sharpe, T., & Watts, M. J. (2012). Policy advice in crisis: How inter-governmental organizations have responded to the GFC. *Journal of Australian Political Economy, 69*, Winter, 103–133.

Smithin, J. (2007). A real interest rate rule for monetary policy? *Journal of Post Keynesian Economics, 30*(1), 101–118.

Smithin, J. (2013). *Essays in the fundamental theory of monetary economics and macroeconomics*. World Scientific Publishing.

Smithin, J. (2016a). Endogenous money, fiscal policy, interest rates and the exchange rate regime: A comment on Palley, Tymoigne and Wray. *Review of Political Economy, 28*(1), 64–78.

Smithin, J. (2016b). Endogenous money, fiscal policy, interest rates and the exchange rate regime: Correction. *Review of Political Economy, 28*(4), 609–611.

Smithin, J. (2018). *Re-thinking the theory of money, credit and macroeconomics: A new statement for the twenty-first century*. Lexington Books.

Smithin, J. (2020). Interest rates, income distribution and the monetary policy transmissions mechanism under endogenous money: What have we learned 30 years on from Horizontalists and Verticalists? *European Journal of Economics and Economic Policies: Intervention, 17*(3), 381–398.

Smithin. (2021). The methodology for assessing interest rate rules: A reply. *European Journal of Economics and Economic Policies: Intervention, 18*(3), 286–292.

Tcherneva, P. R. (2020). *The case for a job guarantee*. Polity.

Tymoigne, E. (2009). *Central banking, asset prices and financial fragility*. Routledge.

Tymoigne, E., & Wray, L. R. (2015). Modern money theory: A reply to Palley. *Review of Political Economy, 27*(1), 24–44.

Watts, M. J. (2010). How should minimum wages be set in Australia? *Journal of Industrial Relations, 52*(2), 131–149.

Watts, M. J. (2021a). The methodology for assessing interest rate policy rules: Some comments. *European Journal of Economics and Economic Policies: Intervention, 18*(3), 275–285.

Watts, M. J. (2021b). *Unpacking the dynamics of fiscal deficits and debt*. University of Newcastle.

Wray, L. R. (1998). *Understanding modern money*. Edward Elgar.

Wray, L. R. (2007). A Post Keynesian view of central bank independence, policy targets, and the rules versus discretion debate. *Journal of Post Keynesian Economics, 30*(1), 119–141.

Wren-Lewis, S. (2020, 14 January). Monetary and fiscal cooperation: The case for a state dependent assignment, Mainly Macro. https://mainlymacro.blogspot.com/2020/01/monetary-and-fiscal-cooperation-case.html

Wright, S. (2021, 20 September). Mortgage stress soars as RBA says tax system pushes up house prices. Sydney Morning Herald. https://www.smh.com.au/politics/federal/mortgage-stress-soars-as-rba-says-tax-system-pushes-up-house-prices-20210919-p58sw3.html

CHAPTER 3

Rules Are Meant to Be Broken: Arguments in Favour of Discretionary Monetary Policy

Sarah F. Small and Bhavya Sinha

1 Introduction

In 1993, John Taylor wrote, "If there is anything about which modern macroeconomics is clear… it is that policy rules have major advantages over discretion in improving economic performance" (p. 197). However, nearly thirty years later, economists and monetary policymakers have *not* reached a consensus in the rules versus discretion debate. John Taylor is the father of the Taylor Rule, a monetary policy rule which has become canonical to the point that, in 2016, three Nobel laureates joined Taylor in signing a letter that urged the United States Congress to mandate that the Federal Reserve explain any future deviations from the Taylor Rule (Kocherlakota, 2016). However, monetary policy practitioners strongly

S. F. Small (✉)
University of Utah, Salt Lake City, UT, USA
e-mail: sarah.small@utah.edu

B. Sinha
Colorado State University, Fort Collins, CO, USA
e-mail: bhavya.sinha@colostate.edu

S. Pressman and J. Smithin (eds.), *Debates in Monetary Macroeconomics*,
https://doi.org/10.1007/978-3-031-11240-9_3

opposed this push for monetary policy to be governed by specific rules. Former chairwoman of the Federal Reserve, Janet Yellen (2015), in correspondence with Speaker of the House Pelosi regarding the Fed Oversight Reform and Modernization (FORM) Act, stated, "[T]he bill would severely impair the Federal Reserve's ability to carry out its congressional mandate and would be a grave mistake, detrimental to the economy and the American people". Ben Bernanke (2015), another former chairperson of the Federal Reserve, also stated that "monetary policy should be systematic, not automatic. The simplicity of the Taylor rule disguises the complexity of the underlying judgments that (Federal Open Market Committee) FOMC members must continually make if they are to make good policy decisions".

Why might Janet Yellen, Ben Bernanke, and many other economists and policymakers be opposed to a rules-based approach to monetary policy? Those in favor of a rules-based approach to monetary policy have proposed a variety of rules (notably Friedman's *k* percent Rule, the Taylor Rule, the Kansas City Rule, the Smithin Rule, and the Pasinetti Rule, among others) and argue that a rule should be chosen and followed to a tee. However, like any public policy, each rule comes with its own political advantages and disadvantages—benefitting one class or another. Those in favor of a discretionary approach to monetary policy have proposed that policy leaders use their own judgment depending on the data and context. They argue that in a dynamic economic and political climate, clinging to strict monetary policy rules can be harmful to economic and social distribution—not stabilizing. In this chapter, we align with the discretionary macroeconomists and argue that rules are meant to be broken. Central banks cannot and should not strictly adhere to monetary policy rules and should instead operate on a discretionary basis.

Section 2 provides a brief review of the rules versus discretion debate on the basis of values, beliefs, and observations of the proponents. In Section 3 we offer criticisms of five notable rules, viz. the Friedman Rule, the Taylor Rule, the Kansas City Rule, the Pasinetti Rule, and the Smithin Rule. We challenge both the plausibility and effectiveness of a rules-based approach and point out their political advantages and disadvantages in Section 4. Section 5 explores the political economy of monetary policy and argues that rules are influenced by political ideologies that may actually deepen economic inequality. Section 6 concludes. Ultimately, a discretionary approach to monetary policy does not mean an unsystematic one; on the contrary, it means a carefully measured, contextualized, and humble approach to monetary policy that can respond to the ever-changing needs of our society and economy.

2 A Brief Review of Rules versus Discretion in Monetary Policy

The dispute over rules or discretion in monetary policy is based on the values, beliefs, and observations of the debating economists and policy practitioners, and their proposed objectives for monetary policy. This extends, of course, to concepts, definitions, and formulations of monetary variables that are contested between the factions of monetary theorists and practitioners. In this section, we briefly discuss the differing values and beliefs of the proponents of rules and of discretion, their proposed objectives for monetary authorities, and perspectives on the existence of a natural rate of inflation and unemployment.

Values Informing Monetary Policy Regimes

John Maynard Keynes wrote in 1930, "it would be much better to leave the management of the reserves of the central bank to its own unfettered discretion than to attempt to lay down by law what it should do or within what limits it should act" ([1930] 1981, 243). Keynes did not believe that rules *could* be laid down: he understood "the immense complexity of its [a central bank's] problems and their varying character in varying circumstances." As Rivot (2015) explains, Keynes argued in favor of long-term guidelines that leave room for short-term adaptations to circumstances, which could contemporarily be construed as a rule but not strictly so. The spectrum of discretionary policy proponents, from complete discretion to policy frameworks, essentially derives from Keynes' notion that a rule would be too rigid to accommodate the complexities of an economy in its context and crises.

With the development of the quantity theory of money, Milton Friedman and the monetarists entered the scene, and the rules versus discretion debate became among the most prominent in monetary policy during the 1960s and up to the 1980s (Argy, 1988). Opposed to Keynes' ideas and in favor of a strict rule for monetary policy, the monetarists believed that the basic economic principles of money and inflation were sufficiently reliable in most circumstances, and ultimately provided a good deal of certainty. They argued that, on average, things would work out the way economic theory suggested as long as governments did not interfere and upset the stable trajectory. Friedman, a leader among the monetarists and on the rules side of the debate, held several beliefs which supported his arguments for static monetary policy with minimal government intervention. First, he had a distinct distrust of policymakers and their political autonomy in their decision-making. Friedman believed monetary policymakers would adopt politically advantageous short-run policies that would operate against long-run stability and predictability for public interest. Second, he valued efficiency in the implementation of monetary policy to ensure the effectiveness of the mandate. Friedman held that with a consistent and unchanging monetary policy in place, any shock in the private sector would naturally smooth out and leave only minimal disruption in its wake (Argy, 1988). Reactionary monetary policies, in Friedman's view, were destabilizing. Much of his argument was informed by his research on the monetary history of the United States (Friedman & Schwartz, 1963). He argued that the lag between problem, implementation, and resolution was too long for reactionary policies to be helpful. In Friedman's view, even well-intentioned policymakers face a series of lags. First, there is a recognition lag in discerning an issue in the economy. Next, there is an implementation lag in deciding and putting into effect a policy. Finally, there is a lag between the action and its effects (Friedman, 1969). Ultimately, Friedman thought a policy reacting to an economic circumstance may no longer be relevant by the time it takes full effect.

More recent proponents for rules in monetary policy take a variety of positions in structuring the monetary policy rule, but many of them are grounded in concerns similar to Friedman's. For instance, proponents of strict monetary rules still argue that rules hold monetary policy practitioners accountable and are good for time consistency and long-run stability. Orphanides (2010, 2) best sums up what many views as the benefits of a rules-based approach: "Policy based on a well-understood rule enhances the accountability of the central bank and improves the credibility of future policy actions. Also, by making future policy decisions more predictable, rule-based policy facilitates forecasting by financial market participants, businesses, and households, thereby reducing uncertainty".

However, recent economists of the post-Keynesian and New Keynesian tradition counter that policy rules are implicitly biased toward the creditor and rentier classes in their valuation of "rational expectations" to maintain predictability and maximize profits. Wray (1998) and Smithin (2007) thus argue for a park-it monetary policy rule that would allow the government to employ a progressive fiscal policy toward achieving greater economic equality. For instance, Wray (2007) strongly argues against the dominance of monetary policy in general, particularly as it prevails in the orthodoxy and in the New Consensus. As he perceives it, monetary policy is not an effective tool for regulating aggregate output and demand. Park-it post-Keynesians argue instead for the increased significance of fiscal policy to achieve macroeconomic objectives of activity and output (Smithin, 2007; Wray, 2007).

Proposed Objectives of Monetary Policy

Supposing that rules make monetary authorities more accountable, what next are the goals for monetary policy against which central banks may be held accountable? Frankly, it depends on who you ask and when you ask. Since the origins of central banks, their roles and goals have changed; from funding governments and wars to simply ensuring price stability (Pollard, 2003). For example, Britain's Royal Charter of 1694, which established the Bank of England, originally decreed that the Bank was founded to "promote the public Good and Benefit of our People" that translated, in actuality, to fund England's war efforts. Today, the Bank of England is less focused on war funding and more focused on monetary stability. In 1913, the United States' Federal Reserve Act chartered the Federal Reserve System with the goal of establishing a national monetary system to provide general financial stability. Later in 1977, it was amended to implement the dual mandate of "goals of maximum employment, stable prices, and moderate long-term interest rates". The evolution of the Bank of England and the Federal Reserve of the United States, as central banks in advanced capitalist economies, only scratch the surface of the complex history of central banking in diverse economies across the world.

Today there are still debates regarding the objectives of monetary policy. The main sides that people take in these debates depend on the priority they place on price stability and inflation versus employment and economic growth. Opponents of discretionary monetary policy argue that discretion is not only open to special interest politics but also biased toward inflation which generates economic instability. In the 1950s and

1960s, monetary authorities were developing reactionary policies that consistently proved to be too late and too much, thus contributing to wild swings in inflation and high levels of instability. In 1966, in an attempt to moderate the price inflation, the Federal Reserve moved in a less expansionary direction but, Friedman (1995) argued, should have done so at least a year earlier. Further, when it did act, it implemented too strong a contractionary monetary policy which resulted in the Great Contraction of 1966. As a corrective reaction, it reverted to a more expansionary policy at the end of the year. Friedman (1995) argued that was rightly done but, again, the Federal Reserve increased the growth of the money supply too much, to the point that led to inflation. Friedman noted similar issues across many decades. He explained that the propensity to overreact can be reasoned as, first, the failure of monetary authorities to account for the lag between action and effect and, second, the compulsion to compensate too much but too late. Hence, in his view, monetary authorities should aim to avoid sharp swings in monetary policy and ensure economic stability by implementing a mechanistic rule that would set a known and static rate of monetary growth (Friedman, 1969, 1995).

Opponents of policy rules that prioritize price stability and low inflation argue that such rules are effectively biased toward the protection of the purchasing power of money, or the rentier class, at the cost of economic growth (Smithin, 2007; Van Lear, 2000; Wray, 2007). They explain that the protection of employment and profits should instead be weighted in policy objectives to expand economic growth for which fiscal policy must be employed. Increased government spending would yield a proportional increase in aggregate output along with modest inflation until the economy closes in on full employment. The implied cost-push inflation effectively has no detrimental impact on employment as increased government spending only slightly increases the general price level. Hence, opponents of such policy rules conclude that central banks should not prioritize a fight against inflation. Proponents of discretion may thus acknowledge the problem of inflation but place it alongside the objective of stimulating an economy to full employment (Van Lear, 2000). To achieve their dual objective of controlling inflation and stimulating aggregate demand, they have proposed incomes policy (Bowles et al., 1990; Cornwall, 1994) and employment buffer stock policies (Wray, 1998). An incomes policy essentially recommends that labor be zapped, either coercively (Cornwall, 1994) by curtailing collective bargaining and increasing workers' sense of employment and security or cooperatively (Bowles et al., 1990) by encouraging social bargaining for a limited capital-labor accord. An employment buffer stock policy would recommend the government guarantee a fixed-wage job to any person willing and able to work (Wray, 1998).

On the Existence of a Natural Rate of Inflation and Unemployment

Some proponents of rules take a different approach. A key difference between the post-Keynesians (such as Wray and Smithin) and the New Consensus (that builds on the neoclassical theory of cumulative inflation) is that the former understands inflation to primarily be cost-determined and, specifically, determined by the conflicting claims of macroeconomic production groups over wealth and income whereas the latter understands inflation to be a monetary phenomenon or excess aggregate demand situation. While post-Keynesians do not believe in the existence of a natural rate of interest as they reject a continuous aggregate production function (Smithin, 2007), the New Consensus believes in a natural rate of inflation and unemployment—a rate of unemployment that maintains price stability and is non-inflationary. Taylor (1993) employed the notion of the natural rate of interest, and argued that economic growth and the inflation rate should inform the monetary authority of the appropriate federal funds rate. Smithin (2007), however, counters that there is no natural rate of interest and, hence, the real rate of interest should be targeted to near zero to account for deflationary pressures.

3 A Selection of Monetary Policy Rules in Theory

In this section, we critically examine five notable monetary policy rules with respect to their theoretical consistency and contextual plausibility. Among the orthodoxy and New Consensus, Friedman (1982) delivered a public lecture that triggered the consideration and practice of a fixed-rule regime from 1985 and up to the early 2000s. More recently, Taylor (1993, 2017) has continued to engage in the debate and demand a return to a strict policy rule from the practice of the dual mandate of the Federal Reserve. We, therefore, consider the Friedman Rule and the Taylor Rule at one end of the spectrum of policy rules. On the other end of the spectrum, among the post-Keynesians monetary theorists, there have emerged two approaches to monetary policy (Rochon & Setterfield, 2007)—one is the activist rule that advocates the setting of counter-cyclical interest rates to ensure low employment and steady growth (Moore, 1988; Palley, 2006, 2007) and the other is the park-it rule that advocates the parking of the interest rate at a determined level, to be revised only sparingly, in order to focus instead on fiscal policy and thus achieve an explicit distributional objective (Smithin, 2007; Wray, 2007). To capture the range and nuance of monetary policy rules, we leave out of consideration the activist rule that ties interest rate policy and the regulation of aggregate demand and unemployment, and instead focus on the rules of Wray, Pasinetti, and Smithin that more distinctly argue against the dominance of monetary policy.

The Friedman Rule

Friedman prescribed a mechanistic rule that would need to be statically followed rather than a policy that reacted to perceived changes in the economy. Friedman (1995) argued that a monetary total would be the best guide or criterion for monetary policy with its relatively efficient time lag and magnitude of impact. He defined this total as the sum of currency and adjusted demand deposits, plus commercial bank deposits, but was open to a broader monetary total. His point was that a monetary total should be chosen; he did not care very much about how the total was calculated. Friedman argued that targeting a steady rate of growth for a monetary total would be a good policy rule and would do away with sharp swings in policy that caused economic disturbances. He explained that the precise rate of growth is less important than pegging a known and stated rate (which he called 'k percent') to ensure economic stability. Friedman's fixed 'k percent' growth rate of the monetary total would achieve stability in the level of prices of final products.

Going further, Friedman (1969) discussed the optimum quantity of money and monetary growth. He noted that optimization of the money supply is key to indirectly, but concretely, obtaining the optimal price level. Emphasizing long-run efficiency rather than short-run adjustments, as was done in the conventional debate of the time, Friedman (1969) arrived at a market measure of the internal rate of discount through a system of equations. He argued that the nominal interest rate should optimally be equal to zero; however, if the central bank cannot peg interest rates, it must control the growth rate of the price level via the control of the growth of the money supply. Any further attempt to control inflation would induce rentiers to hold a stock of wealth so large that it would eventually yield negative returns at the margin and reduce welfare. Thus, at the optimum, each individual and each enterprise would be incentivized to hold a volume of cash balances that would result in a zero marginal yield. The rational individual would optimize its utility, and the enterprise its productive services.

Friedman and many orthodox theorists understood the money supply to be exogenous and argued for fixing a k percent growth rate of money to keep inflation in check as well as for transparency in the economic system. Countering the notion of exogenous money supply, heterodox theory explains that money supply growth is endogenous, since the money growth rate of money depends on private sector credit demand, business activity, and bank lending. This means that the central bank cannot exogenously set the growth rate of money (to, say, k percent). Money supply is endogenous because economic growth stimulates lending. This counters the view that the Federal Reserve is able to push out money into the economy (Moore, 1988). The decision variable for the central bank is thus not the level of reserves or growth rate of money supply, but the short-term interest rate (or the federal funds rate in the United States). Extrapolating, Wray (1998) argues that the interest inelasticity of demand for loans further explains the endogeneity of money supply. Hence, monetary authorities cannot directly control bank reserves or the money supply. As reserves are not independent of money demand, the monetary authority is required to supply reserves, through instruments such as open market operations, to meet money demand in order to maintain a well-functioning financial system.

The Friedman Rule was also based on a broad definition of money (M3) that includes interest-bearing deposits and is also inelastic to changes in the interest rate. Kaldor (1985) countered that there were a few countries (including the United States) that exhibited stable money demand over the 1960s and 1970s using the M3 definition, but that the claim did not hold for a majority of countries and time periods. It definitely did not even hold for the United States, based on the narrow definition of money, M1. Moreover, Friedman based his policy rule on the quantity theory of money, which postulates that money growth rate determines private sector credit demand. However, Kaldor (1985) and Moore (1988) argue that the quantity theory of money was too simplistic in formulating an invariable velocity of money and for missing the reverse causality of private sector credit demand on money growth rates.

The Zero Interest Rate Policy (ZIRP) Rule or the Kansas City Rule

Countering the centrality of the quantity of bank money in monetary policy, Wray (1998) explained that the quantity of bank money is essentially determined by the quantity of bank loans and that the central bank itself does not directly control. Moreover, the central bank exercises little direct influence on the quantity of bank money. Wray (1998) argued that the horizontal money supply is endogenously determined and that it is the short-term interest rate that is exogenously determined. It is essentially the overnight lending rate for reserves in banks that is the policy variable for the Fed, and the Federal funds rate becomes the targeted overnight rate. The overnight lending rate is invariably taken as the instrument for discretionary monetary policy frameworks, and arbitrage then determines the wholesale short-term interest rate. In other words, the short-term interest rate is exogenously determined by the central bank's policy. Then, in order to ensure that the optimal amount of reserves are available to the system of banks, the Fed must coordinate its monetary policy with fiscal policy; Fed policy cannot be independent of fiscal policy (Wray, 1998). Therefore, an activist fiscal policy would work to affect the interest rate in monetary policy; the rule then being that the two branches of policy should be coordinated to keep the nominal interest rate at zero (Wray, 1998, 2007).

The Kansas City Rule dictates that central banks should set the nominal interest rate at zero and leave it be, while shifting the focus to fiscal policy to deal with economic growth (Wray, 1998, 87). Given the dual mandate of the Federal Reserve, the Kansas City monetary policy rule would theoretically yield the highest rate of growth and the lowest rate of inflation because of the high rate of productivity growth. Having satisfied monetary policy demands, the government would use fiscal policy to stimulate effective demand; the impact of this fiscal policy on economic growth would be large because the park-it interest rate is invariant to changes in the growth of labor productivity. Wray (1998) explains that this policy would yield negative real interest rates, thus making this among the most expansionary of monetary policy rules. However, the Great Recession of 2008 pointed out two problems with the ZIRP—the nominal interest rate would have to be set below zero to be an effective expansionary monetary policy during an economic crisis, and the nominal interest rate would have to be higher than zero if the monetary policy needs to be used to offset the bursting of the next financial bubble.

Kregel (2014) explains that the former problem is based on the zero lower bound for nominal interest rates, and not Keynes's liquidity preference and liquidity trap. The perceived limitations of the zero lower bound theory may be overcome with the introduction of progressive policies that would raise the marginal efficiency of capital to offset the liquidity trap. Thus, the Kansas City Rule may not have worked with its narrow application during the recession but could be reconsidered with complementary fiscal policy.

The Taylor Rule

Taylor believed that a rule need not be a mechanical formula and broadened the notion of a monetary policy rule to encompass a nominal income rule, where the central bank targets nominal income but does not exercise pure discretion over this variable. Taylor (1993) advocated monetary policy rules where monetary authorities use the short-term interest rate to maintain output and price stability; specifically putting a positive weight on *both* the price level and real output in the policy rule for interest rates rather than using a pure price rule as is wont to be done for rules that target only inflation.

Taylor (1993) initially formulated the equation for his monetary policy rule as:

$$r = p + 0.5y + 0.5(p - 2) + 2$$

where r is the federal funds rate, p is the inflation rate over the previous four quarters, and y is the percent deviation of real GDP from a target level. He thus argued that the Federal Open Market Committee (FOMC) ought to target the federal funds rate (r)—the interest rate that banks charge each other—in accordance with fluctuations in price levels (p) and output gap (y). The Taylor Rule equation presents the federal funds rate as a function of the inflation rate and output gap. According to the equation, if both the inflation rate and the real GDP are on target, then the federal funds rate would equal four percent in nominal terms or two percent in real terms. If inflation increases above the representative target of two percent or if the real GDP exceeds the trend GDP, then the federal funds rate would need to be increased. The equation essentially suggests that the FOMC should raise the federal funds rate if the output gap increases or if inflation rises faster than the Federal Reserve's target.

Taylor (1993) constructed a nuanced argument for his monetary policy rule that allowed for discretion within the confines of the policy. It encouraged the use of its specific functional form (along with the coefficients) as simply an input in the complex decision-making process of the central bank but also allowed for the complete rejection of the algebraic formula in order to have its general principles considered. Empirically, Taylor (1993) shows that the rule fits actual policy performance and, hence, is desirable on practical grounds.

Over the period of 1987–1992, the United States experienced a crash in its stock market to which the Federal Reserve reacted by easing interest rates. This is similar to what Taylor's policy rule would have directed, thus supporting the role of discretion within the policy rule. However, although the rule may have been shown to be effective in retrospect, when the requisite variables are known, the current output (which would be needed in the calculation of the output gap) is unobservable in the time period when decisions must be made. Further, the concept of the natural or target level of output is a theoretical variable that may be inaccurately measured by monetary authorities, which would also result in an incorrect calculation of the output gap. Thus, there are operational problems with the Taylor Rule (Beckworth, 2017; McCallum, 1999). It has, further, been argued that variables such as the equilibrium real rate of interest are also unobservable (Hummel, 2017).

The Fair Rate Rule or the Pasinetti Rule

According to Pasinetti (1981, 174), the fair rate of interest "stems from the principle that all individuals, when they engage in debt/credit relations, should obtain, at any time, an amount of purchasing power that is constant in terms of labor." The Pasinetti Rule suggests setting the real rate of interest equal to the growth rate of labor productivity. Lavoie (1999, 4) built off Pasinetti's Fair Rate Rule and described how it ought to be put into action: "In an economy where the rate of profit remains constant, this growth rate [of labor productivity] would simply equal the growth rate of real wages. With price inflation, the fair rate of interest would be equal to the average rate of wage inflation; i.e., the growth rate of productivity plus the rate of price inflation". Or, updated by Lavoie (1999), the real rate of interest should fairly equal the real rate of increase in wages.

The Fair Rate Rule, as conceptualized by Lavoie (1996, 1999) and Pasinetti (1981), essentially paints the rentier class as a "necessary evil" and maintains its monetary policy objective neutrally as maintaining the current distribution of income among the production groups of workers, capitalists, and financiers. Linking the rentier classes' income with production and employment advantageously produces incentives that may be beneficial to the working class as well. Additionally, when productivity growth is low, interest rates would also be low; thus, triggering greater borrowing and spending and resulting in stimulated aggregate demand. However, there is mounting evidence that wages do not reflect labor productivity and there is rather a widening gap between productivity and real wage rates (Karanassou & Sala, 2014; Van Ark et al., 2008). There could, thus, be greater labor productivity but suppressed real wages that result in an artificially high interest rate, thereby stifling aggregate demand and the rentiers effectively countering the proposed objective of the rule. Contextualizing the Pasinetti Rule with the dual mandate of the US, a fiscal stimulus would raise economic growth but would also crowd out private investment and credit demand. This is because the fiscal stimulus would increase the interest rate, which would then decrease the investment rate and economic growth.

The Zero Real Policy Rate (ZRPR) Rule or the Smithin Rule

The Smithin Rule, like the Pasinetti Rule, aims to allow individuals and firms to borrow and spend more, thus boosting aggregate demand and, ultimately, employment and wages. However, unlike the Pasinetti Rule and like the Kansas City Rule, it is in the spirit of Keynes' ([1936] 1973) "euthanasia of the rentier" in that it redistributes income away from rentiers and toward workers for consumption (Rochon & Setterfield, 2011). Smithin (2007) formulated the ZRPR Rule by extending ZIRP and considering strong deflationary pressures. The Smithin Rule suggests that central banks should target the *real* interest rate, and not the nominal, at a positive level near zero. This implies that the Smithin Rule, in contrast to Kansas City (ZIRP) Rule, would require decreasing the nominal interest rate during deflationary periods.

Like the Kansas City Rule, the ZRPR Rule would also have the interest rate parked and would have fiscal policy impact economic growth and employment (Rochon & Setterfield, 2011). Collis (2018) has argued that a real interest rate approach, like the Smithin Rule, would be so effective that the Great Depression of the 1930s, the financing of WWII, the stagflation of the 1970s, and the Great Recession of 2008 would not have happened at all. However, concerns about needing economic degrowth for environmental sustainability would suggest that the real interest rate ought to be higher (Pressman, 2020). Smithin (2018) also acknowledges that although this rule would effectively stabilize inflation, it might not make sense in every context and circumstance. Pressman (2019, 2020) delineates the limits to how low interest rates can go before they damage the economy through disintermediation.

4 A Critique of Monetary Policy Rules

A multitude of rules exists without a clear consensus. Which rule should central banks choose? The fact that there is a debate not only on discretion versus rules but also on which rule should be implemented suggests that a strict adherence to a rule is practically unreasonable. The choice of a rule is essentially contingent on the values and politics of the monetary economists and the requirements of the economy at one point in time—both in the short run as well as in the long run. Moreover, all monetary theories and policies offer coarse simplifications of reality: it is not possible for one policy rule to capture all economic variables affecting both inflation and unemployment in diverse monetary economies. Monetary policy rules are limited by factors that are observable and quantifiable. For example, policymakers are unable to observe and measure gaps in ideal/potential output and actual production, as is required by the Taylor Rule. Further, there are challenges in quantifying measures such as societal development, environmental impact, and underemployment—all aspects that are important to consider in a rule but might be weighted varyingly in different circumstances and by different economists.

Simplifying to the United States and the dual mandate of the Federal Reserve, is a rules-based approach the best way to achieve the goals of "maximum employment, stable prices, and moderate long-term interest rates"? The Friedman Rule would not work when dealing with the economic problems in a modern economy. For example, with the bust of the housing market bubble that led to the Great Recession of 2008, the Federal Reserve attempted to revive the economy with an expansionary monetary policy. The k percent rule would have dictated that the money supply growth rate be lowered to match the recessionary economic growth rate to keep inflation in check, thus requiring an increased interest rate. Instead, to spur economic growth, the Federal Reserve reduced interest rates to near zero and implemented a buying program of Treasury bills and securities. This led to a high growth rate of the money supply and to cries by some monetarists that the result of these actions would be inflation. Yet, high inflation failed to materialize. While implementing a ZIRP was not as effective as it could have been, arguably things would have been worse without the expansionary monetary policy (Kregel, 2014).

Practical application of the Taylor Rule has been commented on by several Federal Reserve officials, including Janet Yellen and Ben Bernanke. Internal documents from the 2009 and 2010 FOMC meetings suggest that attempting to follow the Taylor Rule in the 1970s discouraged the FOMC from taking corrective steps that could have sped up the recovery process (Kocherlakota, 2016). Orphanides (2003) argues that attempts to adhere to the Taylor Rule in the 1970s are partly what caused high inflation rates at the time. Bernanke (2015) has argued that monetary policy should be systematic in its economic judgments and policy decisions, and not automatic as the Taylor Rule would suggest. The increasing rigidity of Taylor's arguments to target inflation has been countered by Bernanke (2015), both in its ability to be implemented as well as its overlooking the required balance of maintaining employment in the economy. Yellen (2017) also argued that the prescriptions of the Taylor Rule, or any rule, would not take into account important considerations and outlook of the evolving economy, and may be faulty because estimates of key inputs may vary widely. Interestingly, the Federal Reserve attempted to implement ZIRP during the Great Recession and real interest rates remained positive because of deflation. The central bank then realized that nominal interest rates had to be *negative* to counter deflationary pressures and effectively boost employment and output (Pressman, 2019).

Friedman and the monetarists favored simple instrument-based rules for reasons of transparency and accountability. "Only instruments, not outcomes, are directly controlled by the state and hence government officials can be held accountable for their handling of instruments like the money supply, but not for what happens to outcomes like inflation" (Blinder, 1987, 402). However, Blinder further argued that outcomes such as price levels, unemployment, and output are the variables of ultimate concern to people—nobody directly bothers about an instrument like money supply. For this reason, some rules-based proponents argue that we ought to be "pursuing a rule with feedback from current economic conditions to the money supply" and that "[this] is better than following Friedman's advice" (Sargent, 1981, 553).

Though feedback functions are more developed and more dynamic, they are built on the same objective as a fixed rule: to keep policymakers accountable, to discourage central bankers from making decisions based on short-run circumstances, and to keep monetary outcomes relatively constant. Whether it is skepticism of policymakers intentions or of their know-how, rules proponents dislike discretionary monetary policy because they distrust policymakers. Keynes and Friedman both agreed on the necessity for the central bank to exhibit transparency and accountability. Keynes wrote that "the day-to-day policy of the Bank, its statistics, its technique and its immediate aims and objects should be as public as possible and should be deliberately exposed to outside criticism" ([1932] 1982, 131). Friedman (1960) believed that strict adherence to a rule forces central banks to be accountable in their policy. A fixed rule certainly makes the decisions of a central bank more predictable and accountable but monetary policy rules are rarely so simple. Rule adherence does not necessarily make a central bank's conceptual decisions and practical techniques transparent. Furthermore, a rules approach comes with the danger of framing monetary policy debates around the *rule* itself rather than the *goals* of the policy. Constituents might become more concerned with whether the policymaker is following a rule than whether the policy itself is helping people. Therefore, rule following does not inherently imply more accountability and transparency.

Given these quantification challenges and knowledge gaps, as well as the multitude of rules to choose from and their often-conflicting nature, the implementation of monetary policy rules is a logistical nightmare. If one asks, *can* we practically implement strict monetary policy rules? The answer is surely no. With these problems in mind, we now shift our fundamental question from *can* central banks abide by a rules-based approach to monetary policy, to *should* they?

5 All Rules Are not Made Equal: Political Economy of Monetary Policy

Each monetary policy framework is built on values and beliefs that are political. Rules would benefit certain classes of production at the cost of other classes and are not neutral in their effect on the population. In the orthodox tradition and the New Consensus, monetary policy rules heavily rely on the notion of rational standardized economic agents, but the economy is actually dependent upon the interactions of peoples with varying sets of knowledge and rationality. Hence, rules cannot be justified by appealing to economic rationality. Alternatively, in the tradition of post-Keynesianism, society is formed by a hierarchy of macroeconomic groups that engage in the production process—including financiers, capitalists, and workers. Any construction of a policy framework necessarily reflects the politics of the monetary authority, whether it be of maintaining the status quo or working toward equality. Monetary policy is determined by a political power struggle between the classes of production agents.

Monetary policy rules are not neutral in their effects on individuals and groups. If the central bank were to choose the Kansas City Rule over the Friedman Rule or the Smithin Rule over the Taylor Rule, there would be clear political implications. For instance, the Smithin Rule requires central banks to set the real interest rate near zero, which would imply changing inflation mandates for the central bank that typically dictate annual price increases of around two percent; the low real interest rate that results from this would benefit workers and firms (Pressman, 2020). By prohibiting "usury", or decreasing the scope for interest gains, this squeezes out the rentier class while helping businesses and consumers attain a larger portion of the output (Smithin, 2018, 208). Van Lear (2000) highlights the monetary policy of the late 1990s with high interest rates when the Federal Reserve implemented a high real interest rate policy while the stock market expanded. In this instance, the policy largely favored creditors and big businesses, who could issue stocks, over consumers and smaller firms, who depended on debt to raise funds. Further, Wray (1998) explains that fiscal policy also affects the level of bank reserves and the quantity of money; government spending increases reserves while taxation and sales of bonds in the open market decrease reserves. The Federal Reserve works with the Treasury to maintain positive interest rates through open market operations in order to control inflation. Politically, the Federal Reserve has actively attempted to limit the fiat money created by the government, as it may stimulate the economy to full employment and deficit spending may put upward pressures on the general price level. A fixed-rule policy regime would secure the remunerative returns to finance capitalists at the cost of the borrowers (Wray, 1998). Hansen et al. (2020) argue that central banks should, thus, deliberate on how their decisions affect income inequality. Concern over the winners and losers in the practice of monetary policy gets at the notion that (1) choosing a rule has political implications, and (2) blindly following rules obfuscate important socio-economic outcomes.

Rules that focus on long-run price stability would have socio-economic consequences that would harm vulnerable debtors. As Van Lear (2000, 33) argues, rules that prioritize price stability often "bias policy toward the protection of the purchasing power of money over ensuring sufficient economic vitality, which protects jobs and profits". Proponents of rules argue that these are merely hiccups, and that short-run costs do not exceed the long-run benefits of adhering to rules. But short-run costs *can* exceed long-run gains from rules, particularly when rules do not account for changing circumstances or exogenous shocks. Some rules, such as Friedman's, require monetary policy to be put on a pre-determined path; other rules, such as Taylor's, require the possible contingencies to be pre-determined. However, the social economy of a country is ever evolving and subject to change, which is why the short-run matters with its exigencies and adjustments. Opponents of rules argue that rules are too rigid to address complex politico-economic problems and that they would exacerbate economic inequalities. Brunner and Meltzer (1968) explained that, in ever-changing economies, there are often long-run losses resulting from policy decisions that are made based solely on historical understandings of monetary policy rather than decisions that are updated based on the discretion of the central bank. For example, the Federal Reserve's response to the Great Depression was inadequate primarily due to its reliance on its pre-1929 policy framework (Brunner & Meltzer, 1968). Strict adherence to a rule designed in a specific economic context might prove to be detrimental. Thus, the "short-term pain for long-term gain" argument that ardent rules proponents often tout is more socially stratified than they care to admit.

An alternative to the binary policy regimes of fixed rules and complete discretion would be a policy framework of inflation targeting, combined with a transparent rule as well as the flexibility of discretion. Discretion must be exercised in analyzing the context and requirements of the economy, constantly checking its subjectivity to change, after which a framework of policy rules may be designed to target inflation and unemployment. Rochon and Setterfield (2007) describe the Pasinetti Rule to be the apt high-growth low-inflation monetary policy rule in a high-inflation economy and the Smithin Rule to be the same apt rule, albeit in a low-inflation economy. In a high-inflation economy, the Pasinetti Rule would work to maintain the rentier class by setting the interest rate to the level of labor productivity growth. The Smithin Rule, on the other hand, would work to euthanize the rentier class with a zero real interest rate in a situation of low inflation. Hence, depending on the inflation frontier and the distributional objective of maintaining or destroying the rentier class, an incomes policy could trigger a switch in the monetary policy rule from a Pasinetti Rule to a Smithin Rule, or vice-versa. The maintenance of the rentier class, as supported by the Pasinetti Rule, may be required by certain economies that are dependent on non-capitalist systems of credit and finance. If it is believed that the non-capitalist systems are causing a blockage in capitalist development, then it could be argued that the rentier class needs to be euthanized, as would be the case from following the Kansas City or Smithin rules. Hence, discretion must be practiced in the face of economic context; only then can rules be framed and employed to target stability and economic growth.

6 Conclusion

A discretionary approach to monetary policy does not mean unsystematic or arbitrary policymaking: central bankers do not pull policy levers willy-nilly. There are systematic decision-making processes in which the bank's policy instruments are set to maximize their objectives. In fact, many proponents of discretionary monetary policy still use rules in everyday policy decisions! Rules like the Taylor Rule or the Smithin Rule can serve as useful guidelines for central bankers and allow them to pull from their insights when making policy decisions. As Keynes ([1936] 1973, 297) wrote, "The object of our analysis is not to provide a machine or method of blind manipulation which will furnish an infallible answer, but to provide ourselves with an organized and orderly method of thinking out our particular problems". Rules offer clear and useful intuition and might be worth following in many contexts and circumstances but should not, and logistically cannot, be mandated or blindly followed.

Discretionary policy allows central bankers to take as given current expectations and allows them to consider future expectations/policy as well as evolving socioeconomic circumstances. As discussed, some policy rules are biased toward the rentier class. Strict adherence to such a rule would harm workers with no relief in sight. On the other hand, policies that euthanize the rentier class are not always appropriate either, particularly in a world where climate change may soon require degrowth

(Pressman, 2020). The political economy of monetary policy rules ultimately prohibits class conscious policymakers from strict rule-following.

Ever-changing global economies and diverse political terrains bring about a wide variety of central banking needs. There is surely no "one size fits all" approach to monetary policy. Rules are not worth limiting the flexibility of central bankers to respond to vast economic changes. Rules are fallible and incomplete, and many can deepen economic inequality. Therefore, following a set of rules does not necessarily make central banks more accountable or transparent. In the face of socio-economic changes and updated information, monetary policy rules are simply meant to be broken.

References

Argy, V. (1988). A postwar history of the rules vs discretion debate. *PSL Quarterly Review, 41*(165), 147–177.

Beckworth, D. (2017). The knowledge problem in monetary policy: The case for nominal GDP targeting. *Mercatus on Policy Series*. https://www.mercatus.org/system/files/mercatus-beckworth-nominal-gdp-targeting-mop-2017-v1.pdf

Bernanke, B. (2015). The Taylor Rule: A benchmark for monetary policy? The Brookings Institution. https://www.brookings.edu/blog/ben-bernanke/2015/04/28/the-taylor-rule-a-benchmark-for-monetary-policy/

Blinder, A. (1987). The rules-versus-discretion debate in the light of recent experience. *Review of World Economics, 123*(3), 399–414.

Bowles, S., Gordon, D., & Weisskopf, T. (1990). *After the waste land: A democratic economics for the year 2000*. M.E. Sharpe.

Brunner, K., & Meltzer, A. (1968). What did we learn from the monetary experience of the United States in the Great Depression? *The Canadian Journal of Economics/revue Canadienne D'economique, 1*(2), 334–348.

Collis, R. B. (2018). Three essays on monetary macroeconomics: An empirical examination of the soundness of the alternative monetary model and monetary policy in Canada. Ph.D. Dissertation. York University.

Cornwall, J. (1994). *Economic breakdown and recovery: Theory and policy*. M.E. Sharpe.

Friedman, M. (1960). *A program for monetary stability*. Fordham University Press.

Friedman, M. (1969). The lag in effect of monetary policy. *The optimum supply of money and other essays* (pp. 237–260). Aldine Publishing Company.

Friedman, M. (1982). Monetary policy: Theory and practice. *Journal of Money, Credit and Banking, 14*(1), 98–118.

Friedman, M. (1995). The role of monetary policy. *Essential readings in economics* (pp. 215–231). Palgrave.
Friedman, M., & Schwartz, A. J. (1963). *A monetary history of the United States, 1867–1960*. Princeton University Press.
Hansen, N. J. H., Lin, A., & Mano, R. (2020). *Should inequality factor into central banks' decisions?* International Monetary Fund (No. 2020/196).
Hummel, J. (2017). Central bank control over interest rates: The myth and the reality. Mercatus Working Paper. https://www.mercatus.org/system/files/hummel-interest-rates-mercatus-working-paper-v2.pdf
Kaldor, N. (1985). *The scourge of monetarism*. Oxford University Press.
Karanassou, M., & Sala, H. (2014). The role of the wage-productivity gap in economic activity. *International Review of Applied Economics, 28*(4), 436–459.
Keynes, J. M. [1930] (1981). Minutes of evidence—Committee on Finance and Industry. In The collected writings of John Maynard Keynes (Vol. XX, pp. 38–311). Macmillan.
Keynes, J. M. [1932] (1982). The monetary policy of the Labour Party. In The collected writings of John Maynard Keynes (Vol. XXI, pp. 128–137). Macmillan.
Keynes, J. M. [1936] (1973). *The general theory of employment, interest and money*. In The collected writings of John Maynard Keynes (Vol. VII). Macmillan.
Kocherlakota, N. (2016). Rules versus discretion: A reconsideration. *Brookings Papers on Economic Activity, 2016*(2), 1–55.
Kregel, J. (2014). *Liquidity preference and the entry and exit to ZIRP and QE*. Levy Economics Institute (No. 14-5).
Lavoie, M. (1996). Monetary policy in an economy with endogenous credit money. *Money in motion* (pp. 532–545). Palgrave Macmillan.
Lavoie, M. (1999). *Fair rates of interest and Post-Keynesian economics: The Canadian case*. Presented at the University of Bourgogne.
McCallum, B. T. (1999). Issues in the design of monetary policy rules. *Handbook of macroeconomics* (Vol. 1, pp. 1483–1530). Elsevier.
Moore, B. (1988). The endogenous money supply. *Journal of Post Keynesian Economics, 10*(3), 372–385.
Orphanides, A. (2003). Historical monetary policy analysis and the Taylor rule. *Journal of Monetary Economics, 50*(5), 983–1022.
Orphanides, A. (2010). Taylor rules. *Monetary economics* (pp. 362–369). Palgrave Macmillan.
Palley, T. (2006). A Post-Keynesian framework for monetary policy: Why interest rate operating procedures are not enough. *Post-Keynesian Principles of Economic Policy* (pp. 78–98). Edward Elgar.
Palley, T. (2007). Macroeconomics and monetary policy: Competing theoretical frameworks. *Journal of Post Keynesian Economics, 30*(1), 61–78.

Pasinetti, L. (1981). *Structural change and economic growth*. Cambridge University Press.
Pollard, P. (2003). A look inside two central banks: The European Central Bank and the Federal Reserve. *Federal Reserve Bank of St. Louis Review, 85*, 11–30.
Pressman, S. (2019). How low can we go? The limits of monetary policy. *Review of Keynesian Economics, 7*(2), 137–150.
Pressman, S. (2020). Rethinking the theory of money, credit, and macroeconomics: A review essay. *Journal of Post Keynesian Economics, 43*, 1–13.
Rochon, L.-P., & Setterfield, M. (2007). Interest rates, income distribution, and monetary policy dominance: Post Keynesians and the "fair rate" of interest. *Journal of Post Keynesian Economics, 30*(1), 13–42.
Rochon, L.-P., & Setterfield, M. (2011). Post-Keynesian interest rate rules and macroeconomic performance: A comparative evaluation. In *Credit, Money and Macroeconomic Policy*. Edward Elgar.
Rivot, S. (2015). Rule-based frameworks in historical perspective: Keynes' and Friedman's monetary policies versus contemporary policy-rules. *European Journal of the History of Economic Thought, 22*(4), 601–633.
Sargent, T. (1981). The observational equivalence of natural and unnatural rate theories of macroeconomics. *Rational expectations and econometric practice* (Vol. 2, pp. 631–640). University of Minnesota Press.
Smithin, J. (2007). A real interest rate rule for monetary policy? *Journal of Post Keynesian Economics, 30*(1), 101–118.
Smithin, J. (2018). *Rethinking the theory of money, credit, and macroeconomics: A new statement for the twenty-first century*. Rowman & Littlefield.
Taylor, J. (1993). Discretion versus policy rules in practice. *Carnegie-Rochester Series on Public Policy, 39*, 195–214.
Taylor, J. B. (2017). Rules versus discretion: Assessing the debate over the conduct of monetary policy. NBER Working Paper 24149.
Van Ark, B., O'Mahoney, M., & Timmer, M. P. (2008). The productivity gap between Europe and the United States: Trends and causes. *Journal of Economic Perspectives, 22*(1), 25–44.
Van Lear, W. (2000). A review of the rules versus discretion debate in monetary policy. *Eastern Economic Journal, 26*(1), 29–39.
Wray, L. R. (1998). *Understanding modern money*. Edward Elgar.
Wray, L. R. (2007). A Post Keynesian view of central bank independence, policy targets, and the rules versus discretion debate. *Journal of Post Keynesian Economics, 30*(1), 119–141.
Yellen, J. (2015). Letter to Ryan and Pelosi. https://www.federalreserve.gov/foia/files/ryan-pelosi-letter-20151116.pdf
Yellen, J. (2017). Inflation, uncertainty, and monetary policy. *Business Economics, 52*(4), 194–207.

CHAPTER 4

How and When to Balance the Government Budget

Steven Pressman

1 Introduction

The debate over government debt has a long history within economics. David Hume ([1752] 1985) framed the question in terms of households, arguing that since debt was bad for individuals, it should be bad for the government as well. Adam Smith ([1776] 1937, Book 5, Ch. 3) feared that government debt would take resources away from the private sector, which would have employed them more productively, thereby reducing national wealth and slowing the growth of prosperity. Smith ([1776] 1937, 872) also noted a tendency for governments to run deficits in times of need, yet be 'unwilling and unable to increase their revenue' in normal times. Consequently, national debt (the sum of all past deficits) would grow in bad times and in good times. Smith preferred balanced government budgets, with spending equal to tax collections.

S. Pressman (✉)
Department of Economics, Colorado State University, Fort Collins, CO, USA
e-mail: pressman@monmouth.edu

S. Pressman and J. Smithin (eds.), *Debates in Monetary Macroeconomics*,
https://doi.org/10.1007/978-3-031-11240-9_4

On the other hand, John Maynard Keynes (1936) held that budget deficits were necessary during recessions. Despite a drop in tax revenues and rising debt due to the recession, fiscal policy had to be expansionary. Balancing the budget by cutting government spending, or engaging in austerity policies, would worsen economic slumps by curtailing total spending. The correct policy, Keynes argued, was greater government spending and more debt. Following Smith, Keynes seemed to express skepticism about the wisdom of continued and increasing government debt; instead, he favored the government running deficits during recessions and surpluses during economic expansions. Over the business cycle, the government budget would be balanced.

Since Keynes, many economists have emphasized the negative consequences of deficit spending by the government. One concern has been that expansionary fiscal policy would generate inflation. Another frequent concern is that government borrowing to enact Keynesian policy might reduce or crowd out other types of expenditure—investment, consumption, and foreign. If large enough, the net result will be little or no expansion. If severe, economic growth would fall. The policy implication of these views is that governments should seek to balance their budget and not incur debt.

More recently, modern monetary theory (MMT) has entered the debate on public debt. Like Keynes, MMT economists such as Stephanie Kelton (2020), Bill Mitchell et al. (2019), and Randall Wray (1998) argue that when demand is insufficient, greater government debt would have no negative economic consequences. Rather, it would stimulate the economy and create jobs. But MMT goes beyond Keynes, stressing the ability of governments to increase debt during good economic times in order to deliver things like a Green New Deal. This is possible as long as a country controls its own money supply, or has a sovereign currency, and as long as inflation remains subdued.

Thomas Piketty (2014, 2020) raised yet another concern about continual government debt—its distributional consequences. Seeing inequality as the major economic problem of our time (see Pressman, 2016, Ch. 3), Piketty blames public debt for increasing income and wealth inequality, and wants it eliminated via progressive taxes rather than cuts in needed government expenditures.

This chapter examines these four views regarding government debt. Section 2 looks at Ricardian Equivalence, the doctrine that the government always should balance its budget because deficits crowd out other forms of spending. Section 3 presents the views of Keynes on the need for expansionary fiscal policy. Then, Section 4 examines MMT and Section 5 looks at the work of Piketty. Section 6 concludes with an assessment of these views. It supports both Keynes and Piketty. Budget deficits are necessary during economic crises. At other times, governments should tax the rich in order to generate revenue for necessary government spending and to reduce inequality. And following Keynes, governments should strive for cyclically balanced budgets.

2 Ricardian Equivalence

David Ricardo shared Smith's concerns about public debt, and explained why public debt would hinder economic growth. For Ricardo [1817] (1951), the most important sort of private spending was business investment, as this led to the technological improvements necessary to ward off the stationary state, where economic growth would cease and living standards would stagnate. Public spending could not do this, he thought. It only leads to less private spending—no matter how this spending gets financed.

Ricardo's [1820] (1962) 'Essay on the Funding System' analyzed whether Britain should finance a war with £20 million in new taxes or whether it should borrow £20 million by printing government bonds (i.e. increasing government debt) *with an infinite maturity.* Ricardo assumed that annual interest payments on this debt would require future taxes of £1 million per annum. He did not contemplate the possibility that economic growth would lead to additional tax receipts, which would then be used to repay the debt. Nor did he foresee the possibility of rising government debt, but a constant debt-to-GDP ratio, thereby reducing the burden of public debt. Ricardo only cared about whether it was better to finance government spending now (through taxation) or later (through borrowing now and raising taxes later).

His answer to this question was 'it depends'. What it depends on is the rate of interest. At a rate of 5%, Ricardo concluded that the two alternatives were the same—the loss incurred would be equivalent. Households could give up £20 million now, by paying higher taxes; alternatively, they could take their £20 million and earn 5% interest (£1 million) each year. This interest income would enable households to pay taxes in the future and enable the government to pay interest on its debt. In both cases, government spending would reduce or crowd out other spending. In one case higher taxes would reduce income and spending; in the other case, the need to pay future taxes reduces current spending and increases savings.

In fact, Ricardo ([1817] 1951, 247–249) was skeptical that people would lower their spending by £20 million to pay future taxes if a war was funded with borrowed money. He feared that people would follow the example set by the government and become less thrifty. So Ricardo did not think the two financing methods were actually equivalent. They were also not equivalent at interest rates other than 5%. At rates greater than 5%, households would come out ahead with debt financing; if rates were below 5%, they would come out behind and be better off if they were taxed £20 million one time than to be taxed forever to pay the £1 million of interest on the £20 million debt.

Robert Barro (1979), who is responsible for the modern coinage of the expression 'Ricardian Equivalence', bypassed these nuances in Ricardo. He assumed that people were rational and forward-looking, and wanted to leave money to their heirs. Given these assumptions, rational households would realize that they can pay £1 million in future taxes only if they saved the entire amount that the government borrowed from them rather than taxing them. From the life-cycle theory of consumption (see Modigliani & Brumberg, 1954), which assumes that people want to spread their consumption evenly throughout their lifetime, it follows that when governments run deficits, people spend less now so they will be able to pay their future tax bill. Public spending, financed with borrowing, is countered—dollar for dollar, and pound for pound—by reduced consumer spending.

Budget deficits also crowd out business investment. The economic argument here is straightforward (see Blanchard, 1984; Evans, 1987). When the government goes into debt, it prints bonds and then seeks to sell them. This extra money enables the government to spend more than it collects in tax revenue. As the government sells more bonds, bond prices must fall. Since bond prices and interest rates are inversely related, greater government debt will raise interest rates and reduce investment.

Higher interest rates likewise crowd out foreign spending because they attract capital from abroad seeking higher returns. This appreciates the domestic currency which, in turn, makes imports cheaper and leads consumers to buy foreign rather than domestic goods. It also makes exports more expensive, reducing sales to foreign countries. Even Keynes (1981, 479) recognized this problem and how it limited the ability to effectively employ fiscal policy, noting 'serious limitations to what can be done by a single country which belongs to a world system'.

3 Keynes and the Cyclically Balanced Budget

Despite this proviso, Keynes (1936) made the macroeconomic case for increased government debt during the Great Depression. His theory of effective demand held that spending drove economic growth and created jobs, and that public spending financed by borrowing was needed whenever private spending was insufficient.

Keynes (1936) thought consumer spending was relatively stable because the spending habits of people at the aggregate level determine consumption as a whole, and these habits were largely stable. While some people might change their behavior a little and spend a bit more, others will change their behavior and spend a bit less. These two changes will come close to balancing each other out. The simple Keynesian consumption function, $C = a + bYD$, reflects this. Some consumption, a, is needed to meet the needs of survival. It doesn't depend on one's income, or it is the consumption that needs to take place when income is zero. There is also an increase in consumption as disposable income (YD, or income less taxes) rises, represented by b, which has a value of less than 1. Other factors (both objective and subjective) also may affect consumption, but these are less important than disposable income.

Investment, in contrast, is driven by fickle expectations, which Keynes (1936, 161) called 'animal spirits'. Changes in business confidence regarding the future of the economy would change the level of investment and impact the economy. Moreover, self-fulfilling prophesies come into the picture. When businesses are confident, they invest more and the economy expands. This boom reinforces expectations about profits, leading to greater optimism and investment. Conversely, expectations of a poorly performing economy in the future will lower investment, slow economic activity, and reinforce business pessimism about future profits. When optimism prevails, economies boom; when pessimism sets in, there will be dramatic declines in investment and massive unemployment.

The Keynesian solution to such volatility was to have government stabilize the level of investment. When private investment was low, the government should borrow money and engage in public investments such as building new roads and bridges as well as spending more money on schools and hospitals. This would expand the economy as well as improve expectations regarding the future. In contrast, when business investment was high due to great optimism, the government should stop borrowing, repay past loans, and cut back on public investment. Keynes (1936, 378) mistitled his policy 'the socialization of investment'. He actually sought a 'stabilization of investment' by the government in order to stabilize the economy.

Additionally, government investment spending would have multiplier effects (Keynes, 1936, 115). Individuals receiving more income due to expansionary fiscal policy would spend a large fraction of it—the *b* in Keynes's consumption function. This spending would be another person's income, leading to even more spending, and more income. If expansionary fiscal policy improved business expectations regarding future profits, and so increased business investment, it would have an even larger economic effect as in the multiplier–accelerator model set forth by Paul Samuelson (1939). Likewise, consumer spending will *increase* if government investment improves consumer expectations regarding future income, or generates wealth effects as a result of greater business profits (Keynes 1936, Ch. 8). Also, expansionary economic policy can make the distribution of income more equal. Since spending propensities are likely to be greater for those with lower income, getting more disposable income to those at the bottom half of the distribution (either through tax cuts or expenditure programs) will result in an even greater economic impact (Keynes, 1936, 94–95).

Keynes clearly supported greater government debt during difficult economic times. A little less clear is whether he favored continued budget deficits and rising debt over the long term. Most commentators (Kregel, 1983; Seccarrecia, 1995; Brown-Collier & Collier, 1995) believe that Keynes supported a cyclically balanced budget. Many times Keynes (1980, 225, 277, 352, 406) distinguished between capital government budgets and current government budgets, similar to what business firms do. He maintained that the current budget should be balanced all the time, and that the capital budget should finance government investment. The question is whether Keynes thought that the capital budget should be balanced over the business cycle. In a letter to James Meade, Keynes (1980, 319–320) contended that government capital expenditures would pay for themselves, implying a balanced capital budget over time. And Keynes (1980, 278) called the accumulation of public debt to finance government expenditures 'dead-weight loss'. These remarks suggest that Keynes wanted governments to borrow during bad economic times and spend the borrowed money on public investments that would yield future gains for the nation. In good economic times, governments would run budget surpluses, using their excess tax revenue to pay back prior debt on the government's capital account.

4 Modern Monetary Theory

Modern Monetary Theory (MMT) arose in the 1990s. It conjoins insights from several economists, including Abba Lerner ([1943] 1955) on functional finance (Wray, 1998, 18, 32) and Georg Fredrich Knapp [1924] 1973) on state control of money (called 'chartalism').

Lerner directly addressed the issue of government debt. He wrote at a time when government debt levels were extremely high in developed nations because of the military expenditures necessary to fight World War II. By the end of the war, the debt-to-income ratio was around 120% in the US and 250% in the UK. Moreover, Alvin Hansen (1939) and other economists feared that the world economy would return to depression once the war ended. Businesses would hesitate to invest because without government spending on the war there would be inadequate demand for the goods they produced. This, in turn, would increase unemployment and reduce spending, leading to further reluctance to invest. The result would be 'sick recoveries which die in their infancy and depressions which feed on themselves' (Hansen, 1939, 4). Fiscal policy thus faced a dilemma. Governments could run budget surpluses after the war, and risk worsening a post-war slump, or they could engage in expansionary fiscal policy and risk creating economic problems due to huge government debt.

Paul Samuelson (1948) proposed one way around this dilemma with his balanced budget multiplier. If the government increased taxes and increased government spending by equal amounts there would be no immediate impact on the government budget. However, there would be a *positive economic impact*. Increasing taxes and increasing government spending by an equal amount would raise total spending in the economy because the government would be taxing some income that otherwise would have been saved (since b in the Keynesian consumption function is less than 1), and then spending this money. The economy would therefore grow. Samuelson demonstrated that GDP would grow by an amount equal to the (identical) increase in government spending and taxes. That is, the balanced budget multiplier had a value of 1. Conversely, equal declines in government spending and taxes would reduce GDP by this amount.

Lerner ([1943] 1955) provided another escape route from the debt dilemma. He maintained that as long as someone was willing to lend money to the government, there should be no crowding out. By borrowing money that people already decided to save, the government wouldn't have to accept lower prices for their bonds and offer higher rates of return to obtain funds. Even with little demand for new government bonds, the central bank could monetize the debt by printing money and purchasing government bonds. Lerner noted that functional finance didn't mean governments would always have large debt. Following Keynes, he thought that improved profit expectations can crowd in investment spending and that increased wealth due to greater holdings of government bonds would increase consumption. So, during good economic times more tax revenues would accrue to the government, reducing the debt burden. Finally, if all else failed, the government could tax the rich rather than borrow from them, anticipating Samuelson's balanced budget multiplier.

MMT takes things one step beyond Lerner. It points out that when countries control their own currency (the chartalist point) governments face few constraints on their spending. Unlike the private sector, governments can create money and then spend it. This is possible as long as countries have their own central bank that serves as lender of last resort to the government, and buys the new government bonds that finance greater government spending. Effectively, money gets created by the national central bank to fund government debt. When the government prints bonds and the central bank buys them, government bank balances increase at the central bank (as your bank balance would increase if you borrowed money from a bank). This money will then get spent by the government, putting money into the bank accounts of people and firms, which will then be spent.

Here is another way to look at this solution. Ricardo recognized only two sources for government spending, taxes and borrowing, when arguing that these two financing methods were equivalent in their economic impact. Following Lerner, MMT adds a third way for government spending to increase when necessary—credit and money creation (Mitchell et al., 2019).

This last option is possible only if countries control their own currency, the insight of chartalism. With its own central bank, the USA can create as much money as it wishes as long as monetary policy supports fiscal policy. As a nation, through its central bank, it has the ability to control the amount of legal tender in circulation that can be used to buy things or repay debts. Countries such as Ecuador, El Salvador, and Panama, which use the US dollars for monetary transactions, cannot. Euro nations also cannot create money because they lack a national central bank to serve as lender of last resort and buy government bonds. That decision gets made by the European Central Bank, comprised of representatives from the Euro-using nations. German central bankers, fearing inflation, may not approve buying French government bonds to create more employment in France (and maybe less employment in Germany if Euroland interest rates rise). Or, as with the case of Greece during the Great Recession, a nation may need to spend money to deal with a domestic economic crisis, but can't because European central bankers won't purchase Greek bonds, or help to create more money in Greece (Varoufakis, 2017).

As long as a nation controls its own money supply and interest rates, MMT challenges the standard belief that more government debt will raise interest rates and crowd out other spending. Money creation allows for more government spending; and this government spending provides money to the private sector. Firms and individuals will put their money into the banking system, increasing the ability of banks to lend. Interest rates will not rise. In contrast to the standard crowding out argument, interest rates might even fall as banks seek to make more loans (Connors & Mitchell, 2013).

While MMT and Keynes agree on short-run policy concerning the government budget, they differ when it comes to the long run. Keynes, as we saw, advocated a balanced government budget in the long run. MMT allows for the possibility of continued deficits, as well as government debt that rises in absolute terms and relative to GDP in the long run. The only threat from government debt, according to MMT, is inflation. If this becomes a problem, governments can raise taxes.

Adherents of MMT, however, are skeptical that inflation will become a problem due to large government debt. They point to cases where governments have run large deficits and accumulated massive debt without increasing the inflation rate. Perhaps the best example of this is Japan over the past three decades. Fearing deflation since the 1990s, the Japanese government has been trying to get inflation to rise. Debt has increased and interest rates have been at near zero, in the hope of stimulating the economy (Connors & Mitchell, 2013, 12). Yet, prices have remained stable.

Freed from the constraint of raising revenue by either raising taxes or borrowing, MMT allows national governments to focus on the macroeconomic goals of keeping both unemployment and inflation low. Changes in government spending can deal with the unemployment problem, perhaps with a job guarantee (Tcherneva, 2020). Government spending can also be used to finance a Green New Deal or other economic policies that may be seen as desirable, such as the repair of decaying infrastructure and funding education. Tax policy is left to deal with the problem of inflation.

MMT received considerable attention during the Covid-19 pandemic, when governments abandoned the pretense of needing to balance their budget. Instead, they focused on getting money to people so that they could stay inside, not infect others, and reduce covid-related deaths. Central banks pushed interest rates to zero. Central governments borrowed and spent money unconcerned about crowding out, knowing that central banks would purchase new government bonds if necessary. In the US, several bills threw money at people, including direct payments to individuals[1] and expanded unemployment insurance. The Payroll Protection Plan aided businesses. It gave loans to firms that kept employees on their payroll. These loans would not have to be repaid if firms maintained their payroll. The total amount spent on these programs was enormous in historical terms and relative to the size of the US economy. The US deficit rose from $779 billion (or 3.8% of GDP) in fiscal year 2018 to $2.77 trillion (13.2% of GDP) in fiscal year 2021. The US economy became an MMT experiment. Other nations employed similar policies. Like the Federal Reserve, the European Central Bank sharply increased its bond purchases from Euro nations, enabling governments to borrow and spend more money, thereby helping its citizens survive the worldwide health crisis. The UK Coronavirus Job Retention Scheme provided a form of wage and job insurance for workers; it was funded with money created by the Bank of England.

5 Piketty, Inequality, and Debt

In contrast to Barro, Keynes, and MMT, Piketty is not concerned about macroeconomic issues related to the public debt. Instead he worries about its distributional effects.[2] Like Keynes and MMT, Piketty recognizes that additional government spending is needed in recessionary times. However, Piketty (2014, 567) fears the impact of government debt on inequality and wants government debt 'reduced as quickly as possible', presumably once economic recovery begins. Likewise, Piketty (2014, 564; 2020, 912) wants a quick reduction in public debt that has piled up for many decades because of its impact on income and wealth inequality. He sees tax hikes as a more effective way to euthanize the rentier than Keynes's plan to have government investment stabilize total investment spending.

Similar to Smith and Ricardo, Piketty (2014, 134–135) raises concerns about public debt crowding out investment; and, like Smith, Piketty (2020, 609–610) worries about changes in the stock of national capital. However, this is not his main concern regarding public debt. In *Capital in the Twenty-First Century*, Piketty (2014, 135) criticizes adherents of Ricardian Equivalence for not recognizing that most government debt is owned by the very rich. In addition, he notes that public wealth has remained relatively constant over time as a percentage of GDP and that most changes in national wealth stem from changes in private wealth. However, things did change in the late 2010s due to changes in public wealth. *Capital and Ideology* (Piketty 2020, 610) points out that when *Capital in the Twenty-First Century* was published only Italy had negative net worth given the data available then. As nations recovered from the Great Recession, governments never eliminated their budget deficits; rather, they kept increasing their debt. One of the best examples of this is the 2017 Trump tax cut, which increased US government debt by $2 trillion over 10 years. As a result of such actions, net public capital or wealth in most developed nations is now close to zero (less than 5% of national capital), and both the UK and the US have negative public capital. This means that even if the government sold all its assets, it couldn't repay its creditors. More importantly, the lack of public capital makes it harder for nations to solve key problems such as climate change, and inadequate and unequal educational opportunities (Piketty 2020, 613).

Further, as debt levels rise, more and more tax revenue goes to pay interest on the public debt. This, too, limits the ability of governments to solve national problems. But there is a more important problem according to Piketty. A large majority of government bonds are owned by the very wealthy, and when the government borrows from the wealthy to finance its deficit, wealth accrues to those at the top of the distribution, especially compared to the alternative, which is to increase taxes on the wealthy.

Since the rich receive returns on this wealth, income inequality and wealth inequality both grow.

Worried about the size of government debt and its distributional impact, Piketty looks at four ways governments have historically reduced their debt—inflation, austerity, debt repudiation, and tax hikes.

A first solution is to take the easy way out and sow the seeds of inflation. This is the typical government response to debt problems, according to Piketty (2014, 546). It was the solution the UK government employed to repay the savings it forced on its citizens to pay for fighting World War II. Piketty objects to this solution because of how inflation impacts people. Fearing inflation, he contends, people tend to spend less. He also fears the impact of inflation on bank lending rates. More importantly, there are adverse distributional effects of inflation. The rich, whose wealth consists of largely of real estate and/or financial assets, are better able to escape the real wealth effects of inflation than the middle class or the poor. Piketty (2020, 441) thus sees inflation as 'a regressive tax on wealth'.

Several problems plague this argument. First, many at the bottom of the income distribution are net debtors who gain as inflation reduces their real debt; and those at the bottom half of the wealth distribution have few, if any, assets to drop in value. Second, as Piketty (2014) himself shows, the assets of the middle class are largely real estate holdings; if the rich escape the ravages of inflation because of their real estate holdings, so too should the middle class. Third, Piketty (2020, 442) believes that stock prices rise with inflation. However, a large empirical literature has found an inverse relationship between inflation and real stock prices (see Campbell & Vuolteenaho, 2004). To take one historical example, as US inflation rose during the 1970s, stock prices stagnated. A tiny gain in nominal terms over the decade was overwhelmed by inflation, leading to a nearly 50% decline in real terms. Once the Volker recession of the early 1980s killed inflation, stock prices soared.

Despite the problems with his argument, Piketty's conclusion seems correct—inflation does have undesirable distributional consequences. Frederick Taylor (2013) explains why in his book on German hyperinflation between the two world wars. According to Taylor, businessmen repaid their loans with devalued money, and the price of their finished output rose well above their production costs due to inflation. The rich were able to buy foreign currency and escape the ravages of inflation from a depreciating mark. Farmers were able to sell the food they grew at high prices in cities. Some urban workers had a little bit of protection from inflation, since their wages tended to rise with inflation. The big losers were the middle class (civil servants, teachers, and small business owners). They couldn't hold assets in foreign currencies. Many were on fixed incomes (e.g., war pensions); others, patriotically, lent the government their life savings to support the war effort and then were repaid in worthless marks. This led to other undesirable outcomes. The strongest supporters of right-wing German politicians were those who grew up in middle-class families decimated by the hyperinflation.[3]

A second solution to the debt problem is for governments to pursue austerity, reducing spending and using existing tax revenues to pay down the public debt. Austerity has been a controversial approach to debt reduction. Its supporters claim it boosts confidence in the private sector, thereby increasing investment and offsetting any economic drag from reduced government spending (Alesina & Ardagna, 2010). Paul Krugman (2012) has mocked this view, calling its adherents believers in 'confidence fairies' who will counter the negative economic effects of austerity. Other economists oppose austerity because it kills economic growth (Blyth, 2013; Schui, 2014). Piketty (2014, 542) dislikes the austerity solution for another reason—it abrogates the responsibility of the state to provide health, education, and security to its citizens.

A third way to reduce government debt is through default, or failing to repay bondholders. Piketty (2014, 542) opposes this solution because it is not clear who will lose from it. While it might seem that bondholders will bear the entire cost of a default, since they won't get repaid the money they lent to the government, this may not be true when accounting for ancillary effects. Financial institutions hold a great deal of government bonds and will take a beating. While small depositors are protected by insurance, a government default will reduce bank capital and lending ability. Small and medium-sized businesses typically rely on bank loans for financing. Large firms have retained earnings that they can use for investment purposes, have access to capital markets, and can sell stocks and bonds to raise funds for investment.

Last, but not least, we come to Piketty's preferred solution for paying off the national debt—tax hikes. To reduce the drag on government spending from interest payments on past debt made to the wealthy, Piketty (2020, 444–445) prefers a rapid reduction in public debt. He contends that countries which have done this (via progressive income and estate taxes) have seen large reductions in wealth inequality, along with a subsequent reduction in income inequality. How revenue gets raised is as important for Piketty as paying off the debt. Revenues must come from taxing those most able to pay. *Capital in the Twenty-First Century* proposes a small annual wealth tax of 1–2% to reduce inequality. However, Piketty (2014, 518) doesn't see this as a viable way to finance government spending in the long term because the tax would also reduce wealth inequality (its main purpose), and so reduce the revenues that accrue from the tax. Additional revenue for government expenditures will need to come from income taxes on corporations and wealthy individuals. However, in the short run, before a wealth tax reduces inequality, it can generate a great deal of revenue. For this reason, Piketty (2014, 542) supports a one-time tax on private capital of around 15% in order to pay off most existing public debt.

6 Settling Some Questions About Public Debt

US President Harry Truman used to joke that he was on the lookout for a one-armed economist because, whenever he asked his economic advisors what they thought, they would respond with something like: 'on the one hand, ... but on the other hand ...'. Things are worse with respect to public debt because we have four perspectives here. Each brings something to our understanding of government debt. Keynes explained why balancing the government budget during an economic slump was the wrong policy and would worsen existing macroeconomic problems. The doctrine of Ricardian Equivalence raised concerns about higher interest rates and reduced private spending due to government debt. Emphasizing that government debt can be financed by money creation, MMT answered the crowding out argument and opened policy space for increasing government spending and government debt whenever this was necessary, even during times of economic boom. Piketty raised questions about the sustainability and desirability of large public debt due to its distributional consequences, and suggested how we should go about reducing it.

Each perspective also has limitations. Behavioral economists have questioned the rationality assumption implicit in Ricardian Equivalence. Psychologist Daniel Kahneman (2011) demonstrated that people don't behave this way and won a Nobel Prize in Economics for his efforts. And Hubbard and Judd (1986) note that many people are liquidity constrained and need their current income to meet their daily expenses;

they will spend any additional money rather than save it in order to pay future taxes.[4]

Keynes had no theory to explain the limits of public debt. It is not clear why governments need to run cyclically balanced budgets, why continued debt is problematic, or why public debt can't debt grow in tandem with GDP. Further, after World War II, Keynes himself supported large government spending programs that were likely to be budget busters—child allowances (Pressman, 2014) and the National Health Service (Carter, 2020, 364)—and he was instrumental in getting these programs enacted in the UK. Another problem, raised by Larry Summers (2016) concerns secular stagnation, the issue that worried Hansen. If economies always suffer from insufficient demand, and if Keynesian stimulative policies require greater debt in such circumstances, it is impossible and undesirable to balance the budget over the business cycle. Large government deficits that pile up and increase debt over time will be necessary to deal with persistent tendencies toward recession.

MMT is overly optimistic about its tax solution to inflation. If inflation is a distributional problem as Post Keynesians contend (Lavoie, 2014, Ch. 8),[5] it is not clear how higher taxes might solve this problem. Tax changes would likely favor some groups more than others, exacerbating distributional conflicts. Even if taxes change the income of each group proportionately, this won't resolve the distributional conflict. Since the conflict remains in both cases, inflationary pressures should endure despite the tax changes. On the other hand, if inflation is a demand problem, as MMT seems to imply, raising taxes on the rich won't help much, as the government will mainly be taxing savings. Even taxing the rich indirectly, via higher corporate income taxes, won't help. Large corporations with monopolistic power are likely to respond by raising prices, fueling inflationary pressures. To reduce demand with tax policy it is necessary to tax spenders—the poor and the middle class. Although this will solve the inflation problem, it will worsen the distributional problem pointed out by Piketty and recognized by MMT economists. Finally, there are political economy reasons governments don't raise taxes often—people don't like having to pay higher taxes, and typically they don't vote for politicians who want to raise their taxes or have done so. In 2021, the US economy experienced a 7% inflation rate. Politicians, central bankers, and average citizens all looked at this as a problem. Yet no one was talking about raising taxes to solve the problem. Democrats were talking about increasing spending to create and maintain employment; Republicans opposed this spending, but they were also opposed to raising taxes to deal with this problem or any other problem.

In a similar vein, Piketty is too optimistic about the wealth taxes being able to reduce government debt. Pressman (2016, Ch. 7) identifies several problems with taxing wealth—asset evaluation issues, liquidity issues, security issues, and tax avoidance issues. There is also a practical issue with taxing wealth, especially with Piketty's proposal to eliminate existing public debt with a 15% wealth tax. It cannot be done quickly, as Piketty wants. In the USA, for example, a Constitutional amendment was needed to begin taxing income; the Supreme Court will likely use this as a precedent for taxing wealth. Changes to the US Constitution need a super-majority—two-thirds of the US House and the Senate, as well as three-quarters of US states, must approve any Constitutional change. This will take a very long time to accomplish, especially given the current political situation in the USA and the influence of money on politics. In addition, as Piketty recognizes, a wealth tax must be global in order to keep assets from moving to countries that don't tax wealth and can't report wealth holdings to other nations because they have no records of this. Every nation must quickly pass a wealth tax before any nation can use it to reduce government debt.

At bottom, the issues raised by these different perspectives on government debt are largely empirical. So we should be able to bring some evidence to bear on these positions.

Of all the theories, Ricardian Equivalence has been tested most; the empirical results don't provide much support for it. Even Barro (1989, 49), one of its strongest advocates, notes that the 'results are all over the map'. A meta-analysis by T.D. Stanley (1998) likewise finds great variability in results and little empirical support for Ricardian Equivalence. Many studies have found no evidence that larger government deficits increase household savings rates. Summers and Carroll (1987) found that savings rates tend to *fall* when budget deficits rise (including during times of recession) and take this as a conclusive refutation of Ricardian Equivalence. The same holds for other countries (Masson et al., 1995). Another empirical issue concerns the crowding out of investment. The evidence here indicates that there is little or no crowding out due to government deficit spending. Eisner (1986) and Pressman (1994) find that fiscal policy tends to crowd in rather than crowd out investment. Reviewing the large empirical literature on this topic, Huntley (2014) finds that crowding out is estimated to range from 15 to 50%, with a central estimate of around 33%. Each $100 of additional government deficit spending reduces other spending by $33 and results in $67 of net expenditure, increasing economic growth considerably. Summing up this literature, Stanley (2001, 137) concludes: 'Ricardian Equivalence … is strongly rejected by the empirical literature as a whole'.

The failure of Ricardian Equivalence supports the position of Keynes—in times of recession, expansionary fiscal policy can increase employment with little or no negative macroeconomic effects. The success of Keynesian policies over the past century provides further support for the position of Keynes. The Great Depression did not end while governments attempted to balance their budgets. The New Deal helped mitigate the problem to some extent and it did reduce some of the suffering due to extremely high unemployment, but it failed to end the depression. Unemployment fell sharply only when governments engaged in massive deficit spending to fight World War II. Post-war deficit spending, for example the US GI Bill, propped up demand as military spending fell. It contributed to a post-war boom and prevented the depression that Hansen and others feared (Bennett, 1996). And the world economy did not go into a depression due to the coronavirus pandemic because governments spent money liberally in order to keep households and businesses afloat during a lockdown imposed for health reasons. Immense government spending neither increased interest rates nor reduced consumer spending. Finally, and in accord with Keynes's call for public investment, numerous studies have found that government investment spending increases economy-wide productivity growth, by an amount not that different from private investment (Aschauer, 1989, 1990; Pressman, 1994).

Few direct empirical tests of either MMT or Piketty on the consequences of public debt have been published. Indirectly, the strong evidence against crowding out supports MMT. Also providing some support for MMT is the fact that sharply rising government spending and government debt during the Great Recession did not lead to inflation, although many economists feared this would happen. Finally, there is some econometric evidence showing that increases in government debt don't lead to rising inflation (Hafner & Hein, 1988). On the other hand, rising government debt due to the coronavirus pandemic seems correlated with rising inflation rates. Whether this is due more to demand factors stemming from government stimulus policies or to supply-side factors (such as supply chain problems) remains an unanswered question for now.

Piketty raises an important issue often ignored by the macroeconomists weighing in on the issue of public debt—its impact on inequality. Few studies have looked at this question empirically. Agnello and Sousa (2014) find that it makes a difference whether greater public debt arises from spending increases or from tax cuts. As one might expect, cutting government spending worsens inequality while tax hikes equalize incomes. Other evidence bearing on this question comes from economic history. The world began a tax-cutting experiment in the late twentieth century. USA President Ronald Reagan and UK Prime Minister Margaret Thatcher enacted large tax breaks for the wealthy; they then borrowed this money back from wealthy individuals in order to pay for the tax cuts. In addition, a good deal of government spending was funded by borrowing money from the wealthy rather than taxing them. This ushered in an era of rising inequality, with a larger share of national income going to the very rich. According to Piketty (2014, 300), the share of total income in the USA going to the top 1% rose from 10% (starting in the 1950s and running through the end of the 1970s) and reached 20% by the 2000s. On the other hand, the middle class shrank and went into greater debt, borrowing money for home and auto purchases, a college education and general living expenses (Scott & Pressman, 2013). Similar trends hold for many other high-income nations (Piketty, 2014) and even for many lesser developed nations (Piketty, 2020).

Finally, substantial empirical research is relevant to the question of public debt and inequality. Inequality has large economic costs in terms of economic growth and employment (Charles-Coll, 2013), as Keynes pointed out. It may also be responsible for the problem of secular stagnation. Furthermore, inequality has negative effects on health (Wilkinson, 1996), even controlling for macroeconomic variables, such as economic growth and the rate of unemployment. And, as Wilkinson and Pickett (2009) demonstrate, inequality has large social costs, including an adverse impact on drug use, crime, educational outcomes, and social mobility (also see Payne, 2017).

Two conclusions regarding government debt follow from this. First, there is a strong case for increasing taxes on the rich in order to mitigate inequality and avoid its costs. This supports Piketty's call for reducing public debt by taxing the rich rather than cutting government expenditures or borrowing money from them, and for financing government spending by taxing the rich under normal circumstances, rather than borrowing money from them. While taxing wealth is problematic for a number of reasons, there are a wealth of other options available—raising the corporate income tax, increasing top individual income tax rates, instituting a financial transactions tax, and increasing estate and inheritance taxes, to name a few.

A second conclusion we can draw about public debt concerns Ricardian Equivalence and Keynes. The evidence against Ricardian Equivalence and for the efficacy of Keynesian economic policy during recessions is quite strong. Increasing public debt during bad economic times is essential economic policy. Austerity worsens the immediate economic problem. Things are a bit different in the long run. Besides leading to greater inequality, large and growing deficits and greater government debt may reduce the political will to employ Keynesian policies, and increase deficits and government debt during the next great recession. This supports the remarks by Keynes on the need for cyclically balanced government budgets, or something close to it. Running surpluses in good economic times is one way to ensure that there is little debt when an economic crisis begins and a vigorous policy response is needed.

Combining the insights of Keynes and Piketty, governments should run deficits (to finance government investment spending) during recessions and pay down public debt during economic expansions, when tax revenues from past government investment come into the Treasury and when taxes can be increased on the wealthy without worrying about any negative macroeconomic consequences.

Notes

1. Most people received $1200 from the March 2020 CARES Act, followed by $600 in December 2020 and $1400 in March 2021.
2. Michl (2009, 14, 270) anticipated Piketty here, arguing that government debt redistributes wealth upward, contributing to wealth and income inequality.
3. Keynes (1923) likewise held that inflation after World War I destroyed the British middle class.
4. There is one more flaw in Ricardo—other things being equal (or equivalent), the rich will prefer to be taxed in the future and lend money to the government. This maintains their wealth and power, including their ability to influence future legislation so that (perhaps) they are not taxed in the future.
5. Kelton and Wray both have Post Keynesian leanings, with Wray serving as co-editor of the *Journal of Post Keynesian Economics*. Coincidentally, Piketty

(2020, 442) also sees inflation as a sign that society 'is dealing with a serious distributional conflict'.

References

Agnello, L., & Sousa, R. (2014). How does fiscal consolidation impact on income inequality? *Review of Income and Wealth, 60*, 702–726.

Alesina, A., & Ardagna, S. (2010). Large changes in fiscal policy: Taxes versus spending. In J. Brown (Ed.), *Tax policy and the economy* (pp. 35–68). University of Chicago Press.

Aschauer, D. (1989). Is public expenditure productive? *Journal of Monetary Economics, 23*, 177–200.

Aschauer, D. (1990). Why is infrastructure important? In A. Munnell (Ed.), *Is there a shortfall in public capital investment?* (pp. 69–103). Federal Reserve Bank of Boston.

Barro, R. (1979). On the determinants of the public debt. *Journal of Political Economy, 87*, 940–971.

Barro, R. (1989). The Ricardian approach to budget deficits. *Journal of Economic Perspectives, 3*, 37–54.

Bennett, M. (1996). *When dreams came true: The GI Bill and the making of modern America*. Brassey's.

Blanchard, O. (1984). Current and anticipated deficits, interest rates and economic activity. *European Economic Review, 25*, 7–27.

Blyth, M. (2013). *Austerity: The history of a dangerous idea*. Oxford University Press.

Brown-Collier, E., & Collier, B. (1995). What Keynes really said about deficit spending. *Journal of Post Keynesian Economics, 17*, 341–355.

Campbell, J., & Vuolteenaho, T. (2004). Inflation illusion and stock prices. *American Economic Review, 94*, 19–23.

Carter, Z. (2020). *The price of peace: Money, democracy, and the life of John Maynard Keynes*. Random House.

Charles-Coll, J. (2013). The debate over the relationship between income inequality and economic growth: Does inequality matter for growth? *Research in Applied Economics, 5*, 1–18.

Connors, L., & Mitchell, W. (2013). *Framing modern monetary theory.* Working Paper No. 06-13, Centre of Full Employment and Equity, Charles Darwin University.

Eisner, R. (1986). *How real is the deficit?* Macmillan.
Evans, P. (1987). Interest rates and expected future budget deficits in the United States. *Journal of Political Economy, 95*, 34–58.
Hafer, R., & Hein, S. (1988). Further evidence on the relationship between federal government debt and inflation. *Economic Inquiry, 26*, 239–251.
Hansen, A. (1939). Economic progress and declining population growth. *American Economic Review, 29*, 1–15.
Hubbard, R. G., & Judd, K. (1986). Constraints, fiscal policy, and consumption. *Brookings Papers on Economic Activity* #1, 1–50.
Hume, D. [1752] (1985). Of public credit. In *Essays: Moral, political and literary*. Liberty Fund.
Huntley, J. (2014). *The long-run effects of federal budget deficits on national saving and private domestic investment*. Congressional Budget Office.
Kahneman, D. (2011). *Thinking, fast and slow.* Farrar, Straus & Giroux.
Kelton, S. (2020). *The deficit myth.* Public Affairs.
Keynes, J. M. (1923). *A tract on monetary reform.* Macmillan.
Keynes, J. M. (1936). *The general theory of employment, interest and money.* Macmillan.
Keynes, J. M. (1980). The collected writings of John Maynard Keynes, *Vol. XXVII: Activities 1940–1946: Shaping the post-war world: Rethinking employment and unemployment policy.* Cambridge University Press.
Keynes, J. M. (1981). The collected writings of John Maynard Keynes, *Vol. XX: Activities 1929–1931: Rethinking employment and unemployment policy.* Cambridge: Cambridge University Press.
Kregel, J. (1983). Budget deficits, stabilisation policy and liquidity preference: Keynes's post-war policy proposals. In F. Vicarelli (Ed.), *Keynes's relevance today* (pp. 28–50). University of Pennsylvania Press.
Knapp, G. F. [1924] (1973). *The state theory of money.* Augustus Kelley.
Krugman, P. (2012). Death of a fairy tale. *New York Times*, April 16.
Lavoie, M. (2014). *Post-Keynesian economics: New foundations*. Edward Elgar.
Lerner, A. [1943] (1955). Functional finance and the federal debt. In *AEA Readings in Fiscal Policy* (pp. 38-51). Irwin.
Masson, P., Bayoumi, T., & Samiei, H. (1995). Saving behavior in industrial and developing countries. In *Staff Studies for the World Economic Outlook.* International Monetary Fund.
Michl, T. (2009). *Capitalists, workers and fiscal policy*. Harvard University Press.
Mitchell, W., Wray, L. R., & Watts, M. (2019). *Macroeconomics*. Red Globe Press.
Modigliani, F., & Brumberg, R. (1954). Utility analysis and the consumption function: An interpretation of cross-section data. In K. Kurihara (Ed.), *Post-Keynesian Economics* (pp. 388–436). Rutgers University Press.

Payne, K. (2017). *The broken ladder: How inequality affects the way we think, live and die*. Viking.

Piketty, T. (2014). *Capital in the twenty-first century*. Harvard University Press.

Piketty, T. (2020). *Capital and ideology*. Harvard University Press.

Pressman, S. (1994). The composition of government spending: Does it make any difference? *Review of Political Economy, 6*, 221–239.

Pressman, S. (2014). Keynes, family allowances and Keynesian economic policy. *Review of Keynesian Economics, 2*, 508–526.

Pressman, S. (2016). *Understanding Piketty's capital in the twenty-first century*. Routledge.

Ricardo, D. [1817] (1951). *On the principles of political economy and taxation*. In P. Sraffa (Ed.), The works and correspondence of David Ricardo (Vol. I). Cambridge University Press.

Ricardo, D. [1820] (1962). Essay on the funding system. In P. Sraffra (Ed.), *The Works and correspondence of David Ricardo* (Vol. IV, pp. 143–200). Cambridge University Press.

Samuelson, P. (1939). Interactions between the multiplier analysis and the principle of acceleration. *Review of Economics and Statistics, 21*, 75–78.

Samuelson, P. (1948). The simple mathematics of income determination. In L. Meltzer et al. (Ed.), *Income, employment, and public policy: Essays in honor of Alvin H. Hansen* (pp. 133–155). W.W. Norton.

Scott, R., & Pressman, S. (2013). Household debt and income distribution. *Journal of Economic Issues, 47*, 323–332.

Seccareccia, M. (1995). Keynesianism and public investment: A left-Keynesian perspective on the role of government expenditures and debt. *Studies in Political Economy, 46*, 43–78.

Schui, F. (2014). *Austerity: The great failure*. Yale University Press.

Smith, A. [1776] (1937). *The wealth of nations*. Modern Library.

Stanley, T. D. (1998). New wine in old bottles: A meta-analysis of Ricardian Equivalence. *Southern Economic Journal, 64*, 713–727.

Stanley, T. D. (2001). Wheat from chaff: Meta-analysis as quantitative literature review. *Journal of Economic Perspectives, 15*, 131–150.

Summers, L. (2016). The age of secular stagnation. *Foreign Affairs, 95*, 2–9.

Summers, L., & Carroll, C. (1987). Why is U.S. national savings so low? *Brookings Papers on Economic Activity* #2, 607–642.

Taylor, F. (2013). *The downfall of money: Germany's hyperinflation and the destruction of the middle class*. Bloomsbury Press.

Tcherneva, P. (2020). *The case for a jobs guarantee*. Polity Press.

Varoufakis, Y. (2017). *Adults in the room: My battle with the European and American deep establishment*. Farrar, Straus & Giroux.
Wilkinson, R. (1996). *Unhealthy societies: The afflictions of inequality*. Routledge.
Wilkinson, R., & Pickett, K. (2009). *The spirit level*. Bloomsbury Press.
Wray, L. R. (1998). *Understanding modern money*. Edward Elgar.

CHAPTER 5

The National Debt Is Irrelevant: Some Unsettling Questions Regarding Government Budget Deficits

David Barrows

1 Introduction

According to Aristotle in the *Nicomachean Ethics* 'virtue is a mean between two extremes' (Aristotle, 1998, p. 39). In economics the two extremes are Libertarianism and Marxism. Libertarians believe in the freedom of the marketplace and a minimal state. Marxists believe in the state ownership of the means of production and distribution. Neither Libertarian nor Marxist models exist in reality, but they are helpful to establish the boundaries of relevant public policy. In the real world an important issue is the appropriate mix of public and private goods and services. An essential component of that discussion is how to pay for government spending either via taxation or borrowing, and the effects of public-sector debt.

D. Barrows (✉)
Aurora Philosophy Institute, Ottawa, Canada
e-mail: davidbarrows211@gmail.com

S. Pressman and J. Smithin (eds.), *Debates in Monetary Macroeconomics*,
https://doi.org/10.1007/978-3-031-11240-9_5

The contemporary school of 'modern monetary theory' (MMT) suggests an approach whereby taxation is detached from public-sector expenditures. Taxation would be used to address such things as the distribution of income, to control inflation, and to create a demand for government base money. Public-sector spending would be financed, in part, by the sale of government bonds (Kelton, 2020; Mitchell et al., 2019; Wray, 2012) which implies rising government debt and its economic impact. The genesis of MMT can be found in the writings of Keynes and Lerner. Governments have run large deficits at various times in history, including very recently, but not necessarily informed by MMT. Instead the deficits seem to have arisen spontaneously due to practical necessities.

This chapter evaluates the implications of MMT-style public policy with specific reference to the relationship between national debt and the rate of inflation. For MMT the answer to the question 'Should the central (federal) government always try to balance the budget' is no. The chapter concludes with recommendations for the implementation of a modified version of MMT.

2 The Philosophy of Debt

Analysis of the public debt has two components, scientific and emotional. The emotional component is based upon perceptions concerning the role of the state. On the one hand, the state is seen as an extension of the 'family or community'. In this context, the state is benign, friendly, helpful. The alternative viewpoint portrays the state as distant with dominating and dictatorial tendencies. The argument that governments must 'tighten their (our) belts' as a necessary policy response to higher indebtedness is based upon the fallacy of composition. This assumes national government and household debts are in some sense analogous. There are various reasons why this comparison is incorrect (Kelton, 2020). For example, a household does not have the power to raise money through taxation or by owning a bank and lending money to itself.

Two Harvard philosophers debated the configuration of a just society in the context of inequality. John Rawls was a proponent of contemporary liberalism (Rawls, 1971). Citizens do not 'deserve' to be born into an affluent or low-income family, or to be born more or less gifted than others. The initial distribution of natural assets is undeserved. Wealth creation is a cooperative enterprise, and all social goods are to be distributed equally. Wealth and power should be distributed equally except where inequalities work to the advantage of all. Rawl's theory of justice is within the social contract tradition of Locke, Rousseau, and Kant. Robert Nozick (1974) believed in the minimal state. In this approach, the legitimate use of state power is limited to preventing fraud or the use of force. It does not include the power to tax or to confiscate property. The individual has the right to decide how one's property is disposed of. Taxation without consent is equivalent to forced labour. Socialism and liberalism redistribute wealth to achieve social justice, ignoring how the goods have come to be produced and distributed through trade, labour, gifts, etc. To take goods away from people would be unjust, as long as the initial acquisition of the goods was just. The state should protect property and punish those who violate property rights.

Empirically, however, the elimination of inequality is impossible. Concerning the distribution of wealth in a society, a fitted trend will indicate (history shows) that typically a small fraction of the population holds a large portion of wealth. This 'Pareto distribution' has become known as the Pareto principle, or the 80–20 rule. This rule states that 80% of the wealth of a society is generally held by 20% of its population.

3 Ethical Issues

It can be argued that if the duty to pay a debt is ethical, then the 'ought should imply can' rule applies. There is a difference between borrowing (or taking on debt) and repaying that debt. When money is borrowed, both the borrower and the lender should recognize that the debt can be repaid because lenders ought not lend too much and borrowers should not get in over their head. When it comes to repaying debt, however, sometimes people cannot repay their loans. (This is not a problem for the national government, of course, since they can print money to roll over the debt.) We cannot be morally obliged to do what it is not in our power to do. Thus any obligation to pay is limited by the capacity to pay. Ethically, the obligation to pay a debt may shrink to the obligation to pay what can reasonably be required. However, one person's debt reduction is another person's asset loss. There is context-dependency in relationships of trust, expectation, and obligation implied by the language of 'credit' itself.

The ancient world exhibited a pattern of high-interest loans to subsistence farmers in times of crisis (war, drought, etc.), leading to loss of possessions (and earning potential) and the sale of family members into various forms of slavery. This led to periodic amnesties (such as the Biblical Jubilee) where debts were canceled and slaves returned to their families. This behaviour was not simply a matter of justice, but was undertaken to prevent revolution. In the fourth century BC Dionysus of Syracuse borrowed from the citizens but 'repaid' the loan only by debasing the coinage.

In the pre-commercial feudal era, princes, landlords, and clerics owned estates or sanctuaries that generated income, not unlike a personal business, but by command-and-control operations, with tribute paid by tenant farmers or serfs in return for military protection. Government funds in the feudal era also derived from conquest and war, the sale of offices, titles and indulgences, or debasing coins at the mint. Before the Renaissance, monarchs, princes, and popes borrowed on their own account, pledging personal income and estates as security. They often reneged on their debts. Creditors, initially lured by the prospect of significant financial gains, given their proximity to political power, more often than not were mistreated, whether by defaults, interest reductions, confiscations, or bodily harm.

Governments in ancient and medieval times required funding, as do modern states. But they did not borrow publicly in the sense of drawing funds from a broad populace and making the public ultimately responsible for servicing the debt as a form of deferred taxes. Private borrowing has existed since recorded history and preceded the development of public borrowing by many centuries. Eventually, public borrowing became common but, initially, involved loans in kind (commodities), not money, for shorter rather than extended periods, and for war or personal purposes rather than as a permanent funding source. No debt instruments existed. The notion of sovereign obligation emerged in the late seventeenth century, when the rule of law, security of contract, and parliamentary checks on monarchical power were implemented.

Out of this experience, of the exploitation of the poor by forcing them to borrow to survive a crisis beyond their control, emerged the ancient condemnation of usury, from the criticisms of Aristotle to the censures of Christianity, Islam, and Judaism. From this point of view there is minimal evidence for the utility of the institution of debt and thus limited grounds for an absolute moral obligation to pay in total all interest-based loans. As a result, there is an essential distinction between the legitimacy of 'use' on productive debt and the illegitimacy of extractive and forced debt. This reasoning implies that debt as an institution is morally ambivalent. There may be a 'good' (mutually beneficial) set of debt-related practices. But we cannot insist on an absolute obligation to pay all debt without considering the quality and effects of debt-related activity in society (Salsman, 2017).

Eventually, Aquinas was able to provide a qualified defense of lending, coinciding with the origin and growth of modern private banking and lending, which started in Italy and spread quickly to Spain and Holland. With the Reformation came a defense of usury by Martin Luther. The industrial revolution led to the defense of usury by Jeremy Bentham and his contemporaries in the seventeenth and eighteenth centuries (Smith, Ricardo, Say, and Mill). They argued that the common good is served by the productive activities of entrepreneurs who require start-up capital that must be borrowed (Douglas, 2016).

4 The Psychology of Debt

Max Weber (2002), one of the foundational figures in sociology, argued in his book *The Protestant Ethic and the Spirit of Capitalism* that the development of capitalism in Northern Europe had been profoundly influenced by the Protestant values of prudence and frugality, sometimes referred to as the 'Protestant work ethic'. This 'spirit' of capitalism does not refer to spirit in the metaphysical sense, but rather to a set of values, of hard work, frugality, and progress, that was historically associated with Protestantism. However, it is essential to note that, even in Weber's view, these values are not specific to any one religion. He argues that this spirit emerges wherever traditional forms of capitalism based on interpersonal relationships have been replaced by the rationalized organization of labor. The distinction between the ethical and economic notions of prudence and frugality is often blurred.

In this view, capitalism was believed to embody moral justice, like Adam Smith's 'invisible hand' (Smith, 1776) rewarding those who work hard and save money and punishing those who do not. This belief explains the continued use of morally weighted, if not downright religious, language by some politicians. For example, the prominent German politician, Armin Laschet, wants a return to fiscal orthodoxy and an end to the overly intrusive state that regulates every aspect of people's lives (Financial Times, 2021). He argues that the EU recovery fund, financed by debt taken on by the European Commission, was a one-off and should not be repeated. The EU's fiscal rules must come back into force. And Germany must reinstate its limit on deficit spending.

5 Functional Finance and MMT

While others look at the moral and psychological factors affecting debt, economists tend to focus on the economic factors. According to MMT and 'functional finance' (FF) 'money is a creature of the state' (Lerner, 1947). The state imposes liability in the form of a generalized social unit of account, money, used for measuring obligations. This is based on the ancient Germanic and Anglo-Saxon practice of Wergeld, meaning the amount of compensation paid in law by a person committing an offense to the injured party. The pre-existence of markets is not required. The state chooses and issues the unit of account. The form is determined by the state—gold, base metal, paper, or digitized numbers at the central bank. Inside money is an asset representing, or backed by, any form of private credit that circulates as a medium of exchange. Inside money originated as a transactions cost minimizing innovation.

Central banks were once deemed 'lenders of last resort' to private banks. They now act as lenders of last resort to national governments and the private sector. Some public debt analysts consolidate the balance sheets of central banks and national governments on the argument that the Treasury and the state central bank are effectively a single entity.

To many economists and historians, the spread of central banking and fiat paper money systems in the past century has led to 'market failure' in private-sector banking. However, most central banks originated in a sovereign's need to secure funds that it could not obtain by taxes or voluntary loans. Some central banks began as private banks which were compelled to lend to sovereigns. Upon becoming insolvent due to default, they were nationalized and transformed into government central banks with monopoly control over fiat currencies which eventually displaced gold and silver in private bank reserves. This was the pattern by which most modern central banks were established, including the first two in the late seventeenth century. The Swedish Riksbank was established in 1688 by the takeover of a private bank founded in 1656, which failed. The Bank of England was established in 1694 to finance war with France. England's, and later Britain's, public debt was launched when William III arranged for the sale of public debt through a syndicate of London merchants. In time, this syndicate became the Bank of England.

Keynes

After a decade of budget surpluses in the 1920s the US federal government experienced deficits at the start of the 'Great Depression'. But most politicians and economists believed in the necessity of keeping a balanced budget. In 1931, President Hoover proposed a plan to increase tax revenue by 30%, resulting in the Revenue Act of 1932. The Act increased taxes across the board, rolling back the tax cut reduction programme of the 1920s. Top earners were taxed at 63% on their net income. The Act also doubled the maximum estate tax rate, cut personal income tax exemptions, eliminated the corporate income tax exemption, and raised corporate tax rates. Despite this the USA continued to run budget deficits. Keynes, moreover, put forward a very different view to justify deficits in times of theDepression.

Pigou (1935) published *The Economics of Stationary States* in the static equilibrium tradition of the classical school. When Pigou later wrote against Keynes, in an article using more or less the same analytical setting, Keynes (1937) wrote that this model 'relates to a frozen land remote in its characteristics from all experience'. Pigou's (1943) 'real balance effect' would only work, if at all, in the long term. Keynes made sensible recommendations concerning insufficient aggregate demand to address immediate public policy issues of the 1930s, which Pigou and others had seemed incapable of doing.

Later Friedman and Schwartz (1963) argued that the Great Depression was caused by the fall in the money supply, stating that, 'from the cyclical peak in August 1929 to a cyclical trough in March 1933, the stock of money fell by over a third'. This failure of government policy is consistent with Keynes's analysis of insufficient effective aggregate demand.

Before his death, Keynes maybe had a change of heart and, as quoted by Skidelsky (2001), told Henry Clay of his hope that Smith's 'invisible hand' could help Britain out of post-war economic difficulties 'I find myself more and more relying on a solution to our problems by the invisible hand which I tried to eject from economic thinking twenty years ago'. Shiller and Akerlof (2009) have discussed Keynes's insight on the importance of confidence and expectations in determining the behaviour of business and other economic agents. Meanwhile, Keynes (1919, 235) was always aware of the dangers of inflation:

> Lenin is said to have declared that the best way to destroy the capitalist system was to debauch the currency. By a continuing process of inflation, governments can confiscate, secretly and unobserved, an important part of the wealth of their citizens. There is no subtler, no surer means of overturning the existing basis of society than to debauch the currency. The process engages all the hidden forces of economic law on the side of destruction and does it in a manner which not one man in a million can diagnose.

Functional Finance

Lerner embellished Keynes's theory. However, the logic of a theory does not always lead to policy changes. Lerner translated theory directly into policy and, in doing so, added insight into both theory and policy. But he also often arrived at policy proposals that, at the time, seemed politically impossible. Keynes directed his policies to the political environment of that time. He proposed those policies that in his opinion were implementable.

Lerner (1943) argued that government fiscal policy, spending, taxation, loans and the issue of money, should be based upon results of these actions on the economy, rather than on established traditional doctrine about what is sound or unsound. This principle of judging only by effects has been applied in many other fields of human activity, where it is known as the method of science. The principle of judging fiscal measures by how they work in the economy is called functional finance (FF). The first responsibility of the government is to maintain the total rate of spending on goods and services at a level at which the current prices would buy all the goods that it is possible to produce. If total spending is allowed to go above this level there will be inflation, otherwise there will be unemployment. The government can increase total spending by spending more or reducing taxes. According to Forstater (1999) Lerner's theory includes:

1. Full employment, price stability, and a decent standard of living, and it is the state's responsibility to promote their attainment.
2. Policies should be judged on their ability to achieve the goals for which they are designed and not on any notion of whether they are 'sound', or comply with the dogmas of traditional economics,
3. Money is a creature of the state.

4. Taxing is not a funding operation. The government budget should be judged on its macroeconomic effects. Decisions concerning taxation should be made concerning their economic impact 'not because the government needs to make money payments'.
5. Government borrowing is not a funding operation.
6. The primary purpose of taxation is to influence the behaviour of the public.
7. There are six (or three pairs of) fiscal instruments of government, taxing and spending, buying and selling, and borrowing and lending. 'Printing money' is not independent of these. It is not an instrument of policy. It is only a servant of these policies, just like printing the stationary used in the various government departments.
8. Without a full employment policy, society cannot benefit from labour-saving technological advances. With full employment, labour-saving technical advance is beneficial to society.
9. Without a full employment policy, a country must be concerned with its trade balance. With full employment, here is no need to worry about importing 'too much' relative to exports. In that case exports are a cost, and imports are a benefit.
10. FF is not a policy. It is a framework within which policies may be conducted.

Concerning Keynes, Lerner, as quoted by Colander (1984), noted that;

> I refer to Keynes' timidity. He did not carry his conclusions all the way. I first was hit by this quality—to my great astonishment—when, at a lecture to the Federal Reserve in Washington in 1944, he showed concern that there might be 'too much saving' after the War. When I pointed out that the government could always induce enough spending by incurring deficits to increase incomes, he at first objected that this would only cause 'even more saving' and then denounced as 'humbug' my suggestion that the deficits required to induce enough total spending could always be financed by increasing the national debt. (I must add here that Evsey Domar, at my side, whispered 'he ought to read the *General Theory*'). Colander notes that:

> According to Evsey Domar, Lerner's account underplayed Keynes's violent reaction to Lerner's statement. Not only did Keynes call Lerner's statement

'humbug', he also paraphrased Lincoln's 'you cannot fool all of the people all of the time'.

MMT

Lerner appears to have had no students to continue his work. There is no 'Lerner school'. Lerner never stayed at any one institution for long. He served on the faculties of nearly a dozen universities and accepted over twenty visiting appointments. Nonetheless, today's MMT is to some degree a revival of Lerner's ideas.

Lerner's concept of FF did not receive recognition and acceptance in the mainstream economic literature, although some version of 'Keynesianism' did seem to prevail in the 1950s and 1960s. The 1960s Kennedy tax cuts reinforced the notion of insufficient aggregate demand. However, the current system continues to permit economic and financial crises leading to large deficits with which the mainstream of the economics profession has difficulties. This has led to a revival of FF rebranded as MMT.

Historically, money was a reward for value creation. Today, money is used to *create* value. Consistent with Lerner, MMT argues that a county's currency is a public monopoly for the government. Unemployment is evidence that a currency monopolist restricts the supply of the financial assets needed to pay taxes and satisfy desired savings. Smithin (2022, p. vi) argues that:

> The core argument of MMT rests on the logically unassailable proposition that the central government of an economy with its sovereign currency and a floating exchange rate (to which I would also add a 'fixed but adjustable' exchange rate) faces no binding financial constraints. Under these circumstances, fears about 'unsustainable' budget deficits are nonsense. However, none of this applies to jurisdictions with an irrevocably fixed exchange rate or those embedded in a currency union. Nor does it apply to the individual Provinces or States in a federal system. And by no means does this purely financial insight settle any of the debates about macroeconomic policy alternatives, which must still be debated on the merits of the policies themselves. Critically, the core proposition does not settle debates about the correct level of interest rates or about whether to define interest rates in 'real' or 'nominal' terms.'

Since leaving the gold standard, money has essentially been backed by faith in the issuing government. No longer fearing the shortage of gold, governments are free to print the money needed to assure full employment and pay for resources to do important things like deal with climate change. MMT views currency as a public good rather than a medium of exchange. As a consequence, taxes do not finance spending. Taxes render the money of account chosen by the state as being acceptable for payments. This is consistent with Lerner's concept of FF. The first financial responsibility of the government is to keep the total rate of spending in the country on goods and services neither greater nor less than the rate which at the current prices would buy all the goods possible.

MMT recommends a 'job guarantee' programme as a critical component of its policy package. However, as Barrows (2007) has demonstrated, since the Great Depression of the 1930s no developed economy in the world has utilized a nationwide government program as an 'employer of last resort'. Governments in many transitional economies, however, are reluctantly 'forced' to provide job guarantees to university graduates. At the same time MMT appears disinterested in the composition of public expenditures. In my view, this concept is unviable as public policy. No politician can be elected on a campaign of 'digging holes'. Keynes *was* concerned with public policy implementation. In the *General Theory* digging holes was not a policy recommendation, it was an exercise in hyperbole (which worked well).

Piketty

Thomas Piketty (2014, 2020) takes a different view about debt and deficits from those of Keynes, Lerner, and MMT. His concern in those two volumes is with the distributional consequences of debt, and provides a wealth of empirical data on the topic.

He argues that the new activism of the central banks has also allowed them to buy back a growing share of public debt securities. The most important question is whether we continue along this path. Can we envisage that central banks will in the future hold 50% and then 100% of public debts? From a technical point of view, this would not pose any problem. The difficulty is that by resolving the question of public debt this creates other problems elsewhere, particularly the increasing inequality of wealth. Money creation and the purchase of financial securities lead to an increase in stock and property prices, contributing to the enrichment of the richest. However, if the distribution according to the

80–20 rule is a genuine empirical regularity, as Pareto claimed, Piketty's concerns may seem to be overblown.

6 Does Debt Cause Inflation?

The short answer to this question seems to be no, at least for developed nations. Romero and Marin (2017) employ an annual data set for 52 countries over the period 1965–2014. They utilize a forward-looking model of inflation based on rational expectations, Cagan-type money demand, and a non-Ricardian regime that takes government bonds as net wealth. They conclude that an increase in the debt-to-GDP ratio is not statistically significant as a cause for inflation for developed countries. However, an increase in the debt-to-GDP ratio is strongly associated with high inflation in indebted developing countries, after controlling for money growth and real output growth. Their findings highlight challenges for price stabilization in highly indebted developing countries because the expansion of public debt affects variables sensitive to economic agents' decision-making, such as inflation, income, and interest rates. Moreover, despite the critical role of monetary policy in managing inflation expectations, they argue that fiscal policy may be a dominant factor for the evolution of inflation in highly indebted developing countries. Supporting this work, an analysis conducted by Bilan and Roman (2014) in 22 countries identified the existence of possible inflationary effects of public indebtedness for developing nations. The research could not establish a direct relation in developed countries.

Neo-Keynesian models additionally incorporate forward-looking behaviour and inflationary expectations. The heightened importance of inflationary expectations was initiated and reinforced by the 'Great Inflation' of 1965–1980. Inflation expectations are reflected in financial markets. Adjustments of inflation expectations operate as constraints on the efficacy of countercyclical fiscal policies and straightforward monetary policy (Rockoff, 2021).

Bordo and Meissner (2016) find that the relationship between fiscal deficits and inflation generally holds in wartime when fiscally stressed governments resorted to the inflation tax. In the early twentieth century, there were two peacetime episodes when bond-financed fiscal deficits unbacked by future taxes seem to have significantly contributed to inflation, namely France in the 1920s and the recovery from the Great Depression in the 1930s in the USA. In the post-WWII era, a detailed examination of inflation in the 1960s and 1970s in the US and the UK suggests that fiscal influences on monetary policy were important. Fiscal deficits have been long associated with monetary finance in emerging countries with underdeveloped financial systems and weak budgetary administration.

From this empirical literature we can conclude that the size of the national debt is irrelevant for developed countries. The size and composition of the debt can exert inflationary pressures in developing nations. Keynes concluded that we had reached a condition that might be designated as one of 'true inflation' when a further increase in the quantity of effective demand produces no additional output and entirely spends itself on a rise in costs per unit. What Keynes called true inflation, MMT would call 'demand-pull' inflation.

7 The Political Economy of MMT

In Sect. 6 we noted that MMT seems to work better with respect to inflation in developed nations rather than developing economies. A large part of the reason for this involves political economy, in particular the ability of the central government to collect taxes from the citizens.

Ferguson et al. (2020) argue that development outcomes come in 'clusters' that seem challenging to exit. This is reflected in the interconnection between state weakness and clientelism. State weakness creates the right environment for 'clientelism'. Clientelism sets a structure of incentives for politicians and citizens that is detrimental to building state capacity and encourages tax evasion. These practices become widely accepted in society, resulting in a deeply entrenched relationship of mutually reinforcing influences. A weak state and widespread clientelism are part of a political equilibrium with multiple feedback loops. State weakness particularly with respect to tax collection is a situation that is likely to be very hard to exit. There is no opportunity to apply MMT in those countries in 'weak state traps'.

In general, we can classify economies as (1) high-income, with robust institutions and dominant currency, (2) high-income with efficient government, (3) middle income, (4) weak-state trap countries, and (5) transition/failed states. The amounts and composition of government spending are conditional on the competitiveness of the nation. For those entities classified under (1) national debt is irrelevant. Other developed economies can practice some form of FF but must deal with a number of constraints such as external debt, supply issues, and asset price inflation. Middle income, weak, and failed states are incapable of using FF and MMT.

8 Rules

MMT suggests that national debt which resides in the central banking system is irrelevant. The national government can simply roll over debt and the central bank will accommodate. There are the standard caveats. There can be too much of a good thing, there is always the law of unintended consequences, such as inflation, and unexpected or unforeseen events. Another significant concern is asset-price acceleration. This is especially relevant in the housing markets. Such real estate price inflation is pure economic rent.

The goal of MMT is full employment of domestic resources. That is, domestic resources are not a constraint. Nonetheless, it is possible that combined international demand based on many countries implementing domestic MMT could reach global limits. A coordinated, multilateral response can address this concern.

In our proposal, domestic inflation would not exceed, say, two percent. This represents a clear, consistent, and easily understood target. Keynes, FF, and MMT all agree that inflation is not an acceptable public policy, and to decide whether inflation is excessive or not there has to be accurate measure of inflation including the housing component. In February 2021, the New Zealand government formally added a clause to the central bank mandate, instructing it to consider housing prices in making monetary policy decisions (Powell & Wessel, 2021).

It will be essential to examine the so-called 'Smithin rule'. Smithin (2022) argues for a 'low' real policy rate of interest and 'rules' rather than 'discretion' in monetary policy. A zero real policy rate (ZRPR) would be a 'near-optimal' monetary policy. A commitment on the part of the monetary authorities to a real rate rule of some kind (as opposed to simply setting the nominal policy rate) will cause market participants to change how their expectations are formed. Financial actors will not be able to speculate if there is nothing to speculate about.

9 Conclusion

Personal and public debts are contentious issues. Emotions concerning debt can be powerful. There may be religious connotations. Is debt incurred for consumption purposes or for productive investment? The emotional issues complicate the scientific exploration of private and public obligations. A fundamental philosophical problem is the relationship of public and private debts to the distribution of wealth in society.

The distribution of wealth raises important ethical issues. Has debt contributed to the imbalance of wealth in society? Philosophers have argued that usury is inappropriate from a philosophical and religious perspective. With the onset of the industrial revolution, a consensus emerged to facilitate more public- and private-sector investments necessary to enhance productivity growth. Debt will continue to remain a significant psychological issue. The fallacy of composition occurs when analysts conflate household and state debts. Households do not have access to the money creation process. Politicians continue to invoke the analogy of public debt to household obligations. It is argued that public debt may lead to inflation and contribute to income and wealth disparities. The empirical literature is consistent regarding public debt and inflation. Public-sector debt has no relationship to inflation in developed economies. Public-sector debt in emerging economies does lead to inflationary pressures. The Pareto rule provides an excellent description of wealth distribution over space and over time. This 80–20 rule indicates that 80% of the wealth, generally, is accumulated by 20% of the population. This may render concerns about wealth distribution less relevant.

The Great Depression illustrated the inability of neoclassical economics to develop the appropriate public policy responses. Keynes's contribution was to fully incorporate monetary and real variables. Lerner provided a necessary elaboration with the development of FF. Some would argue that FF-MMT represents a logical extension of Keynesian economics, while others would not agree. MMT builds upon Lerner's FF. But MMT includes policy options that do not follow logically from a Keynes-Lerner analysis, such as the 'zero interest rate policy' (ZIRP), job guarantee, and the Green New Deal. These can all be 'afforded' but must be debated on the merits.

The optimal combination of public and private goods and services is a critical public policy issue. Citizens expect efficient and effective essential public services and insist upon a wide variety of private-sector goods and services. We argue that a modified version of FF-MMT would be an appropriate evolution of the theory of monetary and fiscal policy. This may include the de-coupling of taxation and the resulting revenues from federal government expenditures. In terms of our original question, it may not be appropriate for fiscal policy to always pursue a balanced budget. In particular, the developed nations should borrow and spend what is necessary to achieve full employment, and to meet other important societal goals.

References

Akerlof, G., & Shiller, R. (2009). *Animal spirits: How human psychology drives the economy, and why it matters for global capitalism*. Princeton University Press.

Aristotle (1998). *The Nicomachean ethics* (D. Ross, Trans.). Oxford University Press.

Barrows, D. (2007). Canada's global competitiveness: International trade and investments and public sector management. In T. Wesson (Ed.), *Canada and the new world economic order: Strategic briefings for Canadian enterprise* (pp. 26–28). Captus Press.

Bilan, I., & Roman, A. (2014). Interconnections between public indebtedness and inflation in contemporary economies. *Economics and Sociology, 7*, 59–70.

Bordo, M. & Meissner, C. (2016). *Fiscal and financial crises* (NBER Working Paper No. 22059). NBER

Colander, D. (1984). Was Keynes a Keynesian or a Lernerian? *Journal of Economic Literature, 22*, 1572–1575.

Douglas, A. (2016). *The philosophy of debt*. London & New York: Routledge.

Fergusson, L., Molina C., & Robinson, J. (2020). *The weak state trap* (NBER Working Paper No. 26848). National Bureau of Economic Research.

Forstater, M. (1999). *Functional finance and full employment: Lessons from Lerner for today?* (Working Paper No. 272). The Jerome Levy Economics Institute.

Friedman, M., & Schwartz, A. (1963). *A monetary history of the United States, 1867–1960*. Princeton University Press.

Kelton, S. (2020). *The deficit myth: Modern monetary theory and the birth of the people's economy*. Hachette Book Group.

Keynes, J. M. (1936). *The general theory of employment interest and money*. Macmillan.

Keynes, J. M. (1937). Professor Pigou on money wage rates in relation to unemployment. In D. Moggridge (Ed.), Collected writings (Vol. XIV, pp. 235–238). Cambridge University Press.

Keynes, J. M. (1919). *The economic consequences of the peace*. Macmillan.

Lerner, A. P. (1943). Functional finance and the federal debt. *Social Research, 10*, 38–51.

Lerner, A. P. (1947). Money is a creature of the state. *American Economic Review Papers and Proceedings, 37*, 312–317.

Mitchell, W., Wray, L. R., & Watts, M. (2019). *Macroeconomics*. Red Globe Press.

Nozick, R. (1974). *Anarchy, state and utopia*. Basic Books.

Pigou, A. (1935). *The economics of stationary states*. Macmillan.

Pigou, A. C. (1943). The classical stationary state. *Economic Journal, 53*, 312–317.

Piketty, T. (2014). *Capital in the 21st century*. Harvard University Press.

Piketty, T. (2020). *Capital and ideology*. Harvard University Press.

Powell, T., & Wessel, D. (2021). *Why is the New Zealand government telling its central bank to focus on rising house prices?* Brookings Institute.

Rawls, J. (1971). *A theory of justice*. Harvard University Press.

Rockoff, H. (2021). *Oh, how the mighty have fallen: The bank failures and near failures that started America's greatest financial panics* (NBER Working Paper 28577), NBER.

Romero, J., & Marin, P. (2017). Inflation and public debt. *Monetaria, 1*, 43–100.

Salsman, R. (2017). *The political economy of debt: Three centuries of theory and evidence*. Edward Elgar.

Skidelsky, R. (2001). *John Maynard Keynes: Fighting for freedom 1937–1946*. Viking Penguin.

Smithin, J. (2022). *Beyond barter: Lectures in monetary macroeconomics after 'Rethinking.'* World Scientific Publishing.

Financial Times. (2021, July 21). Interview: Armin Laschet on Merkel, the Greens and fiscal rules. *Financial Times*.

Weber. M. (1930). *The protestant ethic and the spirit of capitalism*. T. Parsons & R. H. Tawney (Eds.), London: George Allen & Unwin.

Wray, R. (2012). *Modern money theory: A primer on macroeconomics for sovereign monetary systems*. Palgrave Macmillan.

CHAPTER 6

What is the Sign of the Balanced Budget Multiplier?

John Smithin

1 Introduction

The purpose of this paper is to discuss Paul Samuelson's famous notion of the *balanced budget multiplier* (BBM) which was a core part of the political economy of the so-called 'neoclassical synthesis' in macroeconomics in the third quarter of the twentieth century. Elsewhere I have called this period an era of 'pseudo-Keynesianism' (Smithin, 2022), and I think that a critical consideration of the various propositions that have been made about the BMM over the years may well serve to explain why this is an accurate characterization.

In the context of the present volume, this paper will deal with the third in our list of 'unsettled questions' namely, 'are tax increases inflationary or deflationary'? Any discussion of the BBM is also bound to address this specific issue, as a consideration of the effects of an increase in taxes is automatically involved. The basic idea of the BBM was that an

J. Smithin (✉)
Department of Economics, York University, Toronto, Canada
e-mail: jsmithin@yorku.ca

S. Pressman and J. Smithin (eds.), *Debates in Monetary Macroeconomics*,
https://doi.org/10.1007/978-3-031-11240-9_6

increase in government spending financed by an equal increase in taxation will cause a net increase in aggregate demand (or 'effective demand') and therefore an increase in real GDP, or in the price level, depending on the circumstances. In short, the sign of the BBM is positive. As far as the effect on the price level (or the inflation rate) specifically is concerned, it was implicit in these sorts of arguments that the effect of an increase in taxation would indeed be deflationary. However, this would be offset by the numerically greater effect of the increase in government expenditure. These sorts of ideas seem to have been very much the conventional wisdom for many years. The logic would be called into question, however, if either the sign of the BBM is negative and/or if the supply-side effects of taxation are properly taken into account, rather than only the demand-side effects.

This paper will argue that the effect of an increase in taxation per se is actually to increase the rate of inflation rather than to decrease it. The ultimate macroeconomic impact of an increase in the average tax rate, taken by itself, would be to cause 'stagflation', an expression which is meant to illustrate 'the worst of all possible worlds'—a combination of higher inflation, lower growth, and higher unemployment. Moreover, as the sign of the BBM does indeed turn out to be *negative*, a balanced budget increase in government spending as a percentage of GDP will have the same effect. In that case (even on the demand side) the effects of the spending increase are more than offset by the increase in the average tax rate.

2 Taxes and Inflation

As just stated, I now think that the correct answer to our 'unsettled question' about taxes and inflation is that tax increases are *inflationary*. However, for those of us brought up in a broadly 'Keynesian' tradition (including, for these purposes, the advocates of the neoclassical synthesis itself) the *tendenz* of most of what we learned in our training, in colleges and universities, was to make this proposition seems quite counter-intuitive. In 'Macroeconomics 101', for example, we would have learned about the effects of changes in both government spending and taxation on aggregate demand. Increases in spending add to the total of aggregate demand whereas increases in taxes reduce it. The impacts were always supposed to be symmetrical. The sign of the balanced budget multiplier therefore turns only on which of these effects is supposed to be the more important quantitatively.

The underlying idea is, obviously, simply that government spending 'puts money into' the economy whereas taxation 'takes money out'. These sorts of ideas, in fact, are more-or-less second nature to most Keynesians and Post Keynesians. In our current volume, for example, Joelle Leclaire, who is a well-known member of the modern monetary theory (MMT) school of Post Keynesian economists, will contribute a paper defending the proposition that tax increases are deflationary. Moreover, this is a key part of the overall macroeconomic policy package that is proposed by MMT. Their view is that the correct role of taxes is *not* to finance public expenditure (and the MMT group is surely correct on this point)[1] but, rather, precisely to restrain aggregate demand should inflation threaten. The argument thus proceeds in what appears to be very much a traditional Keynesian, or Post Keynesian, manner (Kelton, 2020; Mitchell et al., 2019).

On the other hand, in the microeconomic literature in the fields of 'Public Finance' and 'Public Economics' we get a somewhat different take on taxes.[2] In the discussions of tax incidence in that literature, and in the cases of both a specific tax and an *ad valorum* tax, an increase in the tax rate is thought unambiguously to increase the price of any particular good or service, essentially by affecting supply conditions.[3] The most general conclusion reached in the tax incidence literature is (typically) that prices will not increase by the full amount of tax, but nonetheless they will definitely increase. Suppose, then, that we switch the argument back to the macroeconomic level and consider something like an increase in the average tax rate on all the goods and services included in the measure of GDP. Surely something similar to the logic of the microeconomic case must continue to apply, but now as applied to the aggregate price level rather than just to the price level of the individual good or service.

I first became aware of these issues, and the potential conflict between them, a very long time ago during the writing of my doctoral dissertation on the *Financing of Unemployment Insurance* (Smithin, 1982). The unemployment insurance (UI)[4] scheme in Canada in that period was financed by a payroll tax on the entire wage bill. What I wanted to do in that work was to take account of both the aggregate demand and supply effects as just touched on above. One thing that I certainly learned at that time was that these are very difficult topics to get one's head around, and I am therefore very grateful to Joelle for agreeing to present her detailed views on the issue in the current volume. For myself, however, forty or more years later, and in the context of my alternative monetary model (AMM) as set out in *Rethinking the Theory of Money, Credit and Macroeconomics* (Smithin, 2018) and *Beyond Barter* (Smithin, 2022), I have finally come to the conclusion that an increase in the average tax rate will tend both to reduce economic growth and increase unemployment, and also increase the rate of inflation.

3 The Balanced Budget Multiplier and the Genesis of 'Tax and Spend' Policies

The sign of the balanced budget multiplier is therefore yet another of the 'unsettled questions' in monetary macroeconomics and, indeed, we could have also treated this as a separate issue in its own right. In fact, as the reader will see, it does also come up in several of the other contributions to the volume. Samuelson himself thought that the sign of the BBM would be positive and even, at one stage, that it had a value exactly to one. My own view is the opposite. It seems to me that the sign of the balanced budget multiplier is likely to be negative.

I used to think, and even to tell people—without, I am afraid, actually having consulted the original text (*mea culpa*)—that the discussion of the BBM was already present in the very first edition of Samuelson's famous textbook. Now, however, I do possess (a reprint of) the first edition of the text, namely, *Economics: The Original 1948 Edition* (Samuelson, 1997), and it is not there. It *is* in *Economics An Introductory Analysis*, 6th Edition (Samuelson, 1964), which was oldest edition of Samuelson that I actually had on my shelves. In my own defence, I suppose that in the grand scheme of things this was still a relatively early edition. Samuelson's book eventually went into a total of nineteen editions in the sixty-seven years between 1948 and 2009.

In the sixth edition the discussion of the balanced budget multiplier appears in the key Chapter 12, which deals with 'The Theory of Income Determination'. This is the chapter that includes the famous 'Keynesian Cross' diagram, explaining how national income and output are determined. It goes on to work out the value of the various 'multipliers', such as the investment multiplier and the government expenditure multiplier.[5] The investment multiplier and the government expenditure multiplier are positive, but the tax multiplier is negative. At the same time Samuelson also argues that the tax multiplier is less in numerical magnitude than the government expenditure multiplier. Therefore, a 'balanced budget' increase in government spending, offset by an equal increase in taxes, will have an overall positive effect.

Samuelson's theory of the relationship between price level and the level of output was not sophisticated by modern standards, and this turns out to be a key issue in deciding what the sign of the BBM should be. Everything hinged on the somewhat vague concept of a 'full employment' level of output. Before the supposed full employment level is reached, any increase in aggregate demand will feed through directly to an increase in output and has no impact on prices. After full employment, however, output cannot be increased any further, and the whole effect of any demand change would be on prices. In some later textbooks, these assumptions were rationalized/depicted as an 'L-shaped' aggregate supply curve. This would be horizontal before the supposed 'full employment' level of output and vertical thereafter.

As it happens Samuelson's first introduction of the concept of the BBM is in the context of a discussion of 'inflation' (meaning by this precisely the increase in prices after full employment is reached). He writes as follows:

> To offset an 20-billion-dollar upward shift in $I + G$ we must increase tax collections by *more* than 20 billion dollars...[the] needed taxes...[are]...30 billion when the $MPC = 2/3$. This means that (1) when increased government spending is added to a full employment economy with a balanced budget, then (2) taxes will probably have to be increased by *more than enough to balance the budget* if we are determined to avoid an inflationary gap. (original emphasis)

Samuelson then adds a footnote to explain how the argument would work out in the opposite situation of less than full employment. In that case, the whole effect will be on the level of output. Samuelson goes on to say:

> Advanced treatises call this phenomenon the 'balanced budget multiplier theorem'. This very useful, but highly simplified, doctrine says: a *balanced* rise in G and T will raise NNP by just that amount; a balanced cut by \$1 in G and T will cut NNP by \$1. So it is not merely the budget deficit, $G - T$, that has NNP effects. (original emphasis)

In these two quotes the symbols I and G stand for the levels of investment spending and government spending, and T for total tax collection.

The *MPC* is the 'marginal propensity to consume' and NNP represents the measure of output known as 'net national product'.[6]

It has always seemed to me to be somewhat contradictory that the discussion of the BBM should both be reserved for 'advanced treatises' and yet, at the same time, is 'highly simplified'. To my mind the confused wording tends strongly to suggest that something important is missing from the analysis. In practice, though, whether this is really a simple idea or an advanced one, it did become a key part of the new political economy founded by Samuelson, and others, in the years immediately following WW2. In my view, most important implication of this is that what later came to be called 'tax and spend' policies were thought to be a good representation of Keynesian economics. In this way the very notion of 'Keynesian economics' started off on the wrong foot—from the beginning. The potential benefits of increased public spending were recognized but, lurking in the background, there is still the old idea that somehow the spending must be 'paid for' by taxation. This is an erroneous view, which the contemporary MMT school rightly rejects even while (as we have seen) holding somewhat similar views to Samuelson about the effects of taxation on inflation. To me, Samuelson seems to have been trying to present to his readers both the novel idea, for the time, that the increase in government expenditure will have positive effects on economic activity, but is simultaneously seeking to provide reassurance that we need not abandon the traditional idea of 'fiscal responsibility'. The spending is a good thing, he allows, but it must always be paid for.

However, as I have frequently argued elsewhere (Smithin, 2013a, 2014, 2018, 2022) 'tax and spend' was not the policy combination that Keynes argued for in the *General Theory*. He explicitly favoured a policy of 'loan expenditure', which is defined precisely in a footnote to the famous 'banknotes in bottles' passage in Chapter 10, about the 'The Marginal Propensity to Consume'. In that chapter, Keynes points out that the application of what he goes on to call 'strict business principles' to useful public sector projects is likely to cause confusion. According to Keynes (1936):

> It is often convenient to use the term 'loan expenditure' to include the public investment financed by borrowing from individuals and also any other current expenditure which is so financed. Strictly speaking the latter should be reckoned as negative saving, but official action of this kind is not influenced by the same sort of psychological motives which govern

> private saving. Thus loan expenditure is a convenient expression for the net borrowings of public authorities on all accounts, whether on capital account or to meet a budgetary deficit.

There is a very good reason, in my view, for thinking along with Keynes that this *loan* expenditure (i.e., borrowing) is what is really important. Loan expenditure implies credit (and hence money) creation by the banking system which, as I have explained in detail in a number of places (*e.g.*, Smithin, 2016, 2018, 2022), is vital for the realization of monetary profits and hence for the *viability* of a system of 'monetary production' (or 'capitalism') in general. Because of this, the basic idea of 'tax and spend' goes completely against the grain in my opinion, and misses much of the point of the underlying Keynesian argument.

4 Effective Demand Versus Aggregate Supply

Recently, in both Smithin (2018) and (2022) for example, I have used an effective demand/aggregate supply (ED/AS) analysis to show that the sign of the balanced budget multiplier is negative, and that a 'tax and spend' policy leads to stagflation. The same analysis would also lead to the conclusion that an increase in the average macroeconomic tax rate, on its own without there being a corresponding increase in government spending, would have a similar effect.

In *Rethinking the Theory of Money, Credit and Macroeconomics* (Smithin, 2018) I carried out a mathematically rigorous analysis of both issues in the context of the AMM, and also provided graphical illustrations in p, y (inflation/growth) space,[7] where lower-case p stands for the inflation rate and lower-case y for the rate of economic growth. As the original premise of the current volume was to try to avoid formalization as much as possible, I will not reproduce either the algebraic or the graphical argument here. However, in what follows, I will verbally try to explain the underlying logic of the argument as best I can.

The graphical analysis depicted the macroeconomic equilibrium of the system as the confluence of an upward-sloping effective demand schedule (ED), a flat short-run aggregate supply (SRAS), and a positively sloped long-run aggregate supply schedule (LRAS). The LRAS schedule cuts the ED schedule from below. In the given context, ED should be taken to mean the *rate of growth* of effective demand, whereas AS is the *rate of growth* of output supplied.

It will be important to point out the differences between this ED/AS analysis and the aggregate demand/aggregate supply (AD/AS) analysis often found in conventional textbooks. In the textbooks that came immediately after Samuelson's original contribution the aggregate demand schedule (AD) was usually taken to be downward-sloping in *P*, *Y* (price/output) space, with *P* standing for the price level and *Y* for the level of output. The AS schedule depicted in these books meanwhile typically made explicit what had been the implicit assumption in Samuelson. Namely, that the AS schedule will be flat before the full employment level of output is reached and vertical thereafter.

The expression *effective demand* should be taken to mean that at every point along an ED schedule there would be enough credit and money creation to sustain that rate of demand growth in terms of actual purchasing power. This is somewhat different to Keynes's treatment of the issue in the *General Theory*. However it is more consonant, or so I would argue, with the genuine 'monetary analysis' that Keynes claimed he was attempting to put forward. I use this term in the sense employed by Joseph Schumpeter in his posthumously published classic the *History of Economic Analysis* (Schumpeter, 1954). It also represents a slightly different concept of the *difference* between the mainstream notion of aggregate demand (AD) and 'effective demand' (ED) than is sometimes given in the Post Keynesian literature. For example, Victoria Chick(1983) in her authoritative *Macroeconomics After Keynes: A Reconsideration of the General Theory*, writes as follows;

> *effective* demand, in contrast to aggregate demand, is not a schedule – it is the point on the schedule...which is 'made effective' by the firms' production decisions.

Chick is quite correct, of course, in stating that the only actual realization of monetary profits is at the point where the schedules cross. However, the point that I wish to stress in the present treatment is that to be 'effective' the demand anywhere along the schedule must actually be in terms of money. I therefore call the whole schedule—'the ED schedule'.

The fact that the ED schedule is upward-sloping in *p*, *y* space comes about because of the presence in the model of a so-called 'forced saving effect' (Hayek, 1932), or 'Mundell-Tobin' effect (Kam, 2005) as this idea came to be known in the mid-twentieth century literature. (There are also certain analogies albeit with different coordinates, to Keynes's own original analysis using an upward-sloping schedule, to the Post Keynesian *Z*, *N* diagram, and even to Samuelson's own approach before the use of the typical diagram in *P*, *Y* space became standardized.) Whether positively sloped or not, and as I have shown in Smithin (2022), it is an extremely important point that the limiting position of the ED schedule would be vertical. At the aggregate level the ED schedule should never be downward-sloping. As already seen this is a major difference from what became the standard textbook macroeconomic model of the late twentieth century.

The presence of a Mundell-Tobin or 'forced saving' effect is nevertheless an inescapable economic reality, in my opinion, unless the central bank deliberately tries to contradict or counteract it with the application of something like the 'Taylor principle'. (For example, by proactively raising the real policy rate of interest.)[8] There are a number of different ways of demonstrating the existence and relevance of the Mundell-Tobin effect—as a matter of both economic theory and macroeconomic policy. In the world of neoclassical/mainstream economics, for example, this can be achieved by the assumption of an endogenous rate of time preference on the part of economic agents. On this point see Kam (2005) and Kam et al. (2019). Alternatively, and perhaps more simply, by solving the optimization problem of the commercial banks in the overnight market (Kam & Smithin, 2012).

In the end, however, given the realities of today's central bank 'interest rate operating procedures' (Smithin, 2004) the existence of the forced saving effect is really nothing more than simple common-sense. This can be seen, for instance, in the development of the expression for the transmission mechanism of monetary policy as set out in *Rethinking* (Smithin, 2018). This was an empirical analysis with a 'pass-through coefficient' of around 0.7/0.8 in Canada, and similar numbers elsewhere (Collis, 2018; Smithin, 2022). If i stands for the nominal interest rate in the marketplace, i_0 is the nominal policy rate of interest set by the central bank, m_0 is the mark-up between commercial bank deposit rates and lending rates, and m_1 is the pass-through coefficient, the transmission mechanism can then be written as $i = m_0 + m_1 i_0$. Subtracting the currently observed inflation rate, p, from both sides of the expression we obtain $i - p = m_0 + m_1 i_0 - p$. Finally, as $i - p = r$ is the real (inflation-adjusted) rate of interest, and if r_0 stands for the real inflation-adjusted policy rate, $r = m_0 + m_1 r_0 - (1 - m_1)p$. In principle, as $0 < (1 - m_1) < 1$, there is therefore a negative relationship between the inflation rate and the inflation-adjusted real rate of interest. If effective demand growth depends *negatively* on the real rate of interest, this is what ultimately accounts for the *positive* slope of the ED schedule.

On the other hand, the fundamental theoretical reason for the similar upward slope of the LRAS on the supply side, is imperfect competition. (Perhaps somewhat confusingly?) this implies downward-sloping demand curves for the products of each individual oligopolistic firm at the *microeconomic* level, not to be confused with the upward slope of the *macroeconomic* aggregate demand schedule as just discussed. Moving into the macroeconomic context the individual downward-sloping microeconomic *demand* curves translate into an upward-sloping aggregate *supply* schedule.

Interestingly enough Samuelson later admitted that imperfect competition was the unstated basis of his own version of Keynes (see below), although he certainly did not make the point clear at the time. Kaldor (1983) eventually did make this sort of argument explicitly, as did the 'New-Keynesian' economist Mankiw (1985), some two years later. The mathematical details are explained in such sources as Smithin (2013a, 2013b) and (2018). Moreover, the existence of imperfect competition, in this precise sense, is closely connected with the underlying idea that effective demand must be in the form of *money*. In any event, it is important to note that the non-neutrality of both monetary policy and fiscal policy is not ultimately based on the conventional idea of short-run nominal wage rigidity.

The combination of both an upward-sloping ED and also an upward-sloping LRAS schedule is what accounts for the very different results that can be obtained in a true 'monetary analysis' of macroeconomics events as compared to those of the (essentially non-monetary) models of the standard/orthodox economic literature. The latter ultimately rely on one version or another of the assumptions of a 'natural' level of output or 'natural' rate of economic growth. This is exemplified in most of the textbook treatments by LRAS schedules that are ultimately *vertical*. As against this my own basic view about, or orientation towards, macroeconomic theory has always been that a truly 'Keynesian' approach would summarily dispense with all such things as natural rates of growth, natural rates of unemployment, unique NAIRU's,[9] vertical Phillips curves, and so on. The basic analysis should be essentially the same in both the short-run and the long-run. To put it another way, the macroeconomic equilibrium is always a *moving* equilibrium. In principle, therefore, economic growth and the cycle are inextricably interconnected (Smithin, 2018, 2022).

On this subject of imperfect competition, in an interview in a volume by Colander and Landreth (1996), published nearly half a century after the first publication of *Economics*, Samuelson himself plainly states that;

> We always assumed that the Keynesian underemployment equilibrium floated on a substructure of administered prices and imperfect competition.

However, Samuelson clearly failed to incorporate these ideas into the original 1948 edition of his book and thereafter. When asked by the interviewer—why not?—he replied '…there was no need to…'. This seems, in hindsight, to have been a significant tactical mistake on Samuelson's part. The device of the '45° line', inevitably, and in some quarters apparently irretrievably, confused the whole issue of demand *versus* supply, and has led to much misunderstanding and misinterpretation over the years. This statement includes most of the discussions that have taken place about both the BBM and the impact of changes in taxation on prices. Indeed, the whole idea of the so-called 'full employment' level of output, which seems to have played such as important role in Samuelson's political economy and as discussed above, tends to belie the idea that imperfect competition was truly believed to play an important role.

It should be mentioned also that another potential explanation for the long-run *non*-neutrality of monetary and fiscal policy along the LRAS would be the existence of path-dependency/hysteresis in the dynamic process for productivity growth. This is a vehicle favoured by several Post Keynesian economists, and also does check out empirically (Lavoie, 2009). Either of these two options would prove the point, and I would argue that both are likely to be present in reality (Smithin, 2018, 2022).

5 Changes in Government Expenditure and Taxation

How, then, will the analysis of changes in both taxation and government expenditure actually work out in the framework described above? In the context of a macroeconomic model which provides results for both the economic growth rate and the inflation rate, we will consider the effect of a 'balanced budget' increase in government expenditure as a percentage of GDP, offset by an equal increase in the average tax rate.

It will be convenient to consider, first, the effect of the tax increase taken in itself. This speaks directly to our original question about taxation and inflation. As to the underlying question about whether a tax increase is inflationary or deflationary, the original basis for the idea that it is *deflationary* was always that the demand-side effects of tax changes were supposed to be the opposite to those of changes in government expenditure. A tax cut, therefore, would have the same qualitative effect as an increase in government expenditure. It would tend to increase inflation. An increase in taxes, on the other hand, would be considered deflationary. As for a balanced budget change, the only question to ask would be about the relative magnitudes of the quantitative effects. It was not thought to be a question of their algebraic signs.

The most important difference between this kind of traditional analysis and that just sketched out above is that now the supply-side effects of tax changes are taken into account also. On the demand side, the upward-sloping ED schedule will shift back and to the left, because of the tax increase, which would indeed have been allowed for in the conventional analysis. But, at the same time, the increase in the average tax rate shifts the LRAS schedule up and to the left. This supply-side effect would *not* have been present in the conventional model. The flat SRAS schedule also begins to shift upwards.

There are thus both demand-side and supply-side effects of the tax increase, and they are all negative. The first impact will be a recession, but even during the recession there will have already been some increase in the inflation rate. It has not decreased. It is true that in the next phase of the cycle there will be something of a recovery from the depths of the recession. Nonetheless, the inflation rate will keep on rising until it reaches a new higher equilibrium level. In fact, the economy will never be able to return to the original rate of growth. The net effect of the increase in the average tax rate (considered on its own) is therefore higher inflation, lower economic growth, and a higher rate of unemployment.

We have already arrived at the answer to the original question about the effect of an increase in the average tax rate on inflation. Contrary to what sometimes seems to be the consensus view on all sides, an increase in the average tax rate is inflationary, not deflationary. Moreover, it is also one of the possible causes of 'stagflation'. For the purposes of the present paper, however, we are not able just to leave the matter there, even though it does answer the original question. We go on therefore to discuss the sign of the BBM itself. We will discover that a BBM increase in government expenditure as a percentage of GDP also causes stagflation.

If we add in the impact of an increase in the ratio of government spending to GDP, the first thing to remember is that what Samuelson did (the mistake Samuelson made) in the original discussion of the BBM was to focus only on the demand side of the model. The supply-side effect was ignored. Therefore, from his point of view, the increase in government spending would simply tend to increase effective demand whereas the increase in taxes would reduce it. As the effect of the government spending on demand is supposed to be numerically greater than that of the taxes, the net effect on demand would still be positive. In a graphical treatment, the ED schedule would shift out and to the right. If this demand-side impact (a net increase in demand) held good in the case of a BBM increase, what happens in *p,y* space is that the upward-sloping ED schedule shifts out and to right, while the similarly sloped LRAS schedule would shift up and to the left, due to the supply-side effect of the higher taxes. (Unlike in Samuelson this cannot be left out.) The end result will indeed be a higher rate of economic growth (due to the presumed offsetting demand-side effects), but also a higher rate of inflation (because of the supply-side effect of taxation). In terms of the original question about taxes and inflation, the basic notion that an increase in the average tax rate increases the inflation rate is not overturned. I should think that by this stage in the exposition this result is now well established. At the same time Samuelson's original BBM result on output (as translated into the growth context) is preserved. Having got this far, however, I would also strongly argue that the above discussion still remains only what professional economists call a ***partial equilibrium*** analysis, as opposed to a more complete ***general equilibrium*** analysis.

'Partial Equilibrium' Versus 'General Equilibrium' Analysis

In Sect. 2, I already remarked that I thought 'something was missing' from Samuelson's original discussion of the BBM. As has just been argued in detail one such thing was the lack of any coherent treatment of the supply side. It turns out, however, that this was not the only omission from the analysis. We will now go on to argue that even the demand-side analysis was incomplete.

The essential point to be made is that, thus far, we have not really looked at what might be called some of the 'longer-term' effects of a tax increase, not only on the supply side but also on the demand side itself. These should presumably include (I would say *must* include), in particular, the likely effect of a general tax increase in the overall profitability of business firms. At the end of the day, this ultimately has to be one of the most decisive factors in the willingness of the firms to continue making both investment expenditures (and for that matter any other types of spending) that they may otherwise be willing or likely to make.

To help to see this argument, it will be useful to briefly remind the reader of the standard 'expenditure breakdown' of GDP as it appears in the textbooks. This is, namely, $Y = C + I + G + (X - IM)$ where Y stands for real GDP, C for real consumption expenditures, I for real investment expenditure, G for real government expenditure, and $X - IM$ for real net exports (i.e., foreign demand). If, for simplicity, we choose (as did Samuelson in the passage quoted above) to neglect the foreign component of demand, that is, to focus only on the 'closed-economy' case, this reduces to $Y = C + I + G$.

As already discussed, the BBM analysis always did suggest that a government expenditure increase adds directly to effective demand whereas an increase in taxation reduces it, albeit by a somewhat more indirect route (that is, by reducing consumption expenditures). In short, G goes up and C goes down but, because G goes up by more than C, the net effect is positive. As far as investment is concerned, Samuelson's original argument was that investment spending was governed primarily by Keynes's 'animal spirits' (Keynes, 1936), or business confidence. This can be very volatile but, as far as the multiplier analysis is concerned, there is no reason for business confidence to change. Thus I is effectively treated as a constant for the purposes of the BBM analysis. Therefore, G goes up, C will fall but by a lesser amount, and I remains the same. The overall effect on demand is positive.

There is general agreement that animal spirits are a very important factor in making investment decisions. At the same time, however, the firm's actually realized results in terms of profitability must be an equally important factor. This sort of thing was left out of consideration entirely in Samuelson's discussion. Common sense dictates that as well as negatively affecting consumption an increase in the average tax rate must also have a directly negative effect on the overall profitability of business firms. It is therefore a disincentive to continued investment spending. In both *Rethinking the Theory of Money Credit and Macroeconomics* (Smithin,

2018), and *Beyond Barter* (Smithin, 2022), I carried out a formal analysis of this issue along the lines just described. It was discovered that the 'profitability effect' is so pronounced as to more than offset the supposedly positive impact on effective demand that was originally canvassed in Samuelson's BBM analysis.

The general equilibrium analysis of a balanced budget increase in the government spending ratio therefore works out as follows. The increase in the average tax rate still shifts the LRAS schedule up and to the left, as before. But, now, the negative effect of higher taxes on profitability (together with the existing negative effect on consumption) more than offsets any increase in effective demand arising from the increase in government expenditure. Total effective demand *falls*. In short, the ED schedule also shifts back and to the left. The result, once again, is stagflation, a combination of higher inflation, lower economic growth and higher unemployment. And, historically, the 'pseudo-Keynesian' era in the decades immediately after WW2, which was indeed heavily characterized by the 'tax and spend', ethos did come to an end in exactly that way.

The exact date of the end of that era is sometimes given as September 28, 1976 (in the middle of the 'stagflationary' 1970s), on the occasion of a speech given that day by the then British Prime Minister, James Callaghan at the annual Labour Party conference in Blackpool.[10] According to Callaghan, as quoted by Smithin (1990);

> We used to think that you could spend your way out of a recession, and increase employment by cutting taxes and boosting Government spending. I tell you in all candour that that option no longer exists, and that in so far as it ever did exist, it only worked on each occasion since the war by injecting a bigger dose of inflation into the economy, followed by a higher level of unemployment as the next step. Higher inflation followed by higher unemployment.

But according to the above analysis Callaghan got things entirely the wrong way round. He seems to either have misunderstood cause and effect, or perhaps (as a politician) was simply being disingenuous. If his government had indeed pursued a policy of *both* increasing spending and cutting taxes (the *opposite* solution, then and now, to what the conventional wisdom has usually suggested) British economy would have been just fine. There may have been somewhat higher inflation than otherwise (although certainly not 'ever-accelerating' inflation), but also rising economic growth and falling unemployment.[11] It is the 'stag' part of stagflation, after all, that is the main problem, not the 'flation' part. In reality, by 1976, in his former role as 'Chancellor of the Exchequer' (essentially Minister of Finance), Callaghan had already been merrily increasing taxes for quite some time. The real purpose of the speech seems actually to have been designed to justify a forthcoming 'austerity policy'—in the form of still higher taxes rather than serious cuts in spending—again on the principle of 'tax and spend'. In short, higher taxation, in itself, seems in retrospect to have been the main objective. (As is well-known, the main spending cuts did not come until several years later, during the administration of Margaret Thatcher after 1979.)

On a more contemporary note, it is highly ironic in my opinion (but not entirely unexpected given the economic and political events of the last few years) that as these words are being written at end of 2021 the stagflationary conditions of the late 1970s seem to be back with us once again, and with a vengeance. It seems that nothing at all has been learned in all that time—more than 45 years. I hope that Keynes will not have to take the blame once again.

6 Conclusion

In the *General Theory* Keynes (1936) did not advocate a 'tax and spend' policy, but rather explicitly favoured a policy of 'loan expenditure'. He seemed to understand, at least intuitively, and as I have put the point in the past, that 'someone, somewhere, must be willing to continuously go into debt in order to provide profits for others' (Smithin, 2016, 2018). However, essentially because of his (Keynes's) unfortunate decision to 'let technical monetary detail fall into the background' in the exposition in the *General Theory*, it seems that very many of his readers, including Samuelson, did not fully grasp the point.

As I now see it, therefore, it seems that what Samuelson was trying to do in the mid-twentieth century—in the context of what, no doubt, was the very difficult task of interpreting Keynes for an American audience—was to try to *combine* Keynes's message that government spending per se would indeed add to effective demand with the traditional concern for 'sound finance'. The spending must be 'paid for'. But this compromise does not work. It cannot work. The sign of balanced budget multiplier is negative, not positive. In reality, a tax and spend policy will amount to nothing more than one of the possible causes of stagflation. As already mentioned, in the actual historical record stagflation duly arrived in the 1970s. It was responsible for the backlash at the time against what was called 'Keynesian economics' (but, as we have seen, really should have been called Samuelsonian economics) in that time period.

The same analysis answers the question 'are tax increases inflationary or deflationary?' in an unambiguous way. An increase in the average tax rate in the economy can be nothing other than inflationary. Such a change is part and parcel of an overall stagflation scenario.

Acknowledgements I would like to thank Nina Eichacker, Eric Kam, Steve Pressman, Bill Scarth, and participants of the session 'Unsettled Questions in Monetary Macroeconomics' at the Eastern Economic Association annual conference in Boston, February 2020, for helpful comments and suggestions that have improved this paper.

Notes

1. The idea is rather that the purpose of taxation is to create a demand for base money (that is, the liabilities of the state central bank). This is sometimes expressed by the slogan 'taxes drive money'. Elsewhere (Smithin, 2022) I have commented on what I have called 'logically unassailable' nature of the core MMT proposition, namely 'that the central government of an economy with its own sovereign currency, and either a floating exchange rate or a fixed-but-adjustable' exchange rate, faces no binding financial constraints'.
2. I have used capital letters here to emphasise that I am talking specifically about the academic fields of study that go by these names.
3. Barrows and Smithin (2009) explain this argument using a simple diagrammatic analysis.
4. The original idea of the 'multiplier' in Keynes's *General Theory* was to predict by how much the level of GDP would increase for a given increase in the level of spending. If MPC stands for the marginal propensity to consume, then the simplest version of the government expenditure would be $\Delta Y/\Delta G = [1/(1\text{–MPC})]$. If, for example, we have MPC $= 0.8$, the multiplier would be 5. This is to say that an increase in government spending of \$1 million would lead to an increase in GDP of \$5 million.
5. In the more recent textbooks this would be replaced by the concept of *gross* domestic product, GDP, or similar.
6. Samuelson himself, of course, did not include the price level, *P*, in his graphical presentation.

7. See Smithin (2018, 2022) for a discussion of the real world difficulties that this type of response has frequently caused.
8. The 'non-accelerating-inflation rate of unemployment'.
9. In an eerie coincidence, that was 48 years almost to the day after another infamous statement by a hapless British Prime Minister (Neville Chamberlain promising 'peace in our time').
10. For a detailed explanation of these propositions, see Smithin (2018, 2022).

References

Barrows, D. and Smithin, J. (2009). *Fundamentals of economics for business,* (2nd ed.). Captus Press and World Scientific Publishing.

Chick, V. (1983). *Macroeconomics after Keynes: A reconsideration of the general theory*. MIT Press.

Colander, D., & Landreth, H. (1997). *The coming of Keynesianism to America: Conversations with the founders of Keynesian economics*. Edward Elgar.

Collis, R. (2018). *Three essays on monetary macroeconomics: An empirical examination of the soundness of the alternative monetary model and monetary policy in Canada*. PhD thesis in Economics, York University, Toronto.

Hayek, F. A. (1932). A note on the development of the doctrine of 'forced saving'. *Quarterly Journal of Economics, 47*, 123–133.

Kaldor, N. (1983). Keynesian economics after fifty years. In D. N. Worswick & J. R. Trevithick (Eds.), *Keynes and the modern world* (pp. 1–27). Cambridge University Press.

Kam, E. (2005). A note on time preference and the Tobin effect. *Economic Letters, 89*, 137–142.

Kam, E., & Smithin, J. (2012). A simple theory of banking and the relationship between the commercial banks and the central bank. *Journal of Post Keynesian Economics, 34*, 545–549.

Kam, E., Smithin, J., & Tabassum, A. (2019). The long-run non-neutrality of monetary policy: A general statement in a dynamic general equilibrium (DGE) model. *Review of Political Economy, 31*, 202–217.

Kelton, S. (2020). *The deficit myth: Modern monetary theory and the birth of the people's economy*. Hachette Book Group.

Keynes, J. M. (1936). *The general theory of employment interest and money*. Macmillan.

Lavoie, M. (2009). *Introduction to Post Keynesian economics: With a new postface on the subprime financial crisis*. Palgrave Macmillan.

Mankiw, N. G. (1985). Small menu costs and large business cycles: A macroeconomic model of monopoly. *Quarterly Journal of Economics, 100*, 529–553.

Mitchell, W., Wray, L. R., & Watts, M. (2019). *Macroeconomics*. Red Globe Press.

Pressman, S., & Smithin, J. (2022). Some unsettled questions in monetary macroeconomics. In S. Pressman & J. Smithin (Eds.), *Debates in monetary macroeconomics: Tackling some unsettled questions* (this volume). Palgrave Macmillan.

Samuelson, P. (1964). *Economics: An introductory analysis* (6th ed.). McGraw-Hill.

Samuleson, P. (1997). *Economics: The original 1948 edition*. McGraw-Hill.

Schumpeter, J. (1954). *History of economic analysis* (Reprinted by Routledge 1994).

Smithin, J. (1982). *The incidence and economic effects of the financing of unemployment insurance*. PhD thesis in Economics. McMaster University, Hamilton ON.

Smithin, J. (1990). *Macroeconomics after Thatcher and Reagan: The conservative policy revolution in retrospect*. Edward Elgar.

Smithin, J. (2004). Interest rate operating procedures and income distribution. In M. Lavoie & M. Seccareccia (Eds.), *Central banking in the modern world: Alternative perspectives* (pp. 57–69). Edward Elgar.

Smithin, J. (2013a). *Essays in the fundamental theory of monetary economics and macroeconomics*. World Scientific Publishing.

Smithin, J. (2013b). A re-habilitation of the theory of effective demand from chapter 3 of Keynes's General Theory (1936). *International Journal of Political Economy, 42*, 6–24.

Smithin, J. (2014). Economic growth: Free trade, public finance, and the paradox of thrift. *Review of Keynesian Economics, 2*, 456–463.

Smithin, J. (2016). Some puzzles about money, finance, and the monetary circuit. *Cambridge Journal of Economics, 40*, 1259–1274.

Smithin, J. (2018). *Rethinking the theory of money, credit and macroeconomics: A new statement for the twenty-first century*. Lexington Books.

Smithin, J. (2022). *Beyond barter: Lectures in monetary economics after 'rethinking'*. World Scientific Publishing.

Wray, L. R. (2012). *Modern money theory: A primer on macroeconomics for sovereign monetary systems*. Palgrave Macmillan.

CHAPTER 7

Taxes Are Deflationary and Can Be Used as a Deflationary Tool

Joëlle Leclaire

1 Introduction

Taxes, in their many guises, are typically deflationary. This is due to their impact on demand. Higher taxes reduce the income that households have to spend and thereby reduce spending by people. Cuts in consumer spending, in turn, puts downward pressure on prices. This deflationary force is much greater than any possible inflationary pressures that higher taxes might create due to their impact on the cost of producing goods and services, and therefore the price of goods and services. In addition, when taxes are paid to the government, this reduces reserves in the banking system. In the past, this might have put upward pressure on interest rates, which is a component of the price of many goods. Today, however, the

J. Leclaire (✉)
Department of Economics and Finance,
Buffalo State College, Buffalo, NY, USA
e-mail: leclaijj@buffalostate.edu

S. Pressman and J. Smithin (eds.), *Debates in Monetary Macroeconomics*,
https://doi.org/10.1007/978-3-031-11240-9_7

interest rate in the US and Canada, as well as in Europe, is a policy variable determined by the central bank. So, lower reserves should have no direct impact on either the interest rate or on the price of goods.

This chapter begins by outlining different types of inflation and several different types of taxes paid by economic agents. Section 2 explains the three types of inflation—consumer-price inflation, asset-price inflation and "true inflation." Section 3 then looks at eight types of taxes levied by the government. It also examines the extent to which both the US Federal government as well as state and local governments in the US rely on these different types of taxes. It then looks at the impact of each type of tax on prices (and thus inflation).

Deflation due to higher taxes occurs via two related channels—a fiscal channel and a monetary channel. Section 4 looks at the economic impact of taxes through the lens of fiscal policy. It argues that increases in Federal taxes are deflationary, and that state and local tax increases are also deflationary, but less deflationary than hikes in Federal taxes. Much of the fiscal channel takes place directly through a reduction in aggregate demand as taxes take money out of the hands of people and business firms. As a result, people and firms are likely to spend less. Reduced demand, in turn, will lead to higher unemployment, pressures on firms to stop increasing prices, and even pressures on firms to cut prices in order to sell goods and services. There is also an indirect manner in which taxes are deflationary. When taxes (such as VAT or sales taxes) do increase the price of goods, leading to consumer-price inflation, real incomes fall. This leads to a decline in real spending, and puts downward pressure on prices. In this case, the overall impact of the tax is less clear on inflation, as it depends on things such as how much of the cost increase can be passed on to consumers, as well as on how much any reduction in demand leads firms to cut their prices.

Section 5 looks at the impact of taxes through the lens of monetary policy. This monetary channel is the result of how taxes affect bank reserves and net private sector wealth. This section shows that higher taxes remove reserves from the banking system and reduce private sector wealth. It argues that this, in turn, reduces both demand for goods and services deriving from spending out of wealth (a part of consumer-price inflation) and asset-price inflationary pressures.

2 Types of Inflation

There are three types of inflation that need to be distinguished: consumer-price inflation, asset-price inflation, and true inflation. It is important to keep these different types of inflation separate because each type of inflation has different causes and each type of inflation has a different impact on the economy. In addition, different taxes will have different effects on different types of inflation. Consequently, each type of inflation needs to be discussed separately.

Consumer-Price Inflation

Consumer-price inflation is what people are familiar with and worry about. It is a rise in the price of the market basket of goods purchased by a typical household, and is measured in the US by the Bureau of Labor Statistics and similar government statistical agencies in other nations. Economics textbooks usually identify two types of consumer-price inflation—cost-push inflation and demand-pull inflation.

Cost-push inflation is caused by increased costs of producing goods and services. This, in turn, stems from higher prices for factors of production (land, labor, and capital equipment). If those costs are passed on to consumers, which depends on the elasticity of demand for the products in question, then we have cost-push inflation. One example of cost-push inflation was when OPEC raised oil prices in the 1970s. This led to rising production costs because energy was needed to produce things, get parts to manufacturers, and distribute final goods to where consumers bought things.

Demand-pull inflation for consumption goods happens as a result of increased spending for products. In this case, firms see increased demand and respond by increasing their prices and thus their profits. Demand-pull inflation usually occurs during wartime as spending by the Federal government is added to normal spending by consumers and business firms for investment purposes. Governments are reluctant to increase taxes to pay for war, fearing that this might reduce popular support for the war effort. In the US, there were bursts of inflation during World War II, the Korean War, and the Vietnam War.

Regardless of whether inflation is cost-push or demand-pull, increased production of consumer goods will bring prices down to more acceptable levels. When supply factors allow for more production, or demand falls, inflation will return to normal levels. As a result, there is very little need to be concerned with consumer-price inflation as long as we are confident that we can increase employment, labor productivity, and our productive capacity.

Consumer-price inflation may also affect the distribution of wealth and income, but those concerns should be balanced with the distributional effects of deflation. When consumer prices increase, this puts pressure on the purchasing power or consumers and benefits producers, skewing the distribution of income and wealth in favor of firms. On the other hand, when prices fall, consumers may benefit at the expense of producers. In a deflationary environment, the relative purchasing power of household income or wealth increases, as long as income or wealth remains stable in nominal terms.

One way to reduce consumer-price inflation is by raising taxes. There are many ways to go about doing this. The best ways would involve increasing taxes on household incomes, which lower disposable income and household spending. Reduced demand, in turn, puts downward pressure on prices.

Asset-Price Inflation

Asset-price inflation concerns changes in the price of assets or wealth held by people and firms, rather than the price of goods that are consumed by households. While consumer inflation clearly reduces the standard of living of households, this is not the case for asset-price inflation. In fact, just the opposite is true. When stock prices rise, households owning stocks have greater wealth. In addition, this additional wealth will lead to larger returns to households from this wealth in the form of dividends and capital gains. Similarly, when home prices rise, middle-class households, whose wealth is held mainly in the form of home values, will benefit. Some of the increased home value can be borrowed against at low interest rates by taking out home equity loans. This money can then be used for consumption purposes or to reduce other household debt (such as balances on credit cards) that charge much higher interest rates. Moreover, the value of the home can be used to fund the household in retirement—either by enabling them to downsize and receive a large sum of money, or by taking out a home equity loan or reverse mortgage.

Like consumer goods, financial assets can be affected by both cost factors and demand factors. Some financial assets will increase in price when costs associated with holding the asset increase, such as increased fees for example. In this way, financial assets would be affected by cost-push factors. Financial assets might also be influenced by demand-pull factors. When the demand for a particular asset increases, this would tend to increase the price of that asset. One good example of this is higher home prices that are driven by the desire to live in large urban areas and suburban areas with good school districts, and where it is not easy to build additional housing due to zoning restrictions (Glaeser & Gyourko, 2002). Higher financial asset prices are usually desired, given they increase the total value of wealth holdings, but high levels of speculation in financial markets are also linked to instability and financial crises.

There are several ways that financial assets can be taxed in order to reduce asset-price inflation. One way to do this would be to tax the income flows that result from owning these assets. This is done, at present, by taxing people on the stock dividends that they receive because they own shares of stock; it is also done by taxing rent payments that accrue to people from owning land and buildings.

Governments can also tax the value of these assets, or the stock of assets held by individuals. Governments can do this by taxing the value of existing assets through a wealth tax. While these taxes became prominent in Western Europe for several decades following World World II, governments began to abandon wealth taxes in the 1980s. By 2020, only three developed, high-income nations impose a tax on wealth on their citizens—Norway, Spain, and Switzerland. Alternatively, governments can tax the value of these assets when they are sold, which is what capital gains taxes and transfer taxes on real estate seek to do. In these cases, the taxes will reduce the price of the assets that are taxed. For example, a tax on the value of homes owned by people will make home ownership more expensive. As a result of this, people will be less likely to purchase a home, and more likely to purchase homes of lower value. Both of these behavioral responses will tend to reduce home prices on average throughout the economy.

Another way to tax assets is a transfer tax on financial assets or a financial transactions tax. This idea was originally proposed by James Tobin (1978), who argued that a financial transactions tax could be used to moderately increase the cost of trading currency, and thereby reduce the volatility of short-term currency speculation. Since then, this type of tax has been proposed for all financial assets used for speculative purposes. The idea is that adding the financial transactions tax would make it less appealing for short-term speculators by making investment more costly. It is believed that this policy would reduce price volatility in financial markets. It may also reduce asset-price inflation because it imposes costs on buying and selling assets.

If stability in financial markets is what is desired, this might be more easily secured by a market maker, as Paul Davidson (1998) suggests. An appreciation in the price of a financial asset will cause certain investors to increase their purchases of the asset and certain investors to sell their positions. This happens in the market for financial assets because the financial market is designed to increase liquidity for all market participants, and some investors will want to buy (expect the price to increase) while others will take the opposite position (expect the price to fall). The liquidity of the market overall is guaranteed because there are investors on both sides of asset-price expectations. However, under certain conditions, there may be a preponderance of sellers (expecting the price to fall), which makes for an illiquid market, that is effectively, unstable. Davidson suggested that a market maker could provide the solution to this difficult situation when the demand to purchase certain assets is greater than the desire to sell.

True Inflation

In 1929, Keynes wrote an essay entitled "A Programme of Expansion." In this piece he explained that inflation occurs when we push demand beyond our economy's ability to handle that demand immediately. He wrote: "Inflation only results, when we endeavour, as we did in the war and afterwards, to expand our activities still further after everyone is already employed and our savings are being used up to the hilt (Keynes, 1963, 124)." He writes about inflation in *The General Theory* in similar terms: "When a further increase in the quantity of effective demand produces no further increase in output and entirely spends itself on an increase in the cost-unit fully proportionate to the increase in effective demand, we have reached a condition which might be appropriately designated as one of true inflation" (Keynes, 1973 [1936], 303).

Keynes was making the point here that government spending is not always and everywhere inflationary, which counters arguments against government spending. Consumption, investment, net exports, and government spending can increase up to the point where no more employment is possible, and no more production can be turned out given our current productive capacities. At this point, we find ourselves in a state of true inflation, where any increase in spending only goes to raise prices.

Why did Keynes insist on providing us with a third type of inflation, true inflation? He did so because he wanted it to be clear that government spending could increase employment as well as goods and services (somewhat in tandem), and that it could also lead to increases in asset prices. In both of these cases, consumer-price inflation and asset-price inflation, the rise in prices is generally good for the economy. More people have jobs and incomes. Also, the wealth of households (in the form of stocks, bonds, and housing) also goes up, making these households better off.

As with both consumer-price inflation and asset-price inflation, a wide range of taxes can be increased to lower true inflation. The taxes we discuss in Section 3 would all lower demand and thereby exert downward pressure on prices. We now turn to these taxes.

3 Different Types of Taxes

Taxes have always been considered a drain on the economy. Federal taxes, in particular, are a big drain. They take financial resources out of the hands of people and firms, by reducing their bank account balances, which reduces spending in the economy and exerts downward pressure on prices. There are eight main types of tax—(1) individual income taxes, (2) employment or social insurance taxes, (3) corporate income taxes, (4) wealth taxes, (5) financial transactions taxes, (6) excise taxes, (7) sales or value-added taxes (VAT), and (8) property taxes. Only two, excise taxes (taxes on specific goods) and sales/VAT taxes (taxes on all goods bought) will tend to push up prices. But even in these cases, there are deflationary aspects to the tax that counter this. For all the other types of taxes, the impact of raising them will be to reduce demand and put downward pressure on prices.

The first type of tax is the personal or individual income tax. It is paid by most income groups in most countries. Usually, the poor pay little or no income taxes due to a large deduction that is allowed before positive tax rates kick in. People pay income taxes on realized capital gains, on interest and dividend income, on rental income, on employment income, on any taxable transfers such as Social Security payments, and on retirement income taken from accounts where pre-tax income was deposited. The majority of total individual income taxes are paid by higher income households because tax rates are generally progressive. Income taxes reduce the amount of money households have to spend or invest in assets, and therefore exerts a deflationary effect on the economy. This puts downward pressure on both consumer and asset prices. As such, tax increases on individual incomes can be used by governments to respond to rising inflation.

The second type of tax is the employment tax, which is paid by employers and employees, and is assessed on the wages received by workers. Two of the main payroll taxes are retirement and unemployment insurance taxes. Usually these taxes are phased out or eliminated when income reaches a certain limit. For example, in 2021 the US Social Security tax ended at an income of $142,800. While the first $142,800 of wage income was taxed at a rate of 6.2% on the employee, with another 6.2% paid by the employer, higher levels of wage income were not taxed by Social Security. This tax has even been targeted in policy action during times of economic crisis because it can be adjusted quickly and has a direct impact on a large swathe of the working population. During the Great Recession, the Social Security tax rate was reduced by 2 percentage points in 2011 and 2012 for employees and for self-employed workers. This increased spending. A hike in the Social Security tax would have the opposite effect. It would reduce disposable income and reduce consumer spending, and so consumer-price inflation would fall.

The third type of tax is the corporate income tax. It is assessed on the profits of incorporated businesses. Incorporated businesses are supposed to pay Federal income taxes at a rate of 21% in the US in 2021. They also pay state corporate income taxes. In fact, due to various legal tax breaks as well as some tax avoidance schemes, companies pay much lower tax rates on their profits. Some large and profitable companies pay little or none. Since it was enacted in 1894, the corporate income tax rate has increased at times and has fallen at other times. The corporate income tax was at its highest level, 53%, in 1942. It was at its lowest level at its inception of 1% in 1909 (Internal Revenue Service, 2021). The trend since the end of World War II has been to cut corporate income taxes, and this tendency has become more pronounced over time, due to competition among countries in a world of mobile corporate capital and due to conservative Republican tax policy governments that have reduced taxes on the wealthy. Although a matter of some dispute, economists believe that most of the corporate income tax is paid by the wealthy owners of corporate stock (Pechman & Okner, 1974). Just as the individual income tax reduces the amount of money that households have to spend, the corporate income tax reduces the amount of money corporations have to spend and therefore exerts a deflationary effect on the economy. As a result, higher corporate income taxes put downward pressure on prices. Raising the corporate income tax can be used by governments to respond to inflationary pressures

Fourth, there is the wealth tax. This is a tax that is paid on net wealth accumulation above a specific threshold. The aim of this tax is to reduce excessive wealth, although it is erroneously thought by many to be a way of funding various government programs. But there is, in fact, no connection between wealth taxes and spending on government programs. These are two different decisions made by governments. One decision concerns taxing wealth in order to mitigate income and wealth inequality. The other decision concerns how much money the government is going to spend on various programs.

There are actually two main types of wealth tax. One is the sort proposed by Thomas Piketty. Piketty (2014) would apply a 1% annual tax to wealth between 1 million Euros (1.13 million USD) and 5 million Euros (5.7 million USD). Wealth above 5 million Euros would be taxed at 2% annually. The US Federal government does not impose a wealth tax. In fact, very few developed nations do in part because wealth is likely to be moved across borders to avoid taxes. A global wealth tax might be the part of the answer to prevent tax avoidance but how wealth is valued complicates the issue (Pressman, 2016, 139–142). Wealth is held in various forms, some of which are easily valued (like stocks, bonds, property) while others are more difficult to value, business equity being one example.

The second type of wealth tax falls on estates and large gifts. Most estates are not actually taxed in the US because taxes are imposed only at estates and gifts exceeding a value of 11.7 million USD in 2021, and most estates fall below this amount. In addition, there are numerous ways to escape estate taxes. Gifts from wealthy individuals to their heirs would avoid the tax. The taxation of large gifts is thus a necessary complement to taxing large estates.

The failure by nations to tax wealth as well as estates and large gifts means that, in practice, wealth taxes don't reduce inequality by very much. Even if a large wealth tax reduced inequality by a considerable amount, it is not clear that the tax would reduce spending by much or exert a recessionary pressure on the economy. This is because much of what gets taxed with a wealth tax is savings that had been accumulated for many years, and this money is not likely to be spent at all. However, wealth taxes can reduce asset-price inflation, especially if wealth must be sold in order to pay the taxes owed to the government.

Fifth, there are taxes on financial transactions. This is a tax imposed on selling (or the buying) of financial assets. The tax is intended to reduce the frequency of trading in order to promote longer term investment and penalize short-term investment. The tax would increase the cost of the financial transaction and therefore dampens demand for those transactions. Because the elasticity of demand for financial assets is not very dependent on price, and is heavily dependent on expected returns, a financial transactions tax will not reduce the demand for financial assets by very much. So, it will not have much impact on asset-price inflation.

Sixth, there are taxes on specific goods—excise taxes and tariffs. Excise taxes are often applied to undesirable goods like cigarettes, alcohol, and gasoline. In this case the taxes are paid by consumers when they purchase the goods. The goal of the tax is to reduce consumption of that specific good and shift consumer purchases to other goods. Although they may have desirable social ends (better health and cleaner environment), consumers end up paying a higher price for those items that are subject to an excise tax. Excise taxes can also apply to manufacturers and retailers. In these cases, the higher price of goods, due to the excise tax, can generally be passed along to the consumer. The result is that consumers will buy less of the taxed goods. But if they still purchase large quantities of these goods, the higher price due to excise taxes makes it likely that the real value of household income will fall and so consumers will be spending less on output. This is the deflationary aspect of the excise tax.

Similar to the excise tax is a tax on imported goods, or a tariff. Like the excise tax it is imposed on some goods but not others, and like excise taxes it is to a large extent passed on to the consumer in the form of higher prices. This makes it somewhat inflationary in nature. But, as with excise taxes, the loss of purchasing power by households exerts a deflationary force on the economy, and so mitigates the inflationary nature of the tax. Unlike an excise tax, however, tariffs are likely to cause consumers to buy goods that are made at home rather than more expensive imports. To the extent that this happens, a tariff will not reduce household purchasing power as much as an excise tax, and any increase in demand will exert inflationary pressure on the economy.

Seventh, there are sales taxes and value-added taxes. A sales tax is imposed on the final sale of some goods or services to the consumer.

A value-added tax is imposed at every level in the process of producing, transporting, and selling goods and services. Sales taxes, like excise taxes, raise prices. And, like excise taxes, they raise prices for the consumer directly. The higher costs due to VAT at all parts of production process will get passed along the supply chain from one firm to another, until finally the retailer passes most of the tax to the consumer. The end result of a VAT is just like that of a sales tax—higher prices for consumers. But the process is more dispersed over the entire production process. In addition, like the excise tax, the sales tax and the value-added tax will exert recessionary forces on the economy because they reduce the purchasing power of the household and therefore spending. Sales taxes and value-added taxes will lower asset prices only to the extent that lower levels of spending by consumers reduce corporate profits.

The final type of tax is the property tax. This tax is assessed on the value of land and homes owned by people and business firms. In the US typically it is paid to municipal governments based on the assessed value of real estate held and the improvements on that land. This money is then used to fund things like education, police protection, and fire protection for the local community. In other nations, the money is collected by the national government. Like the wealth tax, the property tax is generally not a good policy choice for dealing with the problem of consumer-price inflation. Households may reduce their consumption in order to cover property taxes, pushing demand down. But as it is a tax on assets, increasing the property tax will not reduce spending by much. On the other hand, higher property taxes will mitigate asset-price inflation. Higher property taxes paid to the county, city, or municipality, will reduce new home purchases, other things being equal, leading to deflationary pressure on real estate.

Table 1 shows the amount of money received by the US Federal government from the various types of taxes that we discussed above. It makes quite clear the largest category of taxes paid to the Federal government is the personal income tax, which is followed closely by social insurance taxes. The third largest source of Federal tax is the corporate income tax. These three categories of taxation are all taxes on incomes (either individual income or corporate profits). Together they overwhelm all the other sources of Federal government revenue by a factor of around 30. The majority of Federal government taxes reduce income directly. As a result, they reduce spending and demand in the entire economy. This puts downward pressure on prices.

Table 1 Total US federal tax receipts, 2020

Type of Tax	*Billions of USD*
Personal current income taxes	1679.6
Contributions for government social insurance	1444.6
Taxes on corporate income	192.7
Excise taxes	88.1
Customs duties	68.6
Taxes from the rest of the world	27.4
Other	1.2

Source Bureau of Economic Analysis, 2021. Table 3.2. Retrieved 9/12/21

Table 2 looks at the revenue sources of state and local governments. It should be noted at the outset that the tax collected at these lower levels of government in the US is close to the amount collected by the Federal government. Table 2 shows that the largest categories of state and local government receipts are state income taxes and sales taxes. Two large Federal taxes—corporate income taxes and employment taxes (primarily state unemployment insurance)—are relatively small contributors to state and local government revenues. So, unlike the Federal government, whose main tax is primarily income taxes, state governments rely nearly equally on taxes that are imposed on incomes and taxes that are imposed on the sales of goods and services. Also unlike the taxes imposed by the Federal government, these tax revenues usually lead to greater spending by state and local governments; so state and local government taxes typically return tax revenues to the local economy and to the flow of consumption and income. So, they do not have a large deflationary effect. This is one reason that fiscal policy in the US is usually conducted at the Federal level.

4 Taxes Are Deflationary Due to Their Impact on Spending and Wealth

The key question that needs to be addressed is the following: are taxes deflationary in their overall impact? Secondarily, is the effect greater on the economy from asset-price inflation or the consumer-price inflation? We start with an analysis of all Federal taxes and their effect on aggregate demand for consumer goods and financial assets. Clearly, all Federal

Table 2 Total state and local tax receipts for the US, 2020 (Billions of USD)

Type of Tax	*Billions of USD*
Personal current income taxes	1963.6
Sales taxes	1376.6
Other production and import taxes	615.3
Excise taxes	448.9
Property taxes	202.7
Taxes on corporate income	109.8
Contributions for government social insurance	71

Source Bureau of Economic Analysis, 2021. Table 3.3. Retrieved 9/12/21

taxes are deflationary, partly or entirely, because they draw money out of the economy directly through the various tax channels. In this way aggregate demand for consumer goods as well as the demand for financial assets falls with the amount drawn out of personal income, employment income contributions for social insurance from employees and employers, corporate income and other tax revenue sources such as excise taxes and a wealth tax or a property tax.

Without Federal taxes, US GDP would have been about 12% higher on average from 1947 to 2020 (Bureau of Economic Analysis, 2021, Tables 1.1.5 and 3.2, and author's calculations). Taxes thus represent a considerable drain on the economy. Federal taxes have a major recessionary effect, and this effect reduces both consumer and asset prices from where they would have been without this economic drain. Lower consumer prices in this case reflect lower demand for consumer goods.

Higher taxes will also reduce asset-price inflation. Any tax that falls on asset values or asset sales, such as a financial transactions tax, a property tax, or a wealth tax, will reduce the returns or gains from holding that asset and will thus reduce the willingness of people to buy or hold that asset. This reduced demand for assets will, in turn, lower asset prices or reduce asset-price inflation. In addition, any increase in taxes, also taxes away income that households would have had to spend on goods and services. Any tax on assets also reduces the income that households would have otherwise put toward saving and purchasing assets. This too reduces the demand for assets and the price of these assets. Lower asset prices caused by higher levels of taxation could be construed as positive because they make wealth inequality less unequal.

While taxes are overall deflationary, as we noted above, some taxes tend to push up prices. These are the taxes that impact the cost of producing and selling goods. The main taxes that do this are sales taxes, excise taxes, and value-added taxes. However, as we saw above, these are a very small part of Federal government taxation for the US and their impact is overwhelmed by the deflationary aspect of Federal government taxation.

5 Federal Taxes Are Deflationary Due to Their Impact on Net Wealth

There is another reason taxation is deflationary. It drains reserves out of the national banking system. Through this monetary transmission mechanism, higher taxes (given no change in government spending) will reduce private net wealth and exert downward pressure on both consumer and asset prices. This section explains why this is so, first by explaining how government spending increases the reserves of banks and then how tax increases reduce the reserves of banks.

Reserves are held by banks in order to meet reserve requirements. These reserves never enter into the economy, and therefore they do not affect spending or inflation because they are contained within the banking system.

The central bank sets the discount rate and the overnight lending rate. The discount rate is the interest rate it charges banks for borrowing reserves to meet overnight reserve requirements. The overnight lending rate is the rate the central bank pays on reserves of banks that it holds. The discount rate and the overnight rate paid on reserves by the central bank form a band which contains all the market interest rates on reserves.

Banks needing reserves to meet their reserve requirement can borrow them either from other banks or from the central bank. They will seek to borrow first from other banks at a rate which is below the discount rate. Any banks needing reserves which cannot borrow from other banks, will be forced to borrow directly from the central bank and pay the discount rate.

Banks with excess reserves will seek to lend them at a rate which is greater than the rate paid by the central bank (the overnight rate). Banks will seek to lend out as much of their excess reserves as possible at rates greater than the central bank rate (and lower than the discount rate). Similarly, banks needing reserves will try as much as possible to get them for less than the discount rate. In this way, the central bank rate and the discount rate form a band which contains all the market rates for reserve market transactions (Lavoie, 2011, 11; Wray, 2012, 114–117).

To be clear, when credit-worthy borrowers are given a bank loan, the bank finds the reserves to meet their reserve requirement at the Fed. If bank customers have deposited enough in their accounts, then they may have the right amount of reserves already. If they are short on reserves, the bank will borrow from other banks with excess reserves or from the Fed's discount window. The reserves in the system do not lead to more or less production, lending, or inflation. Reserves are the result of government spending and of private investment decisions made by firms and individuals in coordination with lending decisions made by banks.

New government spending always creates new reserves in the banking system. The government spends by writing checks, which then get deposited into bank accounts. This spending is offset by government bond holdings on the central bank's balance sheet. Central banks (the Federal Reserve in the US) pay a very low interest rates on excess reserves, so banks may choose to lend these excess reserves on the overnight to inter-bank market or use them to buy government bonds.

When business firms and households pay taxes as a part of their regular transactions, the situation we just described works in reverse. Now people and firms write checks to the government, which deposits them into their account at the central bank. In turn, the central bank takes the money away from the bank on which the check was written. A small fraction of the revenue withdrawn reduces required reserves. This will reduce the excess reserves of the bank. This shortage of reserves means that many banks will not be able to meet their reserve requirements. Banks will borrow what they can from other banks and then be forced to pay the bank discount rate. Alternatively, if the rate on Treasuries is lower than the discount rate, banks may choose to sell Treasuries to meet their reserve requirements. This will push the Treasury rate up, and prices down as their supply is fixed in the short term.

However, increasing taxes will not affect the interest rates determined by central bank policymakers, which are the overnight bank lending rate (called the "Federal Funds Rate" in the US) and the discount rate, or the interest rate paid by banks when borrowing from the Federal Reserve. These are controlled by the central bank. It may increase Treasury rates and decrease bond prices in the short term due to a fixed supply of bonds.

Further, in order to pay the taxes that they owe, individuals and firms may need to sell assets, such as stocks and bonds. Through this mechanism, taxes may reduce the demand for these assets, thereby lowering asset prices. Moreover, any consumer spending from wealth would also be reduced as wealth falls. As a result, asset-price inflation will fall in addition to consumer-price inflation because of the reduced spending in the economy.

6 Summary and Conclusion

From the analysis above, we can see that taxes are deflationary through their impact on both aggregate demand, and then the prices of both consumer goods and assets. Federal taxes are more deflationary than state and local government taxes because of the different taxes imposed by these different levels of government. If the goal is to reduce output or economic growth, in order to control inflationary pressures, a very effective method would be to increase Federal taxes on income. Taxes on wealth would also be effective for controlling asset-price inflation.

State and local taxes may also be deflationary though their impact on total demand or spending. However, it must be remembered that the taxes imposed by state and local governments are mainly used to support public infrastructure, public safety, education, and social insurance expenditures. Most of the tax revenues collected by state and local governments quickly return to the flow of spending (consumption and investment) and do not have much impact on the overall economy. In addition, state and local governments also rely proportionately more on excise taxes, sales taxes, and property taxes, and rely proportionately less on income taxes, than the Federal government. The former exerts upward pressure on prices in addition to reducing demand, so the deflationary impact of these taxes is mitigated to some extent. Property taxes imposed by state and local governments reduce home prices, thereby reducing asset-price inflation. It will also reduce demand overall, thus having some effect on consumer-price inflation. Taken as a whole, state and local government taxes have a much smaller impact on prices than Federal taxes.

In addition to the impact of taxes on spending, tax hikes also impact net private sector wealth, because they drain bank reserves. As such, taxes reduce any spending from wealth and put downward pressure on asset prices also.

Overall, taxes cause deflation and Federal taxes in particular should be minimized or even avoided when seeking to enhance and promote higher levels of production and job creation. They are a solution to the problem of inflation.

References

Bureau of Economic Analysis (2021). *National income and product accounts*, 2/25/2021 Release. Available at www.Bea.gov

Davidson, P. (1998). Efficiency and fragile speculative financial markets: Against the Tobin tax and for a creditable market maker. *American Journal of Economics and Sociology, 57*, 639–662.

Glaeser, E., & Gyourko, J. (2002). *The impact of zoning on housing affordability*. NBER Working Paper 8835.

Internal Revenue Service. (2021). *Table 24. U.S. Corporation Income Tax 1909–2010*. Retrieved 11/26/2021.

Keynes, J. M. (1963). *Essays in persuasion*. W.W. Norton.

Keynes, J. M. (1973) [1936]. The collected writings of John Maynard Keynes, Vol. XXX: *The general theory of employment, interest, and money*. Macmillan.

Lavoie, M. (2011). Changes in central bank procedures during the subprime crisis and their repercussions on monetary theory. *International Journal of Political Economy, 39*, 3–23.

Pechman, J., & Okner, B. (1974). *Who bears the tax burden?* Brookings Institution.

Piketty, T. (2014). *Capital in the twenty-first century*. Harvard University Press.

Pressman, S. (2016). *Understanding Piketty's capital in the twenty-first century*. Routledge.

Tobin, J. (1978). A proposal for international monetary reform. *Eastern Economic Journal, 4*, 153–159.

Wray, L. R. (2012). *Modern money theory: A primer on macroeconomics for sovereign monetary systems*. Palgrave Macmillan.

CHAPTER 8

The Ambiguous Effects of Targeting Current Account Surpluses

Nina Eichacker

1 Introduction

The debate over whether economies should target current account surpluses, or an excess of exports over imports, has a long history. Adam Smith and David Ricardo criticized mercantilist practices meant to target trade surpluses, but they advocated for free trade to increase global efficiency and output (Schumacher, 2014). John Maynard Keynes accepted that some economies might have a good reason to generate trade surpluses—to acquire more foreign reserves for fear of constraints on future growth if they ran out of gold—but noted that the end of the gold standard implied that those particular fears were less grounded in practice. While Keynes argued that domestic policies to promote industry and trade advantage could be nationally beneficial, he also argued that these policies were likely to depress global economic prospects (Keynes, 1933, 1964). Joan Robinson (1977) also noted that while export-led growth was a

N. Eichacker (✉)
Department of Economics, University of Rhode Island, Kingston, RI, USA
e-mail: nina_eichacker@uri.edu

S. Pressman and J. Smithin (eds.), *Debates in Monetary Macroeconomics*,
https://doi.org/10.1007/978-3-031-11240-9_8

worthy goal in the long-term, short-term increases in domestic demand for foreign output might likewise promote domestic investment. Despite these ambivalent assessments of trade surpluses, many economies have pursued export-led growth strategies over time and around the world.

In this chapter, I argue that while some global trade leaders appear to be examples to emulate, and although positive net trade balances help increase GDP, maintaining trade surpluses may not be desirable at all times. Though trade surpluses should have positive implications for GDP all else equal, the practice of maintaining and prioritizing trade surpluses may have negative costs for an economy as a whole. This chapter builds upon Keynes and Joan Robinson's 'beggar-thy-neighbor' work to show how competition among trade partners may generate a paradox of thrift, and depress growth throughout the world as a perverse consequence of mercantilist and neomercantilist strategies. Despite the successful track records of particular economies within the global system at preserving positive trade balances, the costs of attempting to prevent trade deficits may be greater than the benefits of the strategy.

This chapter also builds upon Thirlwall's (1980) notion of balance of payments constrained growth (also see Blecker, 2016). It may be rational, even in the absence of a gold standard, for developing economies to target trade surpluses, if their access to foreign exchange reserves may constrain domestic production through various mechanisms. By contrast, large economies that are not vulnerable to the balance of payment constraints may effectively operate as if they were closed in an open system. For these economies, there is no innate advantage to targeting a trade surplus over domestic demand. However, large economies' pursuit of trade surpluses can negatively affect the economic prospects of smaller economies more vulnerable to the balance of payment constraints. This is another route by which targeting trade surpluses can generate negative outcomes at the global level.

Finally, in the era of climate change, targeting trade surpluses might generate negative externalities with domestic and global implications. Given scientific consensus about the negative consequences of climate change for economic output and growth, policies that minimize domestic incentives to transition away from fossil fuels and mitigate environmental damages are shortsighted, for large and small economies. If mitigating environmental degradation raises trade deficits, those priorities should prevail over the desire for surpluses. First, economies considering the cost of transitioning away from the use of fossil fuels and other high-carbon emitting products and practices may require a period of trade deficits in order to make the transition. Over-emphasizing trade surpluses may delay time-sensitive investment and development that relies heavily on imports. Given the diffuse effects of climate change, any possible deterrents to action should be minimized; in this case, accepting deficits en route to transition may be a worthwhile tradeoff. Second, economies that target trade surpluses may face disincentives to transitioning from fossil fuels if many of their exports are fossil fuels or energy intensive in production or extraction. (This problem may likewise affect economies that consume this output at home.) An economy that transitions away from exporting these sorts of goods and services is likely to see a decline in export revenue, and at least a temporary rise in trade deficits. Finally, there is preliminary evidence that countries that generate trade surpluses may also import large volumes of industrial waste, potentially to the detriment of domestic populations (Lee et al., 2020). The challenge of dealing with international waste is beyond the scope of this chapter, but this finding speaks to the value of domestic services, and to the hidden external costs of engendering trade surpluses. The short-term benefits of trade surpluses are outweighed by the global cost of climate change in terms of infrastructure, agriculture, and other forms of production.

The chapter proceeds as follows. Section 2 considers the positive effects of trade surpluses. It walks through neoclassical justifications for free trade, mercantilist justifications for trade surplus, and the infant-industry argument for promoting domestic industry. It provides examples of economies that have successfully (and unsuccessfully) deployed these techniques over time. Section 3 explores the ambiguities of targeting trade surpluses. It begins with the paradox of thrift, and considers Kaleckian theories about how targeting trade surpluses might depress domestic living standards. Next, it considers balance of payment constrained growth, and shows how large economies that successfully target trade surpluses can destabilize conditions for smaller economies—and global growth as a whole. Finally, it considers the potential environmental externalities of targeting trade surpluses. The final section concludes, and provides policy recommendations given the ambiguous desirability of trade surpluses.

2 Positive Effects of Trade Surpluses

This section considers the positive aspects of current account (CA) surpluses. GDP (Y) may be represented as

$$Y = C + I + G + (X - M) \tag{1}$$

$$X - M = CA \tag{2}$$

where C represents consumption, I represents investment expenditure, G represents government expenditure, and X–M represents the current account, or exports minus imports. We assume that an increase in any component of expenditure on domestically produced goods and services, all else equal, will cause GDP to rise. In the case of import demand (domestic expenditure on foreign-produced goods and services) we have the reverse assumption—all else equal, more imports will cause GDP to fall. In this simplified framework, it is easy to see that trade surpluses, all else equal, increase GDP, while trade deficits, all else equal, exert downward pressure on GDP.

GDP accounting identities show that current account surpluses (or deficits) may increase (or deplete in the case of deficits) domestic savings, all else equal. Equations (3) through (7) show this. We may also consider net exports, as equivalent to the difference between national savings (S) and investment (I).

In a closed economy, domestic spending goes toward Consumption, Government, and Investment Expenditure. If national savings is the difference between GDP (Y) and non-investment spending (C + G), then Eqs. (3) and (4) show how national savings should equal investment.

$$Y = C + I + G \tag{3}$$

$$S = Y - C - G = I \tag{4}$$

Allowing international trade, Eqs. (5) through (7) will hold:

$$Y = C + I + G + CA \tag{5}$$

$$Y - C - G = I + CA \tag{6}$$

$$S - I = CA \tag{7}$$

If an economy imports more than it exports, and if investment expenditure is greater than or equal to national savings, it will incur a CA deficit. To account for this difference, economies may see a change in their international balance of payments, demonstrated in Eq. 8.

$$\text{Current Account Balance} + \text{Financial Account Balance} + \text{Official Settlements Balance} = 0 \tag{8}$$

The financial account balance refers to net capital flows, or the difference between domestic financial claims on foreign payments, and domestic financial liabilities, or obligations to pay foreign institutions, as well as the purchase and sale of financial assets across borders. The official settlements balance refers to an economy's holdings of foreign exchange, gold, and other international reserve assets. For large economies that issue vehicle currencies, or currencies widely held around the world, and in the absence of a metallic standard for money, official settlements balances may be negligible. However, smaller economies with less monetary sway may have an incentive to hold more international reserves, or to target current account surpluses, in order to prevent balance of payment crises from ensuing. Under a balance of payments crisis, capital flows between economies may stop or reverse, creating payment and financing problems for the economy in crisis. An economy without adequate reserves of foreign currency may be unable to pay obligations denominated in foreign currency, or may incur rapidly increasing costs of funding trade deficits. Capital outflows of stronger currency may lead to further depreciation of the currency of the economy in crisis. While neoclassical economists generally assume that the depreciation of a nation's currency should lead to a greater trade advantage in global markets, the third section of this paper discusses why there is no guarantee that a balance of payments crisis followed by depreciation should reverse trade flows and improve a deficit economy's trade balance.

Other factors that contribute to the propensity of an economy to experience balance of payment crises, and increase their incentives to hold foreign reserves or maintain trade surpluses, include unrestricted movement of capital and a demonstrated willingness by financial actors to move funds out of a given economy. Both factors contribute to the financial volatility of an open economy. Another factor increasing the potential for the balance of payment crises relates to the relative integration of a small economy in global trade networks. Countries with relatively small export sectors may be more vulnerable to the balance of payment crises than economies with large export sectors; this is because economies with smaller export sectors may face larger opportunity costs in terms of the production of non-tradeable goods and services when trying to increase trade surpluses as a consequence of a balance of payments crisis. Finally, economies with fixed exchange rates, which may be desirable for other reasons, and an absence of capital flow restrictions may be more vulnerable to balance of payments crises because their central banks must also buy and sell foreign reserves in order to maintain their fixed exchange rate. If many of these factors hold, an economy may have a stronger incentive to target trade surpluses than a large economy with a large tradeable sector that is less vulnerable to the opinions of foreign investors and creditors.

Mercantilism is the term used to describe an economic outlook, school of thought, and policies designed to promote national trade interests through several means. While the earliest philosophers and political figures promoting 'mercantilist' ideas may not have used that term, myriad scholars of political economy and philosophy in the seventeenth and eighteenth centuries emphasized the importance of trade, or 'mercantile' affairs, in the promotion of a state's interests (Magnusson, 2019; Viner, 1930). Themes that emerge from ideas and practices deemed later on to be mercantilist include the protection of national economic interests through the acquisition of precious metals and foreign exchange (bullionism), and the general use of state power to promote domestic exports, in order to increase exports relative to imports (Viner, 1930). Viner (1930, 255) has noted the long history of protectionist measures that might be included in mercantilism, including prohibitions on the export of gold and silver bullion and foreign coins, as well as tariffs and prohibitions on imports, citing texts by British mint officials as early as 1381 advising that England import less, and export more in order to accrue more foreign money. By the sixteenth century, British officials routinely referred to the balance of trade, and the desirability of exporting more and importing less (Viner, 1930, 258).

Mercantilists identified several mechanisms by which trade surpluses could generate growth. Mercantilists believed that trade deficits would weaken an economy's standing with rival nations. By contrast, "an influx of bullion resulting from an excess of exports over imports was the common objective both of the earlier and of the later periods" (Viner, 1930, 259). Mercantilists were also sensitive to transaction costs associated with trade—shipping costs and interest on foreign debt—that could further weaken an economy in global standing. Precious metals could also serve as emergency reserves. When other means, such as taxation or borrowing, allowed for the funding of state activity, the importance of trade surpluses declined (Viner, 1930). While some mercantilists used the desirability of trade balances as a support for domestic thrift and saving, this view was not universal. Critics writing in the seventeenth century emphasized the importance of domestic demand as an engine of growth, and contested the notion that individual practices should be applied at the state level (Viner, 1930). Mercantilists also argued that promoting trade surpluses could help increase employment by the logic that imports substituted foreign labor for domestic labor (Viner, 1930, 299).

Another motivation for trade surpluses in the mercantilist framework was greater state power. Viner elaborated on the links between states' political and economic power in his 1948 essay "Power vs. Plenty Under Mercantilism." In the seventeenth and eighteenth centuries, holding extra reserves of wealth could enable attacks on rivals, while simultaneously helping defend against or deter attacks from enemies. Viner (1948) also noted the reinforcing effects of wealth and political power: wealth enabled expansion and defense of interests, which protected national programs that extracted wealth from imperial and colonial holdings; and, at times, governments might prioritize one end—wealth accumulation or national power—over the other depending on historic circumstances.

Throughout history, export-led growth regimes have been popular. Governments in the fifteenth century onward implemented protectionist measures, and engaged in imperialism and colonialism to increase their trade share in the global economy. Imperialism and colonialism also served to decrease production costs and could potentially increase access to bullion, in keeping with mercantilist goals (Horvath, 1972; Mann, 2012; Veracini, 2013). German philosophers and economists in the nineteenth century acknowledged mercantilism's 'state-making' potential: intervention by the state had the potential to modernize economic practices and promote economic growth (Magnusson, 2019). Proponents of mercantilist strategies include Alexander Hamilton, as well as the German economist Friedrich List, who linked British political power with its economic advantage in global trade (Magnusson, 2019). Both Hamilton and List described an arc of national economic development, from low-priced agricultural products to higher-priced industrial output, and argued for policies to develop their respective countries' productive capacity, through a combination of protectionist measures to discourage domestic import of goods from abroad, and to the incubation of infant industries (Magnusson, 2019).

Theorists outside of classical economics have also acknowledged the wisdom of some mercantilist positions. While Keynes was critical of the global consequences of protectionist measures, he acknowledged that governments might have sound reasons to direct economic production in order to maintain security in a volatile world. Keynes also noted that maintaining trade surpluses made sense if there was the potential for changes in the international balance of payments to increase domestic costs of investment through changes in the interest rate (Keynes, 1933, 1964). Proponents of structuralist economics and the protection of infant industries note the links between economic and political power, and the existence of barriers to entry as motivation for actively developing a nation's industrial potential (Thirlwall, 1980; Thirlwall & Hussain, 2004). At the same time, academics focusing on the balance of payments as a constraint on domestic growth recognize that elements of mercantilist emphasis on holding foreign exchange and maintaining positive trade balances may be rational for emerging market economies.

Though classical economists including Adam Smith and David Riccardo rejected the desirability of mercantilism for its conflation of money and value, classical and neoclassical economists have supported trade as a mechanism for growth. Smith argued that trade could provide an outlet for domestic output that is not consumed at home, and classical theorists have argued that production guided by comparative advantage (and later, competitive advantage) should increase global output, efficiency, and well-being. If economies produce the goods and services in which they have comparative advantages, then societal production possibility frontiers expand: by engaging in trade, these economies can theoretically consume more given existing material constraints (Smith, 2003).

An extension of classical and neoclassical economic reasoning for the desirability and trade can be found in the theory of 'competitive advantage.' Michael Porter (1990), who is credited with coining the term, rejected the notion that a nation's trade balance should be assumed to indicate how competitive it was. However, discussions of what propels some countries to generate large trade surpluses often rest on how competitive they are in global markets, whether that is a discussion of the US–China trade balance (Shaikh & Weber, 2021) or the Germany–Greece trade balance in Europe (Naastepad & Storm, 2015). Porter (1990, 10) defines competitive advantage as both the ability to produce goods of higher quality at lower costs and to continually increase efficiency and quality of output over time. Technological progress, access to capital, and the ability to navigate existing barriers to entry all matter for an economy that wishes to increase its competitive advantage compared to rival countries. At the same time, the ability of existing leading producers to erect barriers to entry and to limit the competitiveness of rival producers or different countries can help maintain trade advantages in this framework.

Another route by which export surpluses may lead to growth originates in Keynesian and Post-Keynesian theories stressing the primacy of demand. In the absence of demand, producers have little incentive to invest in order to increase output. Thus, an increase in consumption should provide producers with an incentive to produce more output, and to invest more, with implications for labor markets and income that may further increase demand, output, and so on. In an open economy, trade enables foreign expenditure on domestic output, which provides another source of effective demand. International demand for output measured by exports has the potential to drive growth if it outpaces domestic demand for foreign-produced output. Export-led growth may exist in tandem with domestic aggregate demand, or it may substitute for domestic demand, depending on the mechanism that drives external demand, domestic demand, or both for a given economy's output. Alternately, policies designed to discourage imports—whether through the implementation of tariffs on goods produced abroad, depressed domestic incomes or currency devaluation, or other policies designed to actively discourage domestic consumption of goods produced abroad—limit domestic expenditure on foreign goods, and increase trade balances.

Export-led growth models have retained their appeal over time. Klein and Pettis (2020) describe how the governments of countries such as Korea, China, and Germany have achieved trade surpluses over different time horizons. Germany's model of being an industrial and export center in the Eurozone is often contrasted with Eurozone members that continue to generate persistent trade deficits (Storm & Naastepad, 2015). In the US, Donald Trump campaigned in the 2016 presidential election against long-standing US trade deficits with China and other international trade partners (Swanson, 2019). Critics of President Joseph Biden's policies to increase industrial prowess as a counter to Chinese exports have referred to these policies as New Mercantilism (Hass et al., 2020; Hurlburt, 2021). It is possible, given preferable trade conditions and access to desirable resources that sell for a high price, to maintain trade surpluses for enough time for the strategy to seem worth emulating.

In the German case, supporters of the German model see the government and German firms as having developed a strategy to invest in industrial capacity and technological development. Naastepad and Storm (2015) argue that these supply-side innovations improved firm efficiency, without lowering German workers' living standards, while competitors elsewhere in Europe failed to innovate and maintain higher unit costs of production. By contrast, critics of German 'neomercantilism' have identified German firms' willingness to outsource production, or to threaten to outsource production, to parts of Germany with lower standards of living, such as the old East Germany or post-Soviet Central European nations (Bellofiore et al., 2011). These changes occurred together with labor market reforms that have reduced unemployment eligibility, promoted temporary worker status, and placed downward pressure on domestic wages (Stockhammer, 2016). Klein and Pettis (2020) argue that this depression of German domestic demand can be seen in lower consumption as well as government expenditures supporting large trade surpluses. Braun and Deeg (2020) identify negative spillovers from Germany's export-led growth model for German banks, as German non-financial corporations have increasingly grown to rely on retained earnings to fund development and minimize costs. Though Germany is still a central economic power within Europe, the domestic and international effects of that dominance, which owes much to trade, is ambiguous.

China's trade advantage in global markets has been written about often as a source of Sinophobic sentiment in the US and elsewhere (Moosa, 2011; Negi, 2008; Nyland et al., 2011; Surowiecki, 2003). Klein and Pettis (2020) emphasize the role of wage suppression in Chinese development, along with low welfare expenditure by the government. Palley (2006) identifies the negative effects of Chinese labor laws and working conditions that are hostile to unions. Shaikh and Weber (2021) show that China's trade advantage owes much to both comparatively low labor unit costs, as well as an active state industrial development policy that quickly mobilizes production in fields deemed lucrative. In practice, the trade surpluses that China has developed with countries like the US have given

China a means of resisting externally imposed austerity measures to which other developing or medium-sized economies have fallen victim (Weber, 2020). China has also made substantial moves to restructure its growth from being export-led to being consumption-led. By prioritizing policies that appreciate the Chinese currency and promote domestic consumption and the Chinese service economy, the Chinese government demonstrated a willingness to slow GDP growth in the short run in favor of a different sort of demand-led model. These changes seem to indicate that, despite the success of export-led growth, economies that benefit from export-led growth may prefer alternative models of development (Liu et al., 2019).

Smaller economies have attempted to grow by targeting trade surpluses with mixed results. Success stories include the so-called Asian tiger economies of South Korea, Taiwan, Hong Kong, and Singapore, as well as Ireland. These economies have used an array of strategies including the protectionist measures to foster infant industries, direct government planning, import-substitution policies, and more market-oriented strategies like cutting taxes to encourage foreign firms to relocate (Donovan & Murphy, 2013). Other nations have not succeeded as well. Latin American economies have used both import-substitution policies as well as more neoliberal strategies of attracting foreign capital, prioritizing the output of goods in which economies have comparative advantage, and wage suppression (Amsden, 2004; Kregel, 2008; Moreno-Brid et al., 2004; Teitel & Thoumi, 1986). Smaller economies within the Eurozone have found it difficult to compete with large core economies like Germany, and these dynamics have worsened as governments have implemented restructuring and austerity measures as terms for aid since the 2008 Global Financial Crisis (Bellofiore et al., 2011; Naastepad & Storm, 2015).

The next section of this chapter explores the potential downsides of targeting trade surpluses. It concentrates on the paradoxes of thrift that emerge domestically and globally when economies target current account surpluses, as well as other externalities that emerge from targeting surpluses to the exclusion of other goals.

3 The Ambiguous Effects of Targeting Trade Surpluses

Export-led growth models derive from the Keynesian idea that effective demand is central to growth. Export-led growth regimes have been attractive in open economies where trade and international competition are prominent. The question for policy-makers is whether an increase in net exports may have a larger than unitary effect on GDP—a trade multiplier greater than one—or whether it may result in smaller, or even negative, effects on GDP, which would be the case if the source of the trade surplus is a depression of domestic demand for consumption of domestic goods as well as more imported goods from abroad. The central downside of targeting trade surpluses arises from the paradox of thrift. According to the paradox of thrift, saving generates individual benefits but sacrifices the broader good by reducing total output. In an open economy, the decision by one economy to promote trade surpluses decreases demand for the output of other economies, and may even decrease global output. This effect will be greater if negatively affected economies emulate the example of economies doing lots of saving.

John Maynard Keynes and Joan Robinson wrote extensively about the ambiguous desirability of trade surpluses. Keynes (1933) justified targeting trade surpluses through industrial policy on the basis of increasing an economy's self-reliance, especially given the possibility of global volatility. However, he noted the downsides of elevating national interests over global ones by citing defensive protectionist measures enacted one after another in the interwar period. Though he acknowledged that societies could benefit from having reserves of foreign currency or bullion if there was a chance that global monetary conditions might affect domestic interest rates, he also noted that shifts away from metallic money standards toward fiat systems could obviate that impulse (Keynes, 1964). Finally, Keynes (1964) broadly dismissed targeting trade surpluses as a vehicle for improving domestic saving rates by approvingly citing Mandeville's (1997) *The Fable of the Bees*. Like Keynes, Joan Robinson (1977) acknowledged that there were times when it would be reasonable for economies to target trade surpluses, but that attempts to rapidly increase exports relative to imports through demand-limiting measures were likely to be counterproductive if they worsened global economic conditions.

In "National Self Sufficiency," Keynes (1933) gave a measured assessment of economic self-sufficiency even as he publicly acknowledged that he no longer supported free trade as fervently as he once had. This essay, based on speeches Keynes had given in Ireland during the Interwar period, argued that financial openness had increased volatility and instability, which had exacerbated global economic crises. His strongest recommendation in the piece is for finance, wherever possible, to be home-spun. His next strongest recommendation was for industrial development, as a hedge against constrained access to international markets for physical or economic reasons. He treated protectionism as a dubious practice; while one nation might benefit in the short run, it was bound to worsen the wider good as other nations caught on and imitated the practice. In *The General Theory*, Keynes (1964) noted the destructive consequences of protectionist measures enacted by one government after another between WWI and WWII. Keynes's acknowledgment of trade as a source of volatility also has echoes in the current proliferation of preferential trade agreements as a hedge against international trade volatility. Mansfield and Reinhardt (2008) note that powerful economies like the US and Japan resist eliminating trade barriers when negotiating trade agreements with less powerful partners, while smaller economies must calculate whether the benefits of being in a preferential trade agreement with a stronger partner outweighs the cost of the trade barriers that the stronger partner keeps in place.

Economic assessments of whether trade openness increases economic volatility are mixed. Cavallo and Frankel (2009) use a gravity model of trade to argue that trade openness decreases economies' vulnerabilities to crises, although they acknowledge that emerging economies are more prone to crisis upon liberalizing trade accounts. Lane and Milesi-Ferretti (2012) argue that economies with larger than expected trade surpluses prior to the 2008 Global Financial Crisis were subject to larger reversals in trade accounts after 2008. Historic analyses of the period before WWI indicate that liberalized capital accounts in tandem with unrestricted trade flows created volatility and exacerbated crises (Estevadeordal et al., 2003). Federico and Tena (2013) argue that trade surpluses constituted a small source of Italian growth in the nineteenth century, and that domestic consumption and investment were larger drivers. They also argued that if the sample of polities engaged in trade is increased to include smaller and non-Western economies, that the gains from trade in the late nineteenth and early twentieth centuries were volatile and dispersed. Furthermore, global financial integration preceding the 2008 Global Financial Crisis expanded the scope of failures in Western financial systems (Federico & Tena, 2017).

Export-led growth models might cause perverse outcomes through several mechanisms. Using a one-sector, short-run macro model, Blecker (1989) shows that in a closed economy, capital accumulation and GDP can rise in wage-led regimes, as domestic expenditure by households or the government generates more revenue for firms, and capital accumulation. Opening the economy to trade introduces complications. To compete with foreign firms, domestic firms may attempt to reduce their markups, which has the potential to squeeze firm profits if they cannot reduce workers' wages. If wages fall, the ability of workers to consume goods with relatively higher prices diminishes. As a result, workers may buy relatively more imports from countries with lower production costs. If firms cut wages, or if the domestic currency depreciates relative to one's trade partners, workers' real wages (and standard of living) may fall; however, if firms also increase their reliance on productivity-increasing technology, workers may receive higher real wages (Blecker, 1989). In this scenario, a rising real income may be matched by greater consumption and import purchasing, which may or may not counterbalance the increase in exports. Since export-led growth is likely to be zero-sum, one country's export surplus arises from the decrease in other economies' current account surpluses. As a result, export-led strategies due to "international competition," will tend to "[contribute] to the uneven development of the world economy" (Blecker, 1989, 407).

The size of an economy matters, as well as its relative integration and hegemony in global markets, when considering the desirability of trade surpluses. A large economy that issues a currency in high global demand with an increasing trade deficit is unlikely to experience negative effects, as its domestic interest rates are unlikely to change. By contrast, smaller economies are more vulnerable to interest rate shocks if trade deficits lead to more volatile capital inflows and outflows (Thirlwall & Hussain, 2004). An economy's growth rate is considered to be constrained by the balance of payments if "the growth rate that maintains balance-of-payments equilibrium is less than the growth rate," experienced by an economy if it were closed (Blecker, 2016, 276). Larger economies are less vulnerable to the balance of payment crises if they maintain trade deficits, but the decision by a large economy to target trade surpluses is more likely to generate balance of payments crisis for smaller trade partners. If smaller economies export less, and exchange less domestic currency for the larger economy's vehicle currency, that can decrease the ability of smaller economies to finance imports from larger economies, including capital investments (McCombie, 2004).

Thirlwall's Law, portrayed in Eq. 9, shows that economic growth, export growth, and income elasticity of demand for imports have the following relationship:

$$\dot{Y} = \dot{G}/\pi \tag{9}$$

In this model, $\dot{Y}$ represents the growth rate of GDP; $\dot{G}$ represents the growth rate of exports, and π represents import elasticity of demand. An increase in the growth rate of exports should, all else equal, increase the growth rate of GDP. However, if households purchase more imports as aggregate income rises, growth gains from exports may be counterbalanced by greater domestic demand for foreign output.

Decisions by larger economies to target trade surpluses are likely to decrease smaller economies' export rates, which is likely to further depress growth in those economies. By contrast, in larger economies, the relative standard of living of workers may affect the propensity for households to purchase imports. If economies have prioritized trade surpluses by allowing the stagnation of wages, and imports from abroad are less expensive than equivalent domestic output, then the perverse consequence of targeting surpluses may be yet more import purchasing by households. This may nullify the effect of decreasing deficits or increasing surpluses. Dutt (2002) notes that early econometric analyses by Thirlwall showed that this relationship held for developed economies, but that the results were mixed for developing economies. Dutt argues further that this failure for developing economies is unsurprising, since Thirlwall's Law assumes constant terms of trade, while smaller economies are more vulnerable to volatile capital flows, exchange rates, and interest rates, which underscores the desirability of their holding larger reserves of foreign capital.

Using a panel data analysis of the effects of trade liberalization on export growth, Santos-Paulino and Thirlwall show that regional variation in the price and income elasticity of exports vary considerably around the world, and Latin America and Africa economies that liberalized trade controls were more likely to incur persistent trade deficits than economies in East Asia (Santos-Paulino & Thirlwall, 2004). While this may appear to be an argument for policies designed to promote high-value exports that "are as income elastic as possible in markets outside the region," it is impossible for all economies to successfully produce and market these exports to their neighbors at the same time (Thirlwall, 1980, S94). Liberalized trade and the pursuit of trade surpluses by large economies can thus generate paradoxes of thrift for smaller economies through international capital flows, providing another reason for large economies to avoid targeting trade surpluses.

Hussain and Thirlwall (2004) shows empirically that some countries with large trade surpluses could have lower than predicted economic growth rates according to standard trade multipliers, consistent with the Thirlwall's Law, while different groups of developing economies had divergent growth rates regardless of their trade balances. Countries that predominantly export commodities are more likely to be negatively affected by global economic trade volatility than countries that predominantly export manufactured goods. Hussain (2004) also showed that trade surpluses in commodity exporting countries were less likely to be associated with economic growth than trade surpluses in economies exporting higher-priced goods and services. If countries aspire to grow their economies through positive trade balances, it is imperative for them to shift toward the production and export of goods for which there is relatively low international elasticity of demand, rather than commodities (Araujo & Lima, 2007). This is an argument for active intervention by governments to direct industrial development, though these transition processes themselves may demand periods of trade deficits in the pursuit of surpluses in the longer term.

A different reason to be cautious about targeting trade surpluses stems from the environmental externalities of production for both domestic and foreign consumption. Policies designed to raise output and trade surpluses in the short term may undermine growth in the future if they are environmentally unsustainable. Assuming an economy prioritizes the production of goods and services in which it has a comparative advantage, particularly agricultural or physical commodities as well as other agricultural outputs, extracting or growing those resources to the exclusion of others may have unsustainable consequences. Monoculture, growing one crop to the exclusion of others, may allow for the export of crops in high demand elsewhere in the world, but may open an economy to environmental challenges (Klasen et al., 2016; Zhang et al., 2012). Many high-priced commodities extracted for consumption and export are energy related. The extraction of the commodities themselves may be energy intensive, as in the case of rare-earth metals or tar sands, and the waste products generated as a consequence of extraction have negative externalities related to humans' physical health, the viability of ecosystems, and other consequences that may be poorly understood at the time of their extraction. Similarly, the extraction of certain agricultural products like tropical hardwoods or old growth forests, clearcutting timber, or palm oil extraction can wreak havoc on ecosystems, with long-lasting environmental impacts in the form of lost biodiversity and increased vulnerability to erosion, forest fires, and other natural disasters (Mehlum and Torvik, 2006; Garraín et al., 2016; Riofrancos, 2017).

Trade surpluses may be associated with negative environmental externalities for other reasons. Developed economies pay to export large volumes of physical waste—much of it toxic—to emerging markets (McKee, 1996; Schroeder et al., 2008). Producers in the West have historically exported reserves of products and components that had been banned in domestic markets, and have been associated with environmental, public health, and social harm in those developing economies (Kojima, 2013; Müller, 2019). Lee et al. (2018) show that an unintended consequence of China's export surplus in the recent past has been a tendency for Chinese container ships to return to Chinese ports with containers full of waste. The rationale has been that it is more efficient to bring back a revenue generating 'import' (developed economies' exported waste) rather than sending home an empty ship, or a ship full of imported goods. They argue that these practices depress domestic living standards, regardless of the positive effect on China's trade balance, and propose policies that raise domestic standards of living as a counter to Chinese imports of industrial waste. If developed economies were, instead, to treat waste or reduce waste at home, this could decrease national import balances. While these practices might decrease current account surpluses for economies that import waste, the environmental benefits and health improvements are substantial.

This section of the paper has argued that while trade surpluses can have a positive impact on growth, many other factors render those benefits ambiguous. The relative size of an economy, the form of the policy meant to increase trade balances, the relative need for foreign currency and other monetary reserves, and the environmental externalities associated with trade may all complicate the benefits associated with targeting trade surplus. Any policy meant to increase trade balances by depressing domestic demand for consumption or imports is likely to have broader negative consequences.

4 Conclusion

Ambiguity characterizes the desirability of prioritizing current account surpluses. In a vacuum, trade surpluses should add to GDP. Export-led growth strategies have a long history, from mercantilism to neomercantilism to "America First," as a campaign slogan (Stiglitz, 2017). Governments have long lent their political power to help build domestic industries in the hopes that they will become export powers, or at least to limit domestic dependence on imported capital goods (Magnusson, 2019). Structuralist theories of economic development stressed the potential economic benefits of import-substitution that reduce the dependence of developing economies on expensive imported goods from abroad and diversify economic production for domestic consumption and export (Katzenstein, 2003; Prebisch, 1959).

However, every economy cannot maintain trade surpluses at the same time. At its root, there is a zero-sum element to trade—if any economy exports more than it imports from all of its trade partners, those economies will generate trade deficits. Attempts to increase competitiveness in global markets by lowering costs and wages may lead to diminished aggregate demand for domestically produced goods and services (Blecker, 2013; Stockhammer, 2016). While reduced imports and a potential increase in exports should lead to an increased current account surplus if relative prices fall, these dynamics may not be desirable for other reasons (Klein & Pettis, 2020).

When should economies target trade surpluses? Economies at risk of balance of payment crises have a stronger incentive to target trade surpluses than economies large enough to ignore those consequences. At the same time, if developed economies export goods for which international import elasticity of demand is high, the potential contributions these exports make to GDP may be volatile. Smaller economies that target trade surpluses in the short term may also forgo opportunities to develop industrial capacity, which may be associated with the capacity to export goods and services with a lower international price elasticity of demand. If this is a risk, international organizations should provide greater financial resources to those polities in order to ensure their development, without demanding austerity and structural reform measures likely to depress domestic demand. Blanchard and Milesi-Ferretti (2012) note that trade deficits arising from industry development are likely to serve a larger good, and that developing economies should be supported in how they proceed. Conversely, large economies that issue vehicle currencies, or possess exorbitant privileges, have less reason to target trade surpluses. While these actions may increase domestic output in the short run, they may be matched with an increased domestic demand for imports, which could nullify the intent. Furthermore, attempts by developed economies to increase trade surpluses will likely beggar their neighbors in developing economies and smaller economies in general.

Targeting current account surpluses may slow transitions from carbon-emitting practices. Domestic policies—fiscal, industrial, and monetary—that facilitate a wind-down of fossil fuels and implement renewable energy infrastructure may require inputs from abroad in the short run while economies increase their capacity in renewable energy production and related secondary inputs. Any transition toward a more sustainable future, in carbon emitting terms, will require a reconfiguration of goods produced and goods imported that will likely reduce trade surpluses or increase deficits for some economies, while increasing trade surpluses or reducing deficits for others. China is a large global producer of green energy infrastructure, and other nations should not hesitate to purchase output from international competitors if domestic alternatives are in short supply.

Combining the insights of Keynes, Thirlwall, and others, it is not universally desirable to target trade surpluses. Economies at low risk of balance of payment crises should spend freely on imports, consider the development of domestic service sectors as a substitute for exports with large environmental externalities, and embrace domestic consumption as engines of growth. Constraints on domestic deficit spending—whether fiscal or trade related—are counterproductive at the global level. Policies meant to increase domestic growth via industrial development or the minimization of financial risk are preferable to measures meant to discourage imports, or depress domestic demand. When developing and smaller economies are at risk of balance of payment crises constraining growth potential, international organizations should mobilize resources to alleviate those challenges. This holds especially for economies that were historically colonies or imperial holdings that facilitated developed economies' economic growth and industrialization. On a more structural level, global organizations must commit to better aid infrastructure that eliminates structural contingencies for economies that have been colonized or imperial holdings in the past (Gallagher, 2021). International agreements to curb carbon emissions should continue to provide ample aid to developing economies in this process, to minimize the short-term costs and deficits that arise.

References

Amsden, A. (2004). Import substitution in high-tech industries: Prebisch lives in Asia! *CEPAL Review* No. 82, 75–89.

Araujo, R. A., & Tadeu Lima, G. (2007). A structural economic dynamics approach to balance-of-payments constrained growth. *Cambridge Journal of Economics, 31*, 755–774.

Bellofiore, R., Garibaldo, F., & Halevi, J. (2011). The global crisis and the crisis of European neomercantilism. *Socialist Register, 47*, 120–146.

Blanchard, O., & Milesi-Ferretti, G. M. (2012). (Why) should current account balances be reduced? *IMF Economic Review, 60*, 139–150.

Blecker, R. (1989). International competition, income distribution, and economic growth. *Cambridge Journal of Economics, 13*, 395–412.

Blecker, R. (2013). Long-run growth in open economies. *The Oxford handbook of Post-Keynesian Economics, Volume 1: Critiques and methodology* (pp. 390–414). Oxford University Press.

Blecker, R. (2016). The debate over 'Thirlwall's Law': Balance-of-payments constrained growth reconsidered. *European Journal of Economics and Economic Policies: Intervention, 13*(3), 275–290.

Braun, B., & Deeg, R. (2020). Strong firms, weak banks: The financial consequences of Germany's export-led growth model. *German Politics, 29*(3), 358–381.

Cavallo, E., & Frankel, J. (2009). Does openness to trade make countries more vulnerable to sudden stops or less? Using gravity to establish causality. *Journal of International Money and Finance, 27*, 1430–1452.

Donovan, D., & Murphy, A. (2013). *The fall of the Celtic Tiger: Ireland and the Euro debt crisis*. Oxford University Press.

Dutt, A. (2002). Thirlwall's Law and uneven development. *Journal of Post Keynesian Economics, 24*, 367–390.

Estevadeordal, A., Frantz, B., & Taylor, A. (2003). The rise and fall of world trade, 1870–1939. *Quarterly Journal of Economics, 118*, 359–407.

Federico, G., & Tena Junguito, A. (2013). The ripples of the Industrial Revolution: Exports, economic growth, and regional integration in the early 19th century. *Universidad Carlos II de Madrid* Working Paper 13-02.

Federico, G., & Tena Junguito, A. (2017). A tale of two globalizations: Gains from trade and openness 1800–2010. *Review of World Economics, 153*, 601–626.

Gallagher, K. (2021). The IMF's turn on climate change. *OECD Op Eds*. https://oecd-development-matters.org/2021/03/23/the-imfs-turn-on-climate-change/

Garraín, D., Lechón, Y., & Santamaría, M. (2016). Environmental externalities assessment of a palm hydrotreated vegetable oil. *Clean Technologies and Environmental Policy, 18*(4), 1239–1244.

Hass, R., McElveen, R., & Williams, R. (2020). *The future of US policy toward China: Recommendations for the Biden administration*. Brookings Institution China Center Monograph.

Horvath, R. (1972). A definition of colonialism. *Current Anthropology, 13*, 45–57.

Hurlburt, H. (2021). Inside Joe Biden's foreign policy worldview. *Foreign Policy.* https://foreignpolicy.com/2021/01/15/joe-biden-foreign-policy-relationships-united-states/C

Hussain, M. N. (2004). The balance of payments constraint and growth rate differences among African and East Asian Economies. *Essays on balance of payments constrained growth* (pp. 220–244). Routledge.

Hussain, M. N., & Thirlwall, A. P. (2004). The balance of payments constraint, capital flows, and growth rate differences between developing countries. *Essays on balance of payments constrained growth* (pp. 28–39). Routledge.

Katzenstein, P. (2003). Small States and small states revisited. *New Political Economy, 8*, 9–30.

Keynes, J. M. (1933). National self-sufficiency. *The Yale Review, 22*, 755–769.

Keynes, J. M. (1964). *The general theory of employment, interest and money*. Harcourt, Brace & World.

Klasen, S., et al. (2016). Economic and ecological tradeoffs of agricultural specialization at different spatial scales. *Ecological Economics, 122*, 111–120.

Klein, M., & Pettis, M. (2020). *Trade wars are class wars*. Yale University Press.

Kregel, J. (2008). The discrete charm of the Washington Consensus. *Journal of Post Keynesian Economics, 30*, 541–560.

Lane, P., & Milesi-Ferretti, G. M. (2012). External adjustment and the global crisis. *Journal of International Economics, 88*, 252–265.

Lee, J., Wei S. J., & Xu, J. (2018). An unhealthy trade surplus? *Chinese University of Hong Kong Working Paper*. https://www.econ.cuhk.edu.hk/econ/images/Events/CESI_2019/Xu_Jianhuan_An_unhealthy_trade_surplus.pdf

Lee, J., Wei, S. J., & Xu, J. (2020). The welfare cost of a current account imbalance: A 'clean' effect. *NBER Working Paper* No. 27276. https://www.nber.org/system/files/working_papers/w27276/w27276.pdf

Liu, M., Margaritis, D., & Zhang, Y. (2019). Global financial crisis and the export-led economic growth in China. *The Chinese Economy, 52*, 232–248.

Kojima, M. (2013). Issues relating to the international trade of second-hand goods, recyclable waste, and hazardous waste. *International trade in recyclable and hazardous waste in Asia* (pp. 1–13). Edward Elgar.

Magnusson, L. (2019). Mercantilism. *The Elgar companion to John Maynard Keynes* (pp. 46–60). Edward Elgar.

Mandeville, B. (1997). *The fable of the bees*. Hackett Publishing Company.

Mann, M. (2012). *The sources of social power*. Cambridge University Press.

Mansfield, E., & Reinhardt, E. (2008). International institutions and the volatility of international trade. *International Organization, 62*, 621–652.

McCombie, J. S. L. (2004). Economic growth, trade interlinkages, and the balance of payments constraint: The balance of payments constraint, capital flows, and growth rate differences between developing countries. *Essays on balance of payments constrained growth* (pp. 58–83). Routledge.

McKee, D. (1996). Some reflections on the international waste trade and emerging nations. *International Journal of Social Economics, 23*, 235–244.

Mehlum, H., Moene, K., & Torkvik, R. (2006). Institutions and the resource curse. *The Economic Journal, 116*, 1–20.

Moosa, I. (2011). On the US-Chinese trade dispute. *Journal of Post Keynesian Economics, 34*, 85–111.

Moreno-Brid, J. C., Caldentey, E. P., & Nápoles, P. R. (2004). The Washington Consensus: A Latin American perspective fifteen years later. *Journal of Post Keynesian Economics, 27*, 345–465.

Müller, S. (2019). Hidden externalities: The globalization of hazardous waste. *Business History Review, 93*, 51–74.

Naastepad, C. W. M., & Storm, S. (2015). Europe's Hunger Games: Income distribution, cost competitiveness, and crisis. *Cambridge Journal of Economics, 39*, 959–986.

Negi, R. (2008). 'Beyond the Chinese scramble': The political economy of anti-Chinese sentiment in Zambia. *African Geographical Review, 27*, 41–63.

Nyland, C., Forbes-Mewett, H., & Thomson, S. B. (2011). Sinophobia as corporate tactic and the response of host communities. *Journal of Contemporary Asia, 41*, 610–631.

Palley, T. (2006). External contradictions of the Chinese development model: Export-led growth and the dangers of global economic contraction. *Journal of Contemporary China, 15*, 69–88.

Porter, M. (1990). *The competitive advantage of nations*. The Free Press.

Prebisch, R. (1959). Commercial policy in underdeveloped countries. *American Economic Review, 49*, 251–273.

Riofrancos, T. (2017). Extractivismo unearthed: A genealogy of a radical discourse. *Cultural Studies, 31*, 277–306.

Robinson, J. (1977). What are the questions? *Journal of Economic Literature, 15*, 1318–1339.

Santos-Paulino, A., & Thirlwall, A. P. (2004). The impact of trade liberalization on exports, imports, and the balance of payments of developing countries. *The Economic Journal, 114*, 50–72.

Schroeder, R., St. Martin, K., Wilson, B., & Sen, D. (2008). Third world environmental justice. *Society and Natural Resources, 7*, 547–555.

Schumacher, R. (2014). Adam Smith's 'two distinct benefits' from trade: The dead end of 'vent-for-surplus' interpretations. *History of Political Economy, 47*, 577–605.

Shaikh, A., & Weber, I. (2021). The US-China trade imbalance and the theory of free trade: Debunking the currency manipulation argument. *International Review of Applied Economics, 35*, 432–455.

Smith, A. (2003). *The wealth of nations*. Bantam/Dell.

Stiglitz, J. (2017). The overselling of globalization. *Roosevelt Institute Working Paper*. https://policydialogue.org/files/publications/papers/The-Overselling-of-Globalization_Stiglitz-1.pdf

Stockhammer, E. (2016). Neoliberal growth models, monetary union, and the Euro crisis: A Post-Keynesian perspective. *New Political Economy, 21*, 365–379.

Storm, S., & Naastepad, C. W. M. (2015). Crisis and recovery in the German economy: The real lessons. *Structural Change and Economic Dynamics, 32*, 11–24.

Surowiecki, J. (2003, November 17). Hong Kong hooey. *The New Yorker*. p. 68.

Swanson, A. (2019, November 5). Trump vowed to shrink the trade gap. It keeps growing. *New York Times*.

Teitel, S., & Thoumi, F. E. (1986). From import substitution to exports: The manufacturing exports experience of Argentina and Brazil. *Economic Development and Cultural Change, 34*, 455–490.

Thirlwall, A. P. (1980). Regional problems are 'balance-of-payments' problems. *Regional Studies, 14*, 419–425.

Thirlwall, A. P., & Hussain, M. N. (2004). The balance of payments constraint, capital flows and growth rate differences between developing countries. In *Essays on Balance of Payments Constrained Growth* (pp. 46–57). Routledge.

Veracini, L. (2013). 'Settler Colonialism': Career of a concept. *Journal of Imperial and Commonwealth History, 41*, 313–333.

Viner, J. (1930). English theories of foreign trade before Adam Smith. *Journal of Political Economy, 38*, 249–301.

Viner, J. (1948). Power versus plenty as objectives of foreign policy in the seventeenth and eighteenth centuries. *World Politics, 1*, 1–29.

Weber, I. (2020). Origins of China's contested relation with neoliberalism: Economics, the World Bank, and Milton Friedman at the dawn of reform. *Global Perspectives, 1*, 1–14.

Zhang, D., Min, Q., Liu, M., & Cheng, S. (2012). Ecosystem service tradeoff between traditional and modern agriculture: A case study in Congjiang County, Guizhou Province, China. *Frontiers of Environmental Science and Engineering, 6*, 743–752.

CHAPTER 9

Does a Current-Account Deficit Indicate Bad Economic Policy?

William Scarth

1 Introduction

Many individuals focus on the short-run performance of the economy, in particular on the level of employment. Since exports involve domestic jobs, while imports represent foreign jobs, exports are deemed 'good' while imports are 'bad'. Since a current-account surplus is more likely to exist when exports exceed imports, this short-run focus leads to the verdict that a current-account deficit is 'bad'.

Others take the view that monetary and fiscal policy initiatives can maintain high employment. They think high-employment objectives can be met without focusing on whether exports exceed imports. As a result, they assess the current account by considering long-run, not short-run, issues. Accordingly, when imports exceed exports, the focus is on the fact that we are 'living beyond our means'—financing that overspending by increasing our indebtedness to the rest of the world. The result is that

W. Scarth (✉)
Department of Economics, McMaster University, Hamilton, Canada
e-mail: scarth@mcmaster.ca

S. Pressman and J. Smithin (eds.), *Debates in Monetary Macroeconomics*,
https://doi.org/10.1007/978-3-031-11240-9_9

future generations (who must pay the interest on that debt) need to transfer a fraction of each year's output to foreigners. So current-account deficits involve a transfer in material welfare from future generations (who must service that debt) to current generations (who incur that debt). So whether a deficit is 'bad' or not depends on whether one thinks reducing the living standards of future generations is 'bad' or not.

General views concerning the desirability of transfers from one generation to another usually depend on the nature of the events that communities have to deal with. As a result in Sect. 2 of this essay I describe both the immediate and the lasting effects of several developments that can (and have) confronted economies, indicating how some events make running a permanent deficit in the current account desirable, while others make a permanent surplus appropriate. In Sect. 3, the analysis is extended to evaluate how ongoing productivity growth affects the verdict concerning the current account.

The focus in Sect. 4 shifts to the more general question of whether devoting a higher proportion of a nation's GDP to saving is 'good' or not, since acquiring more claims on foreigners is just one thing people can do with their savings. A second alternative is to buy more machines. Those living later on are wealthier in either case, since both higher interest payments from foreigners, and greater profit earnings from owning more domestically employed capital, make higher living standards in the future possible. Beyond clarifying this point, the purpose of Sect. 4 is to devote more attention to equity issues, by adding the rich-*vs*-poor (within any one generation) dimension to the analysis.

The formal analysis which underpins the discussion in Sects. 2–4 embraces what is referred to as the neoclassical approach within the economics profession. As is the case with all theory, this approach involves many assumptions that are made to simplify the analysis. Neoclassical theory involves the following simplifications:

1. The demand for goods and services is not an issue. The long-run focus is viewed as justification for two assumptions, first that the installation costs that must be incurred to transform consumer goods into capital goods can be ignored (firms are comfortable investing in new capital whatever amount households choose to save). Further, there is sufficient time for prices (wages and interest rates—the returns received by workers and machine owners) to adjust to ensure that full employment of both inputs is maintained.

2. The supply of goods and services is therefore the centre of the analysis. The formal models involve only one type of each input so that an aggregate production (or input–output) function can be involved without encountering internal consistency problems. Along with the assumption that firms maximize profits, the marginal products of each input (which follow from this production function) determine the input prices.
3. Financial considerations are ignored. This assumption is central to ensuring that the model economy converges to the long-run outcome that is the focus of the analysis. For example, such convergence is threatened if interest rates cannot fall enough to ensure that all household saving is invested in capital accumulation. The existence of money as a possible store of wealth for household saving creates a zero-lower-bound on interest rates, and this is one source of a non-convergence problem that is precluded in neoclassical analysis.

Because some economists, and the policy-makers who seek guidance from them, are uncomfortable with these assumptions, I provide some analysis with a short-run focus in Sect. 5 of the essay. After all, if either monetary and fiscal policy—or the economy's self-correction mechanisms that neoclassical analysis depends on to justify the assumption that the economy does eventually get to a long-run outcome—cannot be counted on to maintain high employment, we must confront the possibility that by a wrong verdict concerning the current account might emerge by basing that verdict only on long-run living standards and income-distribution considerations.

Concluding remarks are offered in Sect. 6. The purpose of the essay is to answer the question 'Should trade and financial policies always aim at a current-account surplus?' Our answer is 'no' for two reasons. First, the long-run analysis shows that the desirability of a surplus depends on what shocks confront our economy, which generation we think is more deserving than others, and whether or not we care about within-generation income inequality. Second, the short-run analysis shows that 'yes' a current-account surplus does facilitate building up a potentially useful contingency fund, but there is controversy concerning how much developed economies need such a fund. Since arguments can be made both in favour of, and against, pursuing a current-account surplus, I have to say 'no' to the proposition that it 'always' represents a desirable objective.

2 Long-Run Living Standards

We begin by defining the current account. The current-account balance for a particular country records all exports and imports for that country during a specific time interval, say one year. Some of the exports and imports are goods. For example, Norway imports wine from France and exports oil from its North Sea deposits. Norway's exports enter its recorded current account with a plus sign, while Norway's imports with a negative sign. Its current account is said to be in surplus for that year if the overall number is positive.

There is one category of imports and exports singled out for special attention in a country's current-account measure, lending services. For example, if domestic residents want to spend more than their total income in a particular period, they can borrow from citizens in the rest of the world. This borrowing means that domestic residents have a debt to foreigners (call it F) and in future periods that debt needs to be serviced. If the interest rate paid on that accumulated foreign debt is denoted by r, then the annual debt service obligation is rF. Further, if X denotes the excess of all other exports over imports, the current account, CA, is $X - rF$.

The other relationship we need to appreciate about a country's dealings with the rest of the world is an accounting identity—which states that the country's foreign debt must increase whenever the already existing debt service obligations exceed the revenue received from current net export sales. Using the symbol Δ to denote 'change in', this means $\Delta F = rF - X$. The bottom line is that running a current-account deficit is just another way of saying that we are going more into debt. So, other things being equal, a current-account deficit is 'bad news' for those living later on. But does this mean that such a deficit is bad in some *overall* sense? In what follows, I conclude 'not always', by showing that sometimes a deficit is desirable.

Let us consider several example situations, the first being Norway's discovery of North Sea oil in the twentieth century. This discovery meant that Norwegians could expect higher incomes for a number of years, but they could also anticipate the need to revert to lower incomes later on, after the deposits had been fully mined. Instead of accepting this up-then-down sequence in living standards, Norwegians decided to take a smaller income increase in the early years, and to use the resulting savings to build up a fund that could then be used to augment incomes after the deposits had been exhausted. In the 30 years since the fund has existed, it has built up to 1.2 trillion US dollars. Norwegians have demonstrated that they prefer a smoother time path for their consumption of goods over time, smoother than what they would have had otherwise, and they have accomplished this smoothing by running a current-account surplus for many years while planning to run a current-account deficit for a long time later on. Norwegians would certainly disagree if they were told that running a deficit in future constituted 'bad economic policy'.

Other developments might cause a country's citizens to support a transfer *towards* those living in the present—in the opposite direction compared to the Norway situation. For example, if the current generation is fighting a pandemic, and it is thought to be 'fair' to transfer some of that burden to future generations who are not expected to face such hardship, a current-account deficit during the pandemic is called for. Similarly, a deficit could also be defended if the current overspending involves purchasing a durable item, such as investing in low-carbon-emission infrastructure that will benefit future generations by more than the bequeathed interest-payment obligations.

In the remainder of this section, I consider two other developments. One event looks at the households' optimal response involving a current-account deficit forever, and in the other case, households choose to run a surplus throughout the time sequence following the event. The first event provides another counter-example to the stricture against current-account deficits, while the second provides useful background for later sections of this essay.

The key decision that each individual in the neoclassical model economy needs to make is her consumption-savings plan. That plan is made so that her utility (or satisfaction) is maximized. She gets satisfaction from consuming the goods; saving is valued only because it facilitates future consumption.

There are two important features of each individual's 'utility function' which is the relationship economists use to specify how the consumption of goods generates satisfaction. First, at any point in time, more consumption means more happiness, but there is a diminishing-returns property to this relationship. This means that the first meal in an evening generates more additional satisfaction than would a third meal, if three meals were eaten that same evening. This feature of the utility function leads to the individual wanting to have a smooth consumption path, that is—to avoid being in a situation where she has a period of very high consumption followed by one involving very low consumption, or vice versa. This is because—by switching some consumption from what would otherwise have been a high-consumption period, the individual would suffer a smaller loss of satisfaction than the gain in satisfaction she would acquire by raising consumption in what otherwise would have been a low-consumption period.

Economists refer to this aspect of human nature as the 'diminishing marginal utility of income', and it is important for many issues. For example, it is a necessary (but it turns out, not a sufficient) condition to provide a philosophical underpinning for the proposition that we should redistribute income from rich to poor. In addition, it is a central feature of the models that predict that people are better off when they have freedom to choose different levels of indebtedness to foreigners over time, as a way to smooth their consumption.

The second important feature of the individual's utility function is that it captures a person's preference for consuming sooner rather than later. There are two reasons for incorporating such a preference within the model economy. For one thing, an individual may not live very long; for another she is somewhat impatient. Economists justify assuming that each individual has a positive rate of impatience by noting that observed interest rates are positive. When someone wants to save some of their current income, to lend that spending power to someone else for a period, they expect to receive some interest as compensation for postponing their own consumption. They do not expect to have to bribe the borrower to take the funds off their hands for the period. So there is a discount rate specified in the household utility function in all economic models.

The first development I consider in the model economy is a government decision that some of each year's output be given out as foreign aid. Domestic residents realize that this policy means that they will have to consume less each year—compared to what they had previously planned, since some of the GDP is now going to foreigners. One possibility is to cut annual consumption immediately by the amount that is necessary if the cut is to be the same in every period thereafter. That response is what they would have to adopt if they could not borrow or lend with foreigners. Let us denote that loss in consumption by L. But if they are allowed to borrow internationally, domestic households can do better. Given the discounting aspect of their utility function, future losses are not viewed as important as immediate losses. As a result, when permitted, they choose to borrow to facilitate a drop in consumption that is smaller than L in the early periods, even though that means that their losses will be greater than L in the periods later on. This is an example of a situation in which there would be no basis for saying that the current-account deficit is inappropriate. As long as there are no market-failure problems (such as an externality or asymmetric information) to generate a verdict that what people privately choose is *not* appropriate from a societal point of view, there is no reason to preclude these voluntary and mutually beneficial exchanges between domestic residents and foreigners.

The second event I consider is a rise in life expectancy. With this development, it makes sense for people to save more than before. In the first instance, household income is given, so saving and consumption relate to each other as if each individual confronts a zero-sum game. Higher saving means lower consumption dollar-for-dollar. But as time passes, the higher level of saving means that claims on foreigners are building up. As the current-account proceeds in surplus, interest income is rising, so consumption can start to recover and rise above the level to which it initially fell. It turns out that the new long-run outcome is that annual consumption is not only higher than the initial drop, it is higher than the level that prevailed before whatever the medical breakthrough was that raised life expectancy. The households have chosen to accept some 'short-term pain to achieve long-term gain'. Once again, there seems to be little to recommend that households should not be allowed to use variations in the current account to achieve this outcome—that they prefer to all other responses.

A common feature emerges in both the cases we have just considered. Both scenarios involve households using their ability to save or dissave (by transacting with foreigners) so they can achieve a smooth consumption time-path as their response to each event. Events can cause abrupt changes in their income time-path, but since diminishing marginal utility is part of their inherent make-up, they always try to insulate their consumption time-path somewhat from these irregularities. Since it is consumption (not saving) that generates utility, it is rational to have savings (not consumption) be the shock absorber no matter what the event. Readers who are interested in a more detailed analysis of these two developments can consult Scarth (2014). The first three equations on p. 239 of that book define a system which can be explored using diagrammatic methods to verify what has been reported above.

3 Long-Run Living Standards in the Presence of Productivity Growth

In this section, I extend the neoclassical analysis of the current account by adding ongoing productivity growth. At the beginning of the essay, I summarized the definition of the current account, and how it relates to the change in foreign indebtedness, in the form of two equations, $CA = X - rF$ and $\Delta F = rF - X$. I now add a measure of domestic material welfare. Since imports are goods which domestic citizens enjoy, while exports are domestically produced items that domestic citizens do not get to enjoy, it makes sense to define material-welfare index as total domestic production (the GDP) minus net exports. So, denoting total output and welfare by Y and Z, the living-standards measure is $Z = Y - X$.

Since GDP grows over time with rising worker productivity, it is customary to focus on these measures as ratios to GDP. Let that productivity growth rate be denoted by g. Once we divide all three relationships in the previous paragraph through by Y, use lower-case letters to denote the corresponding ratios to GDP, and recognize that the percentage change in any ratio equals the excess of the percentage change in the numerator over the percentage change in the denominator that is $\Delta f/f = \Delta F/F - \Delta Y/Y$, and replace $\Delta Y/Y$ by g, the relationships become $z = 1 - x$, $ca = x - rf$, and $\Delta f = (r - g)f - x$.

Finally, we restrict our attention to a long-run balanced-growth outcome, a situation in which all aggregates follow the same trend. They are growing at the same rate, g. In that situation all the ratios to GDP stay constant, so Δf is zero. In this case, the three relationships imply two important insights. First, since $ca = -gf$, a current-account surplus exists only if domestic citizens have claims on foreigners (that is, if f is negative). Second, the material-welfare definition becomes $z = 1 - (r - g)f$.

Now let us explore whether a current-account surplus raises or lowers the material-welfare index. Clearly, the answer depends on the sign of the $(r - g)$ term, that is, on the size of 'the' interest rate compared to the growth rate of productivity Which is the bigger of the two? History suggests that on an annual basis 2–3% is a plausible value for productivity growth in many countries. However, we observe many different interest rates, ranging from just 1% on risk-free government bonds in recent years to values around 12%, which firm managers typically use as a minimum internal rate of return that must be expected on contemplated investments before a project is deemed acceptable. The value that is appropriate for calibrating models which involve capital but no government bonds is the investment acceptability cut-off rate, not the government-bond yield.

So let us assume that we 'know' that the appropriate interest rate exceeds the growth rate. When this assumption is inserted into the final expression for our welfare measure, we can see that running a current-account surplus is a good thing. This conclusion follows since with r exceeding g only a negative value for f can make z exceed unity, and ca is necessarily positive if f is negative. All of this makes intuitive sense, since by focusing exclusively on a long-run balanced-growth path we have implicitly decided that the only people we care about are those who live in the future. The only way we can raise their consumption above the nation's future GDP is to ensure that they have financial claims on the rest of the world, and the only way we can bequeath this situation to them is by running a current-account surplus.

Many policy advisors have relied on this result to conclude that *any* pro-savings policy initiative should be recommended. I consider this proposition in the next section of the essay. But first, I consider a little more fully the issue concerning the relative size of r and g.

It is important to appreciate that the claims we have been discussing are paper assets that are best thought of as equities. An equity entitles its owner to receive her share of profits, which are (in turn) the earnings of physical capital in the production process of that period. As long as firms maximize profits, and so hire units of capital up to (but not beyond) the point that the contribution to profits of the last unit hired is just balanced by the rent that must be paid to the capital owner, r stands for *both* the yield earned by each unit of capital and the yield on the associated equity claim.

Armed with this insight, let us recall that, in a long-run balanced-growth setting, g stands for the growth rate observed for GDP as well as all inputs. Using K to denote the capital input, this means that g can be replaced by $\Delta K/K$ in the *r-vs-g* debate—making it an r-*vs*-$\Delta K/K$ debate. Then, we can multiply both sides by K to re-express this contest one more time as an rK-*vs*-ΔK debate. Finally since rK is profits and ΔK is investment (the increase in '*machines*' that takes place during the year) all we have to do is go to a country's national accounts and compare these two numbers. Abel et al. (1989) were the first to point out this very direct way of resolving this debate, and they found that profits exceeded investment *every* year for *every* country for which they could find data. We conclude as before, if enhancing *future* living standards is the goal, more saving is 'good'.

While not the focus of this essay, it may be helpful for the reader's perspective if I refer to two other areas of inquiry that have highlighted an *r-vs-g* debate. One concerns long-run trends in income distribution, while the other concerns whether government budget deficits inevitably lead to a transfer away from future generations in favour of those alive when the deficits are incurred.

In a *New York Times* best-seller, Piketty (2014) stresses what he sees as an important implication of *r* exceeding *g* one that would, if it were true, alarm anyone concerned about income inequality. He assumes that workers' income can be expected to grow at the labour productivity growth rate, and that the income of capitalists can be expected to grow at rate *r*. Piketty concludes that the fact that *r* exceeds *g* (a proposition he assumes since, as we did above, he interprets '*r*' as the marginal product of capital) is sufficient to generate a prediction that the income distribution will become ever more skewed towards capitalists, at the expense of workers, as time passes. It turns out that *if* a second condition is also satisfied, it can indeed be predicted that labour must suffer an ever-dwindling income share. The additional requirement is that it must be particularly easy for firms to substitute capital for labour in their production processes. Specifically, what economists call the elasticity of factor substitution must exceed unity. Unfortunately for Piketty's prediction—but fortunately for workers—the empirical evidence on the substitution elasticity is that it is below unity (Knoblach et al., 2020). There is no denying that we have observed a large growth in income inequality over recent decades, but for the causes of that we must look elsewhere. See, for example, Milanovic (2016) for some explanations.

The other literature that focuses on *r-vs-g* is one that investigates whether the government's debt-to-GDP ratio must inexorably rise forever if the government finances each year's deficit with further bond issue. It turns out that the debt ratio explodes if *r* exceeds *g*, and not so if *g* exceeds *r*. The intuitive reason for this is that with bond-financed deficits the numerator of the debt ratio rises at an annual rate equal to *r*, while the denominator rises at rate *g*. Clearly it is the government bond rate, *not* the marginal product of capital, that should be used for assessing the *r-vs-g* debate in this context. Since this measure of r exceeded g in the 1990s, whereas it is expected to remain less than g after the current pandemic, there is no internal inconsistency in the fact that policy analysts were upset by persistent budget deficits in the 1990s, while these same individuals see no sustainability problem in recent times.

Both the models that I have relied on to examine the current-account question and those used by Piketty to discuss the future of capitalism do not involve a government. Therefore there is no place for considering the government bond rate value for r in our interpretation of those model's implications. Ideally, however, I would prefer to report on research that relies on models that are rich enough to allow savers two ways of holding wealth, capital and government bonds. Early exploration of such models is proceeding. For example, Blanchard (2019) adds uncertainty to the model so that households choose to hold some low-yield bonds despite the fact that an asset with a higher yield, albeit one which involves bearing more risk, is available. Similarly, Ball and Mankiw (2021) add imperfect competition, giving an alternative rationale for the yield on capital to exceed the government bond rate. These analyses show that the feasibility *versus* the desirability of continued bond-financed budget deficits are separate questions. I will make no further reference to this burgeoning literature in this essay, since my focus is on current-account deficit rather than the government budget deficit. This related and developing literature was referenced simply to provide perspective for readers.

4 Equity Considerations Both Within and Across Generations

In the previous section, I narrowed the focus to long-run balanced-growth outcomes. In that setting, we established that higher saving leads to higher material living standards. However, to go further than this, and to conclude that more saving is called for without reservation, we would need to know whether the 'long-term gain' dominates the associated 'short-term pain'. That is the lower consumption that cannot be avoided initially to accomplish the higher saving.

Therefore, we must now assess whether the long-term gain is sufficiently large. The assessment is made difficult by the fact that both historical observation, and simulated versions of model economies, indicate that very many years are involved as we transition from the pain to the gain. The time interval between first embarking on a pro-savings initiative, and the year when we cross over from pain to gain, is a finite number of years. And we also know that after the cross-over—assuming no other developments—there will be an infinite number of years to enjoy the gain. But that simple comparison, by itself, does not provide a compelling basis for saying that the initiative is 'worth it'. Surely we should discount the future gains to some extent. After all, if we believe that governments should make policy decisions that reflect the preferences of their constituents, policy decisions should involve the same discount factor that households rely on when making their own choices that concern the future. In addition, there is the complication that different generations will suffer the pain, compared to those that enjoy the gain. Older individuals may die before the pain years are over, and others will not be born until only the gain years are involved, so a rigorous analysis of pro-savings initiatives requires addressing this issue as well.

In the early days of pro-savings policy analyses, many economists were not familiar with the mathematical tools that are necessary to pursue a formal dynamic analysis to address these challenges. Therefore, a short cut was embraced. This involved appealing to the assumption that everyone—young and old—believe in following the 'golden rule', everyone should 'do unto others' what we would appreciate others doing for us. According to this maxim, even those who lose, the old people in this case, would vote in favour of the pro-savings initiative since it is what these individuals would appreciate old people doing for them if they were young. To support this approach, economists pointed to the fact that there appeared to be a long-standing implicit contract across the generations with each one lowering their own living standard by saving so they could bequeath a higher living standard to their descendants. To honour and continue that implicit contract, each generation has appeared to be comfortable responding to this gift that they received from their ancestors, by extending a similar gift to later generations. This line of reasoning was taken as justification for dropping the 'short-term pain' from the analysis. It was then concluded that the existence of the long-term gain, by itself, was sufficient to recommend that higher saving (and by implication running current-account surpluses) is 'good'.

In more recent years, most economists are trained sufficiently in mathematics to make the short cut unnecessary. However, it remains quite challenging to complete an inter-temporal analysis if households differ very much from one another. The analysis is most manageable if it is assumed that all households are identical. Each one makes decisions on a dynasty basis in the sense that members of succeeding generations are valued just as much as those already alive. So the overlapping-generations family dynasty behaves as if it were just one ever-lasting individual. The benefit of this modelling strategy is that mathematical tractability is achieved, but an obvious disadvantage is that the analysis is unable to address either generational-tension issues, or rich-*vs*-poor issues. For what it is worth, a clear verdict concerning pro-savings initiatives emerges—even when explicitly including both the pain and the gain—more saving (and by implication a current-account surplus) is unambiguously 'good'.

But surely we cannot be satisfied with the underlying assumption that all families are the same. Mankiw (2000) has advocated one way to introduce some heterogeneity among households that I find appealing. He suggests that we think of there being two groups in society. One is wealthy, with parents sufficiently focused on leaving bequests to their offspring, that the ever-lasting dynasty framework is an entirely satisfactory model for interpreting their behaviour. The other group is poor, and cannot afford to save, so they live 'hand-to-mouth' and do not voluntarily save. After studying alternative ways of explaining US data on household consumption patterns, Mankiw argues that a good simplification for macroeconomic modellers to adopt is to assume that each group constitutes half the population. By following Mankiw's suggestion, we achieve both mathematical tractability, and the ability to evaluate the differential effects of pro-savings initiatives on both rich and poor.

To illustrate how things turn out in this framework, I now summarize my analysis of one particular version of a pro-savings initiative contained in Scarth (2014, 282–28). The specific question under study is whether the income tax should be replaced by a consumption tax. Consumption taxes can be avoided if an individual saves their income instead of spending it, while income taxes must be paid whether they spend or save that income, so saving is higher with the consumption tax. As already noted, models that do not permit the existence of a hand-to-mouth group reach an unambiguous verdict. In that case the switch to a consumption tax is supported without reservation.

But the result is different when a hand-to-mouth group *is* part of the population. Both taxes are progressive, since the poor group is exempted from paying either tax. But even with the poor paying no taxes, this group still has to experience a pain-then-gain time sequence, as the rich group chooses to follow this now-familiar pattern, and there is nothing to stop a similar sequence from being imposed on the other group that is part of the same economy. While the rich continue to find that the later gain is worth the earlier pain, the poor are so focused on the here and now that they find that the short-term pain dominates.

To seek an overall verdict, I add a transfer payment to the model, and set it at just what is needed to bring the poor group to the point that those individuals are left indifferent between whether the tax substitution is undertaken or not. I then calculate whether, in present value terms, the rich group—who must finance the transfer payment—remains in favour of the consumption tax. The result is that the rich no longer prefer the consumption tax. The moral of the story is that it is much harder to find an analysis that supports a short-term pain for long-term gain initiative, when the analysis allows for some fraction of the families to discount the future enough to make saving unappealing or impossible.

The application of this insight to the current-account issue is straightforward. If we care about within-generation equity the analytical underpinnings for supporting the claim that running a surplus is 'good policy' is much weaker than it is widely believed to be.

5 Short-Run Concerns

Up to this point in the essay, I have relied on the 'neoclassical' paradigm in economics. As noted in the Introduction, this approach abstracts from such things as sluggish price adjustments, installation costs for capital, financial markets, cyclical unemployment, and concerns about whether it is plausible to believe that the economy eventually reaches an outcome that can be well-described without any reference to the path that is followed earlier on. Critics argue that these abstractions involve such central issues that it is unappealing to apply that analysis to real-world policy debates.

Defenders reply that *all* theory involves 'unrealistic' assumptions. Indeed theory is *designed* to be a simplification, so its relevance should be assessed by comparing its implications—not its simplifying assumptions—to reality. By this criterion, the analysis in earlier sections of the essay does seem useful. To justify this claim further, I briefly focus on the experience of two countries, Canada and China. First, consider Canada in the mid-1990s, when it was the G7 country that was the most indebted to foreigners. At that time, Canadians were transferring roughly 2.5% of each year's GDP to foreigners to finance that debt. Then, a policy of increased national saving was pursued. Canadians suffered lower material welfare for a significant period of time, but a quarter-century later, the previous 2.5 percentage-point gap between GNP and GDP had been eliminated, and Canadians enjoyed higher material welfare as a result. This pain-then-gain outcome is exactly what the neoclassical analysis predicted would result from this pro-saving initiative.

As a second example of the applicability of the neoclassical analysis, consider China. Other countries (in particular, the United States) have long complained that China has been relying on unfair trade practices and policies to maintain a very large surplus in its current account. Why would China want to do this? Our analysis indicates that they would want to pursue this path if their primary goal is to surpass the United States in material living standards as soon as possible, without worrying about the incomes of their poorer citizens (who mainly live in rural areas) along the way. It would seem that this is a pretty accurate description of the Chinese authorities' preferences. I conclude that, despite the long list of simplifying assumptions involved in the neoclassical approach, it does seem to be a useful framework for organizing our thoughts about actual policy choices undertaken in quite different countries.

Despite such reassurance, many analysts want to focus on the short run, not just the long run. I noted in the Introduction that neoclassical economists think such additional analysis is unnecessary since they presume that monetary and fiscal policy can be counted on to keep GDP at its potential. Given this presumption, they feel comfortable ignoring temporary business cycles when discussing issues they feel are of lasting importance, such as average living standards and income distribution. But their critics question the government's ability to pursue stabilization policy sufficiently effectively that short-run issues can be safely ignored. Since the critics have raised some important concerns in this regard, I devote this section of the essay to analysing how our verdict on the current account may need to be modified.

Initially, in the post-WWII years, it was thought that fiscal policy was the appropriate tool to be used for stabilization. with the government running deficits during the recession phase of each business cycle to stimulate demand, and then running surpluses during the over-heated phase of the cycle, to dampen demand and to work back down the public debt that had been accumulated during recessions. However, support for using fiscal policy in this way was undermined when it appeared that governments would embrace only one-half of the advised strategy, running deficits during recessions but refusing to run surpluses during good times. So with *applied* fiscal policy involving what I call 'a legacy problem'—a rising debt-to-GDP ratio—it was decided that monetary policy should replace fiscal policy as the appropriate instrument for pursuing stabilization policy. Only gradually has it become at least partially recognized that this reliance on monetary policy has involved some serious problems.

First, there is the 'lower-bound' issue. Short of eliminating traditional cash and limiting legal tender to appropriate digital entries, it is difficult to have a nominal interest rate much below zero. The novel policies that have emerged in response to this challenge involve either threats to central-bank independence or challenges to their credibility. Second, monetary policy involves its own legacy problem since a *permanent* move to low-interest rates very much threatens the business model of many financial institutions such as pension funds, life-insurance providers, and banks. Finally, there is the debt-trap worry stressed by Minsky (2008) years ago and that White (2021) claims has been under-appreciated. This form of legacy problem involves the tendency for a prolonged period of low-interest rates to encourage people to take on more debt. This is a development that makes it very difficult for central banks to re-normalize the general level of interest rates, since a rise in rates could cause a debt-default crisis.

As evidence that the authorities have felt trapped by this spectre, White notes that the world debt-to-GDP ratio was 280% in 2008, and despite the financial crisis that occurred that year, the debt ratio has been allowed to increase (even before the pandemic) to 330% by 2020. It would appear that monetary policy-making may be open to the same criticism that was levelled at fiscal policy. At least for the last three decades, it has been applied only when expansion is desired. A vicious circle has emerged, the more low-interest rate policy is embraced, the more debt accumulates, so the more 'unthinkable' interest-rate normalization becomes.

It seems inescapable that both fiscal and monetary policies involve limitations that should condition how much we can reasonably expect from stabilization efforts. As a result, it may be risky to base our entire focus of evaluating alternative current-account strategies on long-run issues. After all, if it is unreasonable to presume that we will ever actually get to the long-run outcome envisioned by neoclassical theory, should we not explore the possibility that current-account surpluses may help us during short-run crises? It seems clear that we should, so in the remainder of this section, I do just that. In particular, I explain how the verdict on this score depends on which parts of the world we consider, Europe, the developing countries, or the United States.

European countries are linked through the common currency. Such an arrangement works best when all the member countries share the same goals with respect to national saving objectives. But this consensus is lacking in Europe. Many of the southern countries favour spending beyond current means (transferring income away from future generations), while some of the important northern countries prefer the opposite transfer. Some way of accommodating these different objectives is needed, either some combination of fiscal transfers from one group of countries to the other, some migration of people from one region to the other, or some adjustment in exchange rates. Europe faces a fundamental challenge. There is limited appetite for significant fiscal transfers or migration, and exchange-rate adjustments are impossible if there is only one currency. It will remain a challenge to manage the adjustment frictions that emerge as member states continue to pursue different targets for their current account.

Developing countries have limited resources for insulating their citizens from major shocks, so these shocks can lead quickly to a loss in international confidence in that country's ability to avoid serious recessions. When foreign lenders act on these concerns, they shift their funds to other countries, and this leads to pressure for a big drop in the value of that country's currency. Since that depreciation can lead very quickly to a full-scale domestic banking crisis, the central banks of these countries like to operate in the same manner as all central banks did back in the Bretton Woods era. They want to have sufficient foreign exchange on hand to make it possible to cover some of the withdrawals made by the fleeing foreign investors, without there being as much pressure for domestic-currency depreciation. But to build up that 'rainy day' fund of foreign exchange, the country needs to run a balance of payments surplus. In short, developing countries are less able to base their current-account decisions on long-run considerations.

One reason why widespread bank failures are a particular concern in developing countries is that those institutions bear so much risk. In addition to the usual challenges that confront a bank, such as a term-to-maturity mismatch in its balance sheet, these banks try to bear the exchange-rate risk that their customers wish to avoid. This involves having the loans to domestic households and firms denominated in the domestic currency, while letting the foreign depositors of funds use accounts denominated in US dollars. Therefore, the usual threat to banks of a large deposit withdrawal is magnified by the further immediate deterioration in its balance sheet that occurs when the currency depreciates.

The United States is at the opposite end of the spectrum compared to the developing economies. Their own currency is what is accepted as the international medium of exchange, and essentially everyone assumes that the United States is the supplier of the one (supposedly) 'safe' financial asset in the world, US government bonds. When combined with the fact that it costs the United States very little to print up more physical units of their currency and their bonds, this creates an incentive for Americans to take advantage of their unique situation. If other countries are committed to running current-account surpluses, the United States may as well run a deficit. Instead of the usual signal that a 'belt-tightening' will eventually need to be suffered, the signal that the rest of the world is giving the Americans is that they are happy to exchange real goods and services for essentially costless-to-produce pieces of paper. Why shouldn't the United States take advantage of this unique opportunity? Given how much the Americans have consistently lived beyond their means in this way, it appears that they appreciate this opportunity. They seem to appreciate that most of what has been discussed in this essay does not apply to them.

6 Conclusions

I set out to explore whether trade and financial policies should always aim for a current-account surplus. I conclude that this should *not* always be the focus, for main three reasons.

Firstly, what is desirable depends on the nature of the developments affecting the economy. For example, we found that if we are confronted by a temporary favourable development, it makes sense to pursue a sequence which involves a current-account surplus followed by a current-account deficit. Or, if we are confronted by a permanent unfavourable development, a permanent current-account deficit is recommended.

Moreover, what is desirable depends on which generation we think is more deserving. The more we value future generations compared to those living in the present, and the less we care about income inequality within each generation, the more likely it is that standard economic analysis supports a current-account surplus. But it is not up to economists to advise policy-makers concerning the extent to which different groups within society should be valued.

Finally what is desirable depends on whether or not we need a contingency fund, to help the economy cope with short-run instabilities. The controversies surrounding the effectiveness of standard monetary and fiscal policies that are aimed at stabilizing the level of economic activity in the short run mean that the need for such a contingency fund is very different across countries—with that need being highest for the developing countries and least for the United States.

Since these findings imply that arguments can be made both in favour of, and against, pursuing a current-account surplus, I have no alternative but to say 'no' to the proposition that it 'always' represents a desirable objective.

References

Abel, A., Mankiw, N. G., Summers, L. H., & Zeckhauser, R. J. (1989). Assessing dynamic efficiency: Theory and evidence. *Review of Economic Studies, 56*, 1–20.

Ball, L. M., & Mankiw, N. G. (2021). *Market power in neoclassical growth models* (NBER Working Paper No. 28538). NBER.

Blanchard, O. (2019). Public debt and low interest rates. *American Economic Review, 109*, 1197–1229.

Knoblach, M., Roessler, M., & Zwerschke, P. (2020). The elasticity of substitution between capital and labour in the US economy: A meta-regression analysis. *Oxford Bulletin of Economics and Statistics, 82*, 62–82.

Mankiw, N. G. (2000). The savers-spenders theory of fiscal policy. *American Economic Review Papers and Proceedings, 90*, 129–125.

Milanovic, B. (2016). *Inequality: A new approach for the age of globalization*. Harvard University Press.

Minsky, H. P. (2008). *Stabilizing an unstable economy*. McGraw Hill.

Piketty, T. (2014). *Capital in the twenty-first century*. Harvard University Press.

Scarth, W. (2014). *Macroeconomics: The development of modern methods for policy analysis*. Edward Elgar.

White, W. (2021). *It's worse than 'reverse': The full case against ultra-low and negative interest rates* (Institute for New Economic Thinking Working Paper No. 151). Institute for New Economic.

CHAPTER 10

The Case for Fixed Exchange Rate Regimes: What for and in What Form?

Adrien Faudot and Nikolay Nenovsky

1 Introduction

The debate about exchange rate regimes is currently an unresolved issue in macroeconomics. The issue has divided all schools of thought: from neoclassical to post-Keynesian economists. For instance, the Mont Pelerin Society members were divided on whether they should support floating or fixed exchange rate regimes, which gave rise to fierce disputes (Schmelzer, 2019, 211). The disagreement has also caused a schism between the different streams of neoliberal economists. For their part, post-Keynesian economists also disagree on the constraints induced by fixed regimes and

A. Faudot (✉)
Universitie Grenoble Alpes, Grenoble INP, CERAG, Grenoble 38000, France
e-mail: adrien.faudot@univ-grenoble-alpes.fr

N. Nenovsky
LEFMI, University of Picardy Jules Verne, Amiens, France
e-mail: nenovsky@gmail.com

National Research University Higher School of Economics, Moscow, Russia

S. Pressman and J. Smithin (eds.), *Debates in Monetary Macroeconomics*,
https://doi.org/10.1007/978-3-031-11240-9_10

the alleged benefits of floating rates as shock absorbers (Bougrine & Seccareccia, 2004; Lopez & Perrotini, 2006).

During 1930, and until circa 1950, most economists supported fixed (albeit adjustable) regimes (Irwin, 2017). For around two decades after this, the majority opinion, including official and heterodox economists, supported floating or managed floating (Guzman et al., 2018; Ocampo, 2017). Proponents of fixed exchange rate regimes are currently seen as cranks or nostalgic for the gold standard. The literature on exchange rate regimes is abundant and continues to grow. A large part of it is now conducted on an empirical basis, outside any theoretical system, which tends to obscure the fundamental issues at stake.

Two facts will be highlighted in this chapter. The first is that the main discussions regarding the subject are focused on a few issues that have been at the centre of economic debates since the 1930s, although financialisation and globalisation have dramatically accentuated these issues. The second is that a popular contemporary approach to heterodox economics—the Modern Monetary Theory (MMT)—supports floating rates, based on the argument that floating is necessary for currency sovereignty, the latter being key to expansionary Keynesian fiscal policies (Kelton, 2020; Sardoni & Wray, 2007; Tcherneva, 2016). In doing so, MMT allows us to study exchange rates and propose an alternative view.

While recognising the fragility of fixed regimes in the context of the current financial globalisation, this chapter attempts to demonstrate that fixed exchange rate regimes are still appropriate exchange rate arrangements and preferable to floating regimes. The first argument is that businesses and, more generally, all economic agents that trade with non-residents need exchange rate stability, which leads them, in our current system of floating rates, to adopt the US dollar for a wide range of cross-border operations. As examined below, US dollar dominance in trade invoicing and settlement dramatically reduces the benefits of floating and is a significant source of financial problems. Secondly, the alleged advantage of the leading alternative to fixed rates—floating rates—is that the central bank and the government enjoy a policy space that does not exist under fixed exchange rates. Both empirical-based and theoretical arguments have increasingly challenged this assumption. The third argument extends the second one, asserting that floating rates relying on exchange rate adjustments in case of external disequilibrium (currency depreciation) tend to follow uncooperative behaviour, a beggar-thy-neighbour policy that is harmful for international stability. On the other hand, under specific conditions, fixed rates can pave the way for international stabilisation and multilateral cooperation. The last section (Sect. 4) reviews these conditions and examines two fixed regimes with very different properties: (1) currency boards and dollarisation, and (2) a fixed regime with capital controls. Both allow for exchange rate stability and are, to some extent, preferable to floating rates. However, both have been criticised for causing macroeconomic problems. The paper goes on to examine a third option—which is admittedly "politically naïve" (Moore, 2004)—an International Clearing Union.

2 Fixed Parities as a Public Good

The main argument in favour of fixed exchange rates is that it is far more convenient for producers located in a particular currency area to express the price of their exports in terms of local currency, regardless of the currency used for settlement. This argument relates to the fundamental issue of accounting and economic calculation. All economists accept the assumption that exchange between individuals is hardly possible without a standard unit of account. Every trade area—whatever its size—rests on an established standard and stable unit of account. International trade is no exception in this regard; at a minimum, it needs a common accounting standard, and accounting needs stability. From this point of view, fixed exchange rates are preferable to floating ones, as they facilitate traders' expectations (Lavoie, 2014, 495). Fixed exchange rates not only stimulate foreign trade, but they are also a key mechanism for attracting foreign capital, ensuring security for investment and profits. For peripheral and developing countries, where there are no domestic savings and the fiscal base is weak, external capital is the primary institutional lever for development and catching up to more developed nations (Gerschenkron, 1962).

Until the 1950s, the consensus was that central banks should preserve stable parities (Irwin, 2017). Fluctuating exchange rates were already discussed in academic circles and practised by a handful of countries. Most economists tolerated them only as a temporary adjustment phase to a new set of parities according to macroeconomic fundamentals and the real exchange rate. As a result, fluctuating exchange rates "turned out to be part of the journey to a fixed exchange rate" (De Vries, 1969, 152).

Generalised floating was conceived as disorder and the most uncoordinated response to the failed Bretton Woods agreement. New problems would arise with floating. For instance, Kindleberger believed that transaction costs would threaten the flexible exchange rate system. "Finally, the many academic economists who recommend separating international money and capital markets by a system of flexible exchange rates between national currencies in effect call for a return to Babel, with foreign languages used by none save professional interpreters. This maximises transactions costs and minimises international discourse" (Kindleberger, 1967, 11).[1]

The reality was slightly different. After the gold window closed in 1971, the system did not explode. Foreign exchange markets developed new hedging instruments to adapt to the changing environment of fluctuating rates. Nevertheless, floating introduced new costs associated with the rise of uncertainty (Davidson, 2006, 262). On the one hand, the adoption of flexible exchange rates bolstered speculation and financialisation. On the other hand, it did not prevent private actors from remaining pegged to the US dollar. As Kindleberger (1976, 61) wrote: "When the 'public good'—international money—is not available, companies have to provide for themselves".

The argument that commensurability is crucial for international trade may seem trivial. However, it has probably been overlooked by most economists discussing exchange rate regimes. As a result, exchange rate regimes are often considered in the literature merely as alternative options with their specific properties, advantages, and disadvantages (Murau et al., 2020, 771). For example, they are compared as shown in Table 1:

Table 1 Exchange rate regimes compared: advantages and disadvantages. The authors, adapted from Obstfeld and Rogoff (1995)

	Fixed	*Floating*
Monetary policy	Constrained	Unconstrained
International integration	Encouraged with the anchor country and its currency area	Complicated by fluctuations and risk premium
Currency crisis	Not prone to currency crisis when credibly fixed to the anchor	Not prone to currency crisis due to foreign exchange market equilibrium
Inflation	Low, although this depends on the anchor economy	Imported inflation caused by depreciation

As Rossi (2007, 101) points out, the fact that exchange rates are constantly fluctuating or expected to move in the future brings the world to a state of disorder in which currencies are bartered. In practice, however, as one can imagine, international trade does not tolerate barter as a *modus operandi*. In a sense, multinational corporations (MNCs) have overcome this problem by adopting the US dollar as their international currency, regardless of their parent countries. Hence, they do have a common monetary standard for trade and accounting by necessity. MNCs have used the same functional currency—the US dollar—for decades, for most international transactions. This private expediency has not gone without raising several significant issues.

The (partial) dollarisation of MNCs is causing a large part of the world to adhere to the dollar standard. Since the US dollar is the global funding currency, MNCs' debt is often denominated in US dollar (Adler et al., 2020). The role of the dollar in invoicing (as a unit of account) and settlement in international trade, has led to the dollarisation of a substantial part of worldwide bank deposits (Gourinchas et al., 2019, 9). The US dollar can only be spent in the US banking system, forcing non-US businesses to hold their export earnings in the US banking system instead of converting them into domestic currencies. These businesses have to use the liabilities of the US banking system, including so-called shadow money (Tokunaga & Epstein, 2018). The US dollar banking system has deployed new banking instruments to meet the global demand for safe US dollar assets. Such a demand has resulted primarily from the accumulation of dollars in institutional cash pools (Pozsar, 2013; Tokunaga, 2019, 34).

The shadow banking system makes US dollar instruments available to non-residents and develops new instruments: "money-like claims" (Pozsar, 2014; see also Murau et al., 2020). Shadow banks create claims that cannot be used for settlement purposes but promise to convert *at par* against bank deposits.[2] Several studies mention that the US dollar shadow banking system has an international dimension (Poszar, 2013), although this dimension remains understudied. While the global economy is currently characterised by various types of exchange rate regimes—from pure floating to dollarisation—private actors have developed a financial architecture that reconstructs a system with a stable unit of account (i.e. the US dollar). As a result of the development of these financial instruments, coupled with growing international trade, the use of the US dollar increased in the post-Bretton Woods era (Gourinchas et al., 2019).

What is the link between the dominant role of the dollar in invoicing and settlement in international trade, and the discussion of exchange rate regimes? For the country of origin, having a fixed exchange rate against the US dollar does not exempt its MNCs from using and accumulating US dollars. There are still transaction costs that push MNCs to use the US dollar rather than a smaller currency, even if the latter is credibly anchored to the US dollar. One may argue that MNC's preference for stability is of secondary importance to the choice of exchange rate regime. However, depending on their degree of openness and, more generally, the dependence on international factors, monetary authorities, and governments of many countries may prefer to stabilise the exchange rate to avoid the destabilising effects of exchange rate movements on profit margins and/or on domestic prices of imported goods (i.e. the pass-through effect).

It is generally believed that the era inaugurated by Nixon in 1971 after the closing of the gold window is one of the worldwide free-floating exchange regimes. This is not true. Fixed exchange rates are a reality shared by many countries in the world, especially developing countries. Ilzetski et al. (2019) find that 59% of the world's countries are pegged to the US dollar (see IMF 2020 for a classification of countries' de facto exchange rate regimes). Free-floating rates are only possible in a few large and advanced currency areas, with a few exceptions. For developing countries, free-floating is considered dangerous for domestic stability. Even one of the most prominent proponents of flexible regimes, Milton Friedman, does not believe that floating rates are appropriate for developing countries (Edwards, 2020). The size of countries also matters: a floating rate regime is unthinkable in small countries.[3] For these reasons, small open economies have a vested interest in joining monetary blocs. The construction of European monetary integration and the continuing enlargement of the area have been undertaken following these principles. Large economies tend to aggregate peripheral economies and form monetary blocs that have a lower degree of openness (taken as a single bloc) and are thereby better prepared for the consequences of floating.

Hence, it would be wrong to argue that all countries can let the foreign exchange markets determine the rate at which the national currency will be exchanged for another currency. The more open the economy is to international trade, the more appropriate a fixed exchange rate regime is. In practice, MNCs and, more generally, all companies involved with activities abroad lobby to peg the domestic currency to socialise this cost

(Broz & Frieden, 2006, 592). If this is so, the central bank would have to bear the cost of maintaining the peg. Note that this argument is not valid for the US economy. As we live in a world where the US dollar is the dominant currency, the US economy does not and cannot have an anchor. McKinnon (2005, 244) defines three rules that the anchor economy should follow: the US capital markets should be open to foreigners; the US should abandon any exchange rate policy, and the Federal Reserve should pursue an independent monetary policy to preserve the purchasing power of the dollar. Therefore, when speaking about fixed exchange rates, we also assume that the dominant currency has no anchor. Only a reform of the international monetary system implementing a currency union or a clearing union (see proposals below) would emancipate the dominant currency issuer from these rules.

3 Do Fixed Exchange Rates Hinder Currency Sovereignty?

Notwithstanding the above arguments, economists may recommend governments adopting flexible regimes because the national currency depreciation against other major currencies serves as a shock absorber to external imbalances. If governments in different countries choose to pursue different policies, it seems easier to let the market "discover" the appropriate exchange rate level. Otherwise, there is a risk of widening disequilibrium. The central bank will find it increasingly difficult to deal with it, and dealing with exchange rates will come at a growing cost.

The other argument in favour of flexible regimes is that floating exchange rates are preferable to fixed exchange rates because of the policy space provided (Kam & Smithin, 2008; Sardoni & Wray, 2007). This argument has been particularly emphasised by post-Keynesian authors highlighting the need to preserve monetary independence and reject hard pegs, currency boards, and currency unions. For instance, Bougrine and Seccareccia (2004, 674) argue that floating regimes "equip policy-makers with a wider capacity to conduct stabilisation policies independently of the rest-of-the-world environment". A country could decide its economic policies leaving aside the international dimension, thanks to the absorptive properties of floating exchange rates. Following this approach, if a country experiences a current account deficit, its government should let the currency depreciate instead of implementing austerity policies.

The depreciation of the national currency can be compared to a general subsidy from the domestic sector to the export sector, as it reduces relative export prices (in terms of foreign currency) while relative import prices increase (in terms of local currency).[4] On the one hand, it reduces real wages. On the other hand, however, it helps domestic producers gain market shares. Depreciation is considered a less painful way of adjusting to external constraints. In practice, governments try to avoid depreciating national currencies because depreciation can spark a number of macroeconomic problems, including imported inflation. As Moore (2004, 632) notes in a thought-provoking article: "The current floating exchange rate system prevents most countries from aggressively pursuing expansionary domestic policies".[5]

Several arguments counter the view that the floating regime is stabilising.

First, the free-floating regime relies excessively on speculative self-equilibrating movements. Speculative movements follow boom-bust cycles, which often bring the exchange rate permanently to an unacceptable level (Ocampo, 2017, 105). It is even uncertain that exchange rate movements eventually reach any equilibrium at all. In the meantime, it may have unintended consequences for domestic producers, consumers, and financial stability. Carry trade is a speculative practice that amplifies exchange rate fluctuations and undermines financial stability, reflecting the fact that exchange rate flexibility does not necessarily lead to an equilibrating exchange rate. Flexibility can become a means to profit from speculative activities, as McKinnon (2011, 774) highlights.

Rey (2016) updates an old criticism by arguing that floating rates do not protect against the consequences of US Federal Reserve decisions.[6] The Mundellian trilemma, which concludes that independent monetary policy can be achieved with flexible exchange rates, has lost much of its relevance due to cross-border capital flows (Eichengreen, 2021). According to Rey (2016) the trilemma has become a dilemma: on the one hand, to follow the US Federal Reserve's monetary policy and, on the other hand, to implement capital controls to obtain monetary policy autonomy. The transmission of US monetary policy to the rest of the world is a fact, so that everyone now recognises that the countries that have opted for flexible rates are nonetheless constrained to follow the US Federal Reserve more or less.

In practice, emerging market economies are most vulnerable to the accommodative US monetary policy (Carstens, 2019). However, even advanced economies pursue externally constrained monetary policies. For instance, Switzerland is said to be "sovereign"—i.e. it issues its own currency and its debt is denominated in the national currency. Negative interest rates are designed to combat appreciation pressures on the Swiss Franc, although they do put pressure on financial stability in Switzerland (Rossi, 2019). We can also mention China, which is not yet a mature economy, but is engaged in a liberalisation process and is seeking a more market-led exchange rate. McKinnon and Schnabl (2014) highlight that China has been impacted by the quantitative easing policy in the US and, more generally, in Western countries. Therefore, China has chosen to discourage hot money inflows by following the Federal Reserve policy and cutting its central bank rate.

All proponents of fixed rates acknowledge that exchange rate pegging entails a partial abandonment of national self-determination. However, this abandonment is implicit in any open economy. As Davidson (2006, 272) points out:

> The loss of complete economic self-determination is the cost of any permanent trading relationship. Economic independence must always ultimately mean either complete economic isolation or complete dominance of others. Autarky and independence can only be purchased at some cost. Once a nation decides to join a community of nations for both political and economic reasons then interdependence and feedback effects among the trading partners are inevitable. The trick is to make these feedbacks provide for economic stimulus as much as possible before global full employment is achieved.

It is true that under a fixed exchange rate regime, monetary policy is ultimately balance of payments constrained (Hanke, 1999, 337). However, monetary policy is balance of payments constrained regardless of the exchange rate regime. "Market" balance of payments (i.e. the balance resulting from supply and demand in the foreign exchange market) should be distinguished from the accounting balance of payments (i.e. the balance of goods, services, and capital recorded within a given period). At freely floating exchange rates, the market balance of payments is necessarily at equilibrium, since the foreign exchange market (supply and demand for the domestic currency) determines the market equilibrium exchange rate. Although market balance is guaranteed, the current account could suffer from exchange rate misalignment even at floating rates. This could generate persistent disequilibrium. The problem arises from the fact that no country can escape balance of payments (i.e. current account) constraints. As Vernengo and Caldentey (2020, 336) show, developing countries cannot in practice sustain current account deficits for prolonged periods.

In case of recurrent current account disequilibrium, real adjustments must eventually be made. A country that has chosen a floating exchange rate regime and is experiencing currency depreciation is certainly not constrained from defaulting in its own currency. It can, however, be forced to default on foreign obligations—not to mention the fact that currency depreciation usually leads to a reduction in imports whose price has increased. In order to prevent such a default, it may be forced "to adopt contractionary fiscal policies to curtail imports and/or increase interest rates, and deal with the outflows of capital and loss of reserves" (Vernengo & Perez-Caldentey, 2020, 337). In other words, a floating regime does not relieve any country from the balance of payments constraints.

4 The Objective Of International Monetary Coordination

Obstfeld and Taylor (2017, 21) recognise that "While floating exchange rates can allow individual countries to stabilise to a degree, they also raise the age-old problem of competitive currency depreciations, in which demand is just being shifted between countries". This age-old problem is that of beggar-thy-neighbour policies caused by exchange rate depreciation as a balance of payments adjustment tool. Countries may be tempted to rely on currency devaluation or depreciation to boost the domestic economy. As is well-known, currency devaluation can contribute to an increase in exports while reducing imports. This issue was raised after the Great Recession in 2008. Blanchard (2017), for example, reminds us that the monetary policy in advanced economies after 2008 led to currency appreciation in emerging market economies, which shrunk their competitiveness and triggered complaints. The desired currency depreciation leads to a reduction in real wages (in terms of imported goods) and can increase domestic employment. As such, it belongs to beggar-thy-neighbour policies (Davidson, 1992). As Robinson (1969, 87) pointed out in 1937:

> For every increase of employment at home there is a corresponding increase of unemployment abroad, where export industries have lost their markets and home industries are exposed to competition from cheap imports. For the rest of the world slump conditions become still more severe. From a purely nationalist point of view this in itself is of no importance – if the unemployed are foreigners they are no concern of ours – but it leads to consequences of which the most hard-bitten nationalist must take account. For other countries, finding them-selves in a more wretched plight than ever, will have still stronger motives for protecting themselves, by tariffs, devaluation or wage cuts.

Depreciation may result in retaliation. For this reason, the International Monetary Fund (IMF), set up at Bretton Woods in 1944, had as its primary task to "exercise firm surveillance over the exchange rate policies of members" (Article IV). Any substantial currency movement required that the IMF be notified. This rule has been violated by several countries. The most significant departure from this rule was by the US in 1971. Trade conflicts and the belief that the US dollar was overvalued led to exchange rate adjustments instead of trade restrictions (James, 2019, 268–269).

Most proponents of fixed exchange rates are not necessarily hostile to changes in parities (Heilperin, 1955, 83), especially when the old parities are inappropriate and even impede domestic adjustment.[7] Nevertheless, any change in parities does not relieve the domestic economy from the real adjustments that must be made. Heilperin (1939, 168) points out that the process of international re-equilibrium must take place regardless of the exchange rate regime. In case of a deficit, the country will have to choose one or more options from the following list: stimulating exports; restricting imports; encouraging inward foreign investment and the entry of foreign short-term deposits; discouraging national investments abroad; and purchasing short-term deposits abroad. In case of a surplus, the country will have to re-equilibrate through the same tools in the opposite direction: stimulating imports; discouraging exports; discouraging foreign investment in the country, or encouraging investment abroad.

A significant difference between fixed and flexible regimes is that the process of re-equilibrium can take place under an organised monetary system compared to a disorganised monetary system. This led the classical faction of the Mont Pelerin Society (including Hayek, Mises, and Heilperin) to reject floating rates on the pretext that they would encourage disorder and monetary nationalism. Fixed exchange rates can facilitate a forum for discussing international monetary coordination. A fixed regime can be considered the first step towards monetary integration (as opposed to disintegration) and further international cooperation. Outside this logic of cooperation, small countries often decide to fix their exchange rate against a regional or global hegemon because they take into account the peculiarities of the domestic economy, including geo-economic and geopolitical linkages.

Among the above-mentioned external adjustment tools, some are expansionary and others are deflationary. To avoid the deflationary ones, which are very painful (as Krugman 1989 admits), a deficit country should avoid contracting its imports, while a surplus country should increase its imports and encourage investment abroad. In the next section, we examine a proposal aimed at international monetary coordination with stable exchange rates *and* expansionary adjustment mechanisms.

5 Three Proposals to Make Fixed Exchange Rates Sustainable

Three proposals seem appropriate for maintaining fixed exchange rates over time. The first two (currency boards, on the one hand, and capital controls, on the other) have been often tried, while the third one (the International Clearing Union) has remained at the draft stage.

Currency Boards or Dollarisation (or Unilateral Euroisation)

Proponents of currency boards or dollarisation (or unilateral euroisation) agree with proponents of floating, and recognise that pegged rate regimes are unsustainable. They are incompatible with pursuing an active monetary policy (through sterilisation attempts), because this sooner or later leads to a crisis.

> Discretionary monetary authorities such as Central Banks have generally been unsuccessful at maintaining rigid exchange rates because they have done so in an inconsistent way. An analysis of the supply and demand for money shows the contradiction in using sterilized intervention to simultaneously target the exchange rate and the nominal supply of money, as almost all central banks do sometimes and many do most of the time. (Schuler, 1999, 85)
>
> Pegged rates invariably result in conflicts between exchange rate policies and monetary policies. [...] Balance-of-payments crises erupt as a monetary

authority increasingly offsets the reduction in the foreign component of the monetary base with domestically created base money. (Hanke, 2002, 91)

Unlike pegged regimes, currency boards and dollarisation are based on automatic monetary *rules*, and monetary policy is delegated to a credible foreign central bank. This eliminates currency risk; reduces the risk premium; strengthens trade with the anchor area, and attracts foreign capital. Currency boards, in addition to legally pegging the exchange rate to a stable foreign currency, also institute a legal 100% (or sometimes less) coverage of the central bank's monetary base and core liabilities with highly liquid foreign currency assets (Schwartz, 1993).[8] Convertibility is complete. In this case, the central bank's balance sheet eliminates domestic sources of monetary base and abandons active monetary policy. The monetary base is determined endogenously by the demand for money (Hanke, 2002). In this configuration, the central bank cannot influence the system's liquidity, nor can it conduct open market operations or act as a lender of last resort (LOLR). In each particular national case, residual options for influencing liquidity can be found, but these are rather exceptions. The currency board is considered sustainable due to the strong credibility effect (generated by the anchor currency) and as a consequence of the "discipline effect" and the systemic nature of tight budgetary constraints (austerity) (for more details see Desquilbet & Nenovsky, 2004). Friedman, who is often considered the guru of floating exchange rates, actually favours currency boards (or as he calls them, "unified currency") for small and peripheral economies:

[A] unified currency assures a maximum degree of integration of the country in question with the greater world. [...] So I believe there is no conflict between wholehearted advocacy of floating rates for major countries and the existence of currency blocs of smaller countries attached to the major countries. (cited in Edwards, 2020, 14–15)

There have been various institutional departures from the classical principles of currency boards (Camillieri Gilson, 2002). As shown by Nenovsky and Hristov (2002), the new generation of currency boards, unlike the colonial versions of currency boards (often referred to as first generation), allows some flexibility to implement modern monetary policies (reserve requirements, partial LOLR, presence of a government deposit on the central bank balance sheet). It is worth noting that cross-border capital movements nowadays lead to instability, both in the direction of speculative credit growth and of rapid withdrawal of foreign capital in times of crisis. This instability manifests itself both through the banking system and through other types of external capital inflows, such as EU funds in European countries. This also applies to dollar countries. This is why, especially after 2008, most currency boards and dollarised countries have been pursuing active regulatory policies, especially with respect to foreign banks.

Dollarisation is a regime in which a foreign currency is officially adopted as legal tender and the national currency is completely abolished (with some exceptions where small-value national coins are in circulation) (Bogetić, 2000).[9] Unilateral euroisation, which is not agreed upon, is a form of dollarisation involving the European currency instead of the US dollar. Unilaterally euroised countries should be distinguished from euro area members, as they do not participate in the governing institutions of the euro area. Just as the dollarised economies did with the US dollar, the euroised economies have unilaterally adopted the euro as legal tender. In this extremely dependent monetary form, monetary authorities do exist which, however, can only provisionally be called central bank (e.g. the Central Bank of Montenegro, Fabris et al., 2004). Convertibility is complete. There is no monetary policy. It is necessary to put foreign currency banknotes into circulation, which is done by a one-time conversion of foreign reserves into banknotes or their purchase. This regime ultimately links the dynamics of monetary processes to that of the leading centres and is extremely disciplining for public finances.

Dollarisation or currency boards are generally supported by orthodox economists and monetarists, but not only. Basil Moore, a well-known post-Keynesian, argued in 2004, after the Argentina debacle, that dollarisation was the second-best option to stabilising exchange rates since the long-awaited international monetary reform was not taking place. Dollarisation has the great advantage of being a "bottom-up" option, as its implementation does not require a new Bretton Woods-type conference. In comparison, the top-down solution of creating an International Clearing Union (see below) is highly unlikely and politically naïve. According to Moore, dollarisation is superior to fixed rate regimes precisely because it avoids the risk of breaking the fixed rates through devaluation and at the same time integrates the monetary systems of different countries. Eventually, the countries adopting the US dollar would increasingly be led to share seigniorage incomes and even be represented on the Federal Reserve Open Market Committee (Moore, 2004, 652).

The choice of a currency board and dollarisation is most often the result of geopolitical choice and self-imposed strategic dependence. For example, the choice of a currency board in the Baltic countries in the early 1990s, and later the choice of the German mark as official legal tender in Montenegro and Kosovo, is a visible manifestation of the desire by the national elites to replace the geopolitical anchor: in the first case to replace USSR/Russia with Germany and the EU, and in the second case to replace Yugoslavia/Serbia with Germany. We should also add the consideration that for small countries the political cycle leads to extreme instability of their monetary regimes, which become hostage to the political struggle and most often lead to inflation, devaluation, and financial crisis (often referred to as "financial and inflationary trauma"). This means that in small countries the dependence of the monetary regime on domestic factors is relatively greater and more harmful than their external dependence. Informal monetary practices that are also part of a country's monetary system, the most common form being "currency substitution", are also important. It is expressed in the preferences of consumers and producers in the small and peripheral country to pay, measure, and save in a stable foreign currency. Both monetary regimes fit into the model of "dependent capitalism", which in principle can be quite successful (Magnin & Nenovsky, 2020).

The currency board and dollarisation are also criticised from a technical point of view: the anchor country's monetary policy is transmitted passively; there are no instruments to react to asymmetric shocks; there is no LOLR, and competitiveness is lost because the exchange rate is overvalued. The proponents of these regimes respond that the goal of these regimes is passive behaviour (following the lead anchor) and that another type of regime would likely be less successful. They also argue that the economy can adjust to any level of the nominal exchange rate. The absence of nominal depreciation of the national money has a stimulative effect, forcing firms to increase their productivity and governments to maintain strict fiscal discipline.

Proponents of currency boards or dollarisation acknowledge that such exchange rate arrangements entail real adjustments that *have to be made* in case of external disequilibrium, meaning deflationary policies in the event of a current account deficit. In practice, this is painful. Deflation can hardly be avoided in the case of an external deficit, whatever the exchange rate regime adopted. Two alternative policy options do mitigate recourse to deflation.

Introduction of Capital Controls on Short-Term Capital Flows

One of the arguments in favour of flexible rates is that the central bank, by giving up support for official parity, avoids a costly battle with foreign exchange speculators. However, this battle can be better avoided by introducing controls on hot money flows (Vernengo & Rochon, 2003). The grounds for refraining from controlling capital movements are usually that they will lead to misallocation and serious problems arising from this.[10] These arguments rest on the fact that capital market regulations segment domestic markets from international markets (Guzman et al., 2018, 58). However, it can be seen as a policy option, a policy of selective capital controls that permit most capital inflows and outflows while preventing some categories of volatile capital flows with low social utility. This implies screening of capital flows.

Financialisation has reinforced the need to discuss capital controls. Since the 2008 financial crisis, economists from various schools of thought have recommended implementing capital controls, and it is not only heterodox economists who have traditionally supported these instruments (i.e. post-Keynesians, Latin American structuralist schools). For example, McKinnon and Schnabl (2014) recommend introducing capital controls in response to the troublesome inflows resulting from expansionary monetary policies in advanced economies and demand for higher interest rates in emerging economies. Even official economists such as those of the IMF have proposed capital controls as a policy option to stabilise national economies (Ostry et al., 2011). In practice, since WWII, the number of countries applying foreign exchange controls or selective short-term capital controls has declined dramatically, but, as Ilzetsky et al. (2019, 635–637) note, since mid-2014 many developing and emerging country governments have moved towards capital controls.

This solution is probably limited in its time and scope. Capital controls gradually lose their effectiveness once capital flows find other routes to reach their destination. Over the past two decades, investors and speculators in China have used various channels to circumvent existing controls, including trade mis-invoicing and non-repatriation of profits. Despite capital account regulations, the 2014–2017 period saw massive capital flight from China, which was only, and not completely, stopped by tighter controls. Ideally, to be effective in the long run, capital controls should be applied "at both ends", with central banks communicating cross-border capital flows to each other (Helleiner, 2015). Such a scheme requires international cooperation and could represent another path towards a more integrated international monetary and financial system.

Establishment of a Clearing Union and an International Investment Council

The very mention of the International Clearing Union immediately evokes Keynes' post-war plan prepared for the Bretton Woods conference. Working on a post-war international monetary order scheme, Keynes (1980, 33) called its first draft in 1941 "Proposals for an International Currency Union". Only subsequent drafts were renamed "Proposals for an International Clearing Union". Keynes wanted a unification of the world monetary system on the model of national monetary systems. Many economists after him followed this route, and have made extensive use of comparing national and international monetary integration (Davidson, 2006; Moore, 2004; Triffin, 1964).

Let us assume a monetary economy similar to ours in which commercial banks issue bank money through decentralised credit policies. Each commercial bank issues its own bank money and is ultimately overseen by the central bank. The role of the central bank, by issuing central bank money, is to unify the monetary system. As a result, a commercial bank issuing bank money does not have to devalue (revalue) its exchange rate when it registers an interbank deficit (surplus). This problem does not exist because the interbank money market, supervised by the central bank, recycles surpluses towards deficit banks. The central bank compensates for interbank money market failure in the event of general distrust and a credit crunch. As a result, thanks to the central bank's daily operations, commercial bank liabilities (i.e. bank deposits) are means of payment *at par.* Commercial bank liabilities are not bartered among customers as long as the parity is reliably provided by these modern banking system's mechanisms. Keynes' Clearing Union sought to replicate the banking system at the international level. It is essentially a blueprint for fixed exchange rates.

As McKinnon (2011, 760) notes, foreign exchange markets should no longer exist within the International Clearing Union, as they will be replaced by central banks' mutual clearing in the International Clearing Union. Consequently, currencies cease to be bartered in the foreign exchange markets. As Keynes (1980, 33) writes, "Central banks will buy and sell their own currencies among themselves only against debits and credits to their accounts at the Clearing Bank...Each national currency will have a fixed value...determined at the creation of the Currency Union in Clearing Bank money". National currencies will remain convertible as long as the par value system is backed by the International Clearing Union, just as in national banking systems a customer of one bank can have his deposits converted into deposits of another bank.

Such a plan implies integration and unification of national banking systems. Fixing parities and creating an international currency unit is only one aspect of this ambitious international integration. Monetary unification should also include the integration of trade and capital markets if it is to be sustainable over time. This means that countries should recycle trade surpluses in deficit regions through financial transfers in an orderly and sustainable way. During the wartime discussions on the post-war monetary order, Oxford economists Kalecki, Balogh, and Schumacher proposed a plan to improve on Keynes' plan in this direction with the creation of an International Investment Council alongside the International Clearing Union (Toporowski, 2018). In fact, Keynes' plan was mainly concerned with the current account and did not adequately address international investment. Kalecki, Balogh, and Schumacher therefore envisioned an International Investment Council under the auspices of the United Nations, which would deal separately with countries in need of investment for post-war reconstruction purposes. This International Investment Council would help developing countries and countries with short-term deficit issues. This would allow cross-border investment flows, especially to underdeveloped countries. This scheme was intended to promote full employment policies, as well as economic development and fixed parities.

Keynes' Plan, combined with the proposals of Kalecki, Balogh and Schumacher, could solve the main problem of the current international monetary (non-)system. Under such conditions, monetary plurality—i.e. the coexistence of many national currencies—would cease to be a problem, as national currencies would be part of a truly international currency system. The remaining sensitive issues in such an organisation would be arbitrage between rules and discretion (Keynes, 1980, 116). Mutual commitment is necessarily rules-based: it limits discretion to preserve the Clearing Union's cohesiveness.

6 Concluding Remarks

Although most economists acknowledge that fixed exchange rates are a desirable goal for facilitating trade and integration, maintaining exchange rate parity can be a difficult objective. This paper does not demonstrate that a fixed exchange rate regime is a panacea in the current global economy, as many variables can undermine fixed regimes and cause severe constraints on economic policies.

However, the chapter supports the case for fixed rates and the case against floating rates. We begin by showing that any trading area must have stable exchange rates. The unit of account is the heart of any monetary system and is justified by the need for stable exchange rates to enable economic calculations and subsequent trade operations. Therefore, by maintaining fixed exchange rates, monetary authorities would be doing a great service to internationally oriented companies. The rest of the article attempts to debunk the idea that, on the one hand, fixing the exchange rate would mean a complete abandonment of monetary policy, and on the other hand, pure or managed floating exchange rates would give the central bank discretion. Some policy measures may preserve policy space under fixed rates; however, policy space is externally constrained under all exchange rate regimes, especially in the current financial globalisation environment. As a result of all this, the supposed advantages of flexible rates diminish, while fixed rates still have the advantage for facilitating integration.

The paper then discusses three policy options that enhance the sustainability of fixed rate regimes: the adoption of a rules-based currency board (or dollarisation), the introduction of selective capital controls, and the creation of an International Clearing Union. These policy options are very different as they have different impacts and focus on different issues (the instability caused by monetary policy vs. that caused by cross-border capital flows). The first two—currency boards or capital controls – can be implemented unilaterally (although their effectiveness improves with international cooperation). An international clearing union is a much more ambitious plan that preserves both international integration and macroeconomic stability, but we have to recognise that such a cooperative scheme raises the eternal issue of political feasibility.

Notes

1. In this essay, Kindleberger compared international money and international language.
2. "These instruments have one common attribute, which is that they promise to trade *at par* on demand. This makes them money" (Pozsar, 2014, 9).
3. Keynes (1971, 16) also argued that smaller countries should be pegged to a major currency issuer with an international financial center.
4. Here, we assume that once the currency depreciates, the price of imported goods will rise accordingly and will not follow pricing-to-market strategies.
5. Friedman (1966) argues that floating rates aim to stabilise exchange rates.
6. This echoes Hayek (1937, 73), who argues that "the belief that by maintaining an independent national currency we can insulate a country against financial shocks originating abroad is largely illusory".
7. An eloquent example is the common currency of the CFA area, created in 1948 and devalued in 1994 by 50%, and since then the new parity of the fixed exchange rate has been maintained.
8. The currency boards of recent decades, some of which still exist today, are Hong Kong (since 1983), Estonia (1992–2011), Lithuania (1994–2015), Bulgaria (since 1997), Bosnia and Herzegovina (since 1994/1998), Argentina (1991–2002), and Djibouti (1949).
9. Among the examples of dollarisation, we note Panama (1904), Ecuador (since 2000), El Salvador (2001), and as Euroisations—Kosovo (1999) and Montenegro (1999).
10. The other objection is that capital controls are challenging to implement in practice. "After a while people find loopholes, hidden capital flight occurs, and the central bank again faces a drain of foreign reserves" (Schuler, 1999, 98). This argument is consistent with the experience of many countries in the twentieth century.

References

Adler, G., Casas, C., Cubeddu, M. L. M., Gopinath, G., Li, M. N., Meleshchuk, S., Buitron, C. O., Puy, D., & Timmer, M. Y. (2020). *Dominant currencies and external adjustment* (IMF Staff Discussion Note No. 20/05). International Monetary Fund.

Blanchard, O. (2017). Currency wars, coordination, and capital controls. *International Journal of Central Banking, 13*(2), 283–308.

Bogetić, Ž. (2000). Official dollarization: Current experiences and issues. *Cato Journal, 20*(2), 179–213.

Bougrine, H., & Seccareccia, M. (2004). Alternative exchange rate arrangements and effective demand: An important missing analysis in the debate over greater North American monetary integration. *Journal of Post Keynesian Economics, 26*(4), 655–677.

Broz, J. L., & Frieden, J. (2006). The political economy of exchange rates. In *The Oxford handbook of political economy* (pp. 587–597). Oxford University Press.

Camillieri Gilson, M.-T. (2002). *Policy pre-commitment and institutional design: a synthetic indicator applied to currency boards* (OECD Working Paper No. 330). OECD.

Carstens, A. (2019). *Exchange rates and monetary policy frameworks in emerging market economies*. Public lecture at the London School of Economics, London, May 2. https://www.bis.org/speeches/sp190502.htm

Davidson, P. (2006). A framework for analysing dollarization. In *Monetary integration and dollarization: No panacea* (pp. 259–275). Edward Elgar.

Davidson, P. (1992). Reforming the world's money. *Journal of Post Keynesian Economics, 15*(2), 153–179.

Desquilbet, J.-B., & Nenovsky, N. (2004). *Credibility and adjustment: Gold standards and currency boards compared* (William Davidson Institute Working Paper No. 692). William Davidson Institute.

De Vries, M. (1969). Fluctuating exchange rates. In *The International Monetary Fund. Vol. II: Analysis* (pp. 152–173). International Monetary Fund.

Edwards, S. (2020). *Milton Friedman and exchange rates in developing countries* (NBER Working Paper No. 27975). NBER.

Eichengreen, B. (2021). Bretton Woods After 50. *Resview of Political Economy, 33*(4), 552–569.

Fabris, N., Vukajlovic-Grba, D., Radunović, T., & Janković, H. (2004). *Economic policy in dollarized economies with a special review of Montenegro* (Working Paper No 1). Central Bank of Montenegro.

Friedman, M. (1966). *Essays in positive economics*. University of Chicago Press.

Gerschenkron, A. (1962). *Economic backwardness in historical perspective*. Harvard University Press.

Gourinchas, P. O., Rey, H., & Sauzet, M. (2019). *The international monetary and financial system* (Working Paper No. w25782). National Bureau of Economic Research.

Guzman, M., Ocampo, J. A., & Stiglitz, J. E. (2018). Real exchange rate policies for economic development. *World Development, 110*, 51–62.

Hanke, S. (1999). Reflections on exchange rate regimes. *Cato Journal, 18*(3), 335–344.

Hanke, S. (2002). Currency boards. *Annals of Academy of Political and Social Science, 579*, 87–105.
Hayek, F. A. (1937). *Monetary nationalism and international stability*. Longmans, Green.
Heilperin, M. A. (1939). *International monetary economics*. Longmans, Green.
Heilperin, M. A. (1955). Fixed parities and international order. *PSL Quarterly Review, 8*(33), 80–85.
Helleiner, E. (2015). Controlling capital flows "at both ends": A neglected (but newly relevant) Keynesian innovation from Bretton Woods. *Challenge, 58*(5), 413–427.
Ilzetzki, E., Reinhart, C. M., & Rogoff, K. S. (2019). Exchange arrangements entering the twenty-first century: Which anchor will hold? *Quarterly Journal of Economics, 134*(2), 599–646.
IMF. (2020). *Annual report on exchange arrangements and exchange restrictions 2019*. International Monetary Fund.
Irwin, D. A. (2017). The missing Bretton Woods debate over flexible exchange rates (NBER Working Paper No. 23037). NBER.
James, H. (2019). The multiple contexts of Bretton Woods. In *The Bretton Woods agreements: Together with scholarly commentaries and essential historical documents* (pp. 254–272). Yale University Press.
Kam, E., & Smithin, J. (2008). 'Unequal partners': The role of international financial flows and the exchange rate regime. *The Journal of Economic Asymmetries, 5*(1), 125–137.
Kelton, S. (2020). *The deficit myth: Modern monetary theory and the birth of the people's economy*. Public Affairs.
Keynes, J. M. (1971). The collected writings of John Maynard Keynes: *Vol. V: A treatise on money: The pure theory of money*. Macmillan.
Keynes, J. M. (1980). The collected writings of John Maynard Keynes: *Vol. XXV: Activities 1940–1944 shaping the post-war world: The clearing union*. London: Macmillan.
Kindleberger, C. P. (1967). *The politics of international money and world language*. Princeton University Department of Economics.
Kindleberger, C. P. (1976). Lessons of floating exchange rates. *Carnegie-Rochester Conference Series on Public Policy, 3*, 51–77.
Krugman, P. (1989). The case for stabilizing exchange rates. *Oxford Review of Economic Policy, 5*(3), 61–72.
Lavoie, M. (2014). *Post-Keynesian economics: New foundations*. Edward Elgar.
Lavoie, M. (2015). The Eurozone: Similarities to and differences from Keynes's plan. *International Journal of Political Economy, 44*(1), 3–17.
Lopez, J., & Perrotini, I. (2006). On floating exchange rates, currency depreciation and effective demand. *BNL Quarterly Review, 59*(238), 221–242.

Magnin, E., & Nenovsky, N. (2020). Dependent monetary regimes in the Balkans: Enlarging the "varieties of capitalism" hypothesis. *International Journal of Public Administration, 44*(14), 1216–1230.
McKinnon, R. (2005). *Exchange rates under the East Asian dollar standard: Living with conflicted virtue*. MIT Press.
McKinnon, R. (2011). Beggar-thy-neighbor interest rate policies. *Journal of Policy Modeling, 33*(5), 759–775.
McKinnon, R., & Schnabl, G. (2014). China's exchange rate and financial repression: The conflicted emergence of the RMB as an international currency. *China & World Economy, 22*(3), 1–35.
Moore, B. J. (2004). A global currency for a global economy. *Journal of Post Keynesian Economics, 26*(4), 631–653.
Murau, S., Rini, J., & Haas, A. (2020). The evolution of the offshore US-dollar system: Past, present and four possible futures. *Journal of Institutional Economics, 16*(6), 767–783.
Nenovsky, N., & Hristov, K. (2002). The new currency boards and discretion: Empirical evidence from Bulgaria. *Economic Systems, 26*(1), 55–72.
Obstfeld, M., & Rogoff, K. (1995). The mirage of fixed exchange rates. *Journal of Economic Perspectives, 9*(4), 73–96.
Obstfeld, M., & Taylor, A. M. (2017). International monetary relations: Taking finance seriously. *Journal of Economic Perspectives, 31*(3), 3–28.
Ocampo, J. A. (2017). *Resetting the international monetary (non) system*. Oxford University Press.
Ostry, J. D., Ghosh, A. R., Chamon, M., & Qureshi, M. S. (2011). Capital controls: When and why? *IMF Economic Review, 59*(3), 562–580.
Pozsar, Z. (2014). *Shadow banking: The money view* (Office of Financial Research Working Paper No. 14–04). https://doi.org/10.2139/ssrn.2476415
Pozsar, Z. (2013). Institutional cash pools and the Triffin dilemma of the US banking system. *Financial Markets, Institutions & Instruments, 22*(5), 283–318.
Rey, H. (2016). International channels of transmission of monetary policy and the Mundellian trilemma. *IMF Economic Review, 64*(1), 6–35.
Robinson, J. (1969). *Introduction to the theory of employment* (2nd ed.). Macmillan.
Rossi, S. (2007). *Money and payments in theory and practice*. Routledge.
Rossi, S. (2019). The dangerous ineffectiveness of negative interest rates: The case of Switzerland. *Review of Keynesian Economics, 7*(2), 220–232.
Sardoni, C., and Wray, L. R. (2007). *Fixed and flexible exchange rates and currency sovereignty*. (Levy Economics Institute of Bard College Working Paper No. 489). Economics Institute of Bard College.

Schmelzer, M. (2019). What comes after Bretton Woods? Neoliberals debate and fight for a future monetary order. *Nine Lives of Neoliberalism* (pp. 197–218). Verso Press.

Schuler, K. (1999). The problem with pegged exchange rates. *Kyklos, 52*(1), 83–102.

Schwartz, A. (1993). Currency boards: Their past, present, and possible future role. *Carnegie Rochester Conference Series on Public Policy, 39*, 147–187.

Tcherneva, P. R. (2016). *Money, power, and monetary regimes* (Levy Economics Institute of Bard College Working Paper No. 861). Levy Economics Institute of Bard College.

Tokunaga, J. (2019). The comparative advantage of the US shadow banking system and the role of the US dollar. *The Japanese Political Economy, 45*(1–2), 20–42.

Tokunaga, J., & Epstein, G. (2018). The endogenous finance of global-dollar-based financial fragility in the 2000s: A Minskyan approach. *Review of Keynesian Economics, 6*(1), 62–82.

Toporowski, J. (2018). Multilateralism and regional trade and payments. *Financialisation in Latin America: Challenges of the export-led growth model* (pp. 13–22). Routledge.

Triffin, R. (1964). *The evolution of the international monetary system: Historical reappraisal and future perspectives*. Princeton University Department of Economics.

Vemengo, M., & Rochon, L. P. (2000). Exchange rate regimes and capital controls. *Challenge, 43*(6), 76–92.

Vernengo, M., & Pérez Caldentey, E. (2020). Modern money theory (MMT) in the tropics: Functional finance in developing countries. *Challenge, 63*(6), 332–348.

CHAPTER 11

In Defence of Flexible Exchange Rates in a Small Open Capitalist Economy

Eric Kam

1 Introduction

The rise to dominance of neoclassical theory and its obsession with constructing general equilibrium models based on optimization underpinnings has accomplished little to quiet the debate regarding the key importance of selecting an appropriate exchange rate regime for a small open economy (SOE). Economists have mostly agreed that the proper choice of exchange rate regime is a necessary but not sufficient condition for growth and at least saddle-path stability. However, the past century of research and real-world data has failed to generate consensus regarding the optimal exchange rate regime. Across theorists, there is support for one of two choices: a fixed or flexible exchange rate. Recently, the literature has seen growing support for a hybrid version of the two regimes such as a 'fixed-but-adjustable' nominal exchange rate or, at the other extreme, an irrevocable 'hard' nominal exchange rate peg or accession to

E. Kam (✉)
Department of Economics, Toronto Metropolitan University, Toronto, Canada
e-mail: erickam@torontomu.ca

S. Pressman and J. Smithin (eds.), *Debates in Monetary Macroeconomics*,
https://doi.org/10.1007/978-3-031-11240-9_11

a currency union. The different theories allow for various hypothetical expositions, but have offered little insight into how a capitalist economy actually operates.

The thesis of this paper is simultaneously 'simple' and yet, at another level, complicated and powerful. In a capitalist economy operating in the real world of financial and monetary markets, the only stable and viable exchange rate regimes are either ones with floating exchange rates or, at a minimum, fixed-but-adjustable exchange rates. Why then are so many theorists in favour of such things as hard pegs or currency unions? The answer is that each of these systems only performs well in strongly abstract theoretical terms which fail to translate into the real world. In reality, such systems are fundamentally unstable. In effect, they are nothing more than an attempt to (incorrectly) label what are predominantly 'monetary' variables as 'real' variables. This resembles the way in which 'real business cycle' theorists, for example, incorrectly argued that interest rates are not a monetary phenomenon. In reality, macroeconomic stability rests on the benefits of exchange rate flexibility.

The crux of the argument lies in the failure of many economic theories to properly model the macroeconomy. Contrary to neoclassical theories of the open economy, there has never been any such thing as an exogenously fixed natural rate of interest, or a 'world' rate of interest, in any capitalist economy. These concepts are relevant only to a hypothetical barter or 'real exchange' economy. These are popular in the literature only because they are convenient mathematical simplifications to create closed form solutions. Assuming a fixed natural rate of interest, or a fixed world interest rate, satisfies the goal of ensuring closed form mathematical solutions. But at the same time it induces a bias in favour of fixed exchange rates in defiance of many of the realities 'on the ground'. Neither device bears any relation to how a capitalist economy really functions in our society.

Almost all monetary theorists invoke the Mundell-Fleming-Dornbusch (MFD) model to examine monetary policy in the SOE, but argue that MFD suffers from a lack of microeconomic underpinnings. This paper demonstrates an alternative to *both* MFD and the more recent open-economy models with micro-foundations. I start by modelling an individual economy which does have intertemporal optimization underpinnings, and then extend the model to the open economy. The novel contribution, which turns out to be critical, is to model an endogenous rate of time preference. This eliminates the terminal results of a natural rate of interest or world rate of interest. Moreover, it is no longer prone to counterintuitive preference assumptions that have weakened previous attempts.

Section 2 discusses the relationship between the rate of time preference and the exchange rates. Section 3 asks what may be learned by studying the various interest rate parity conditions. Section 4 then discusses the prospects for economic stability in the various alternative exchange rate regimes. Sections 5 and 6 introduce the 'Tobin effect' which is then applied to a single economy characterized by endogenous time preference. Section 7 extends the model to the context of an SOE with flexible exchange rates. Section 8 reveals what 'modern monetary theory' (MMT) can teach us about the exchange rate regime choice. The final section offers a summary.

2 Time Preference and Exchange Rates

When applied to an SOE, optimization models with time-additive preferences confront a potentially terminal problem. To generate a well-defined, stable steady state, theorists like to assume that the rate of time preference and the discount rate applied to future utility streams is equal to a 'world' interest rate, which is fixed and exogenous. However, there is no consistent explanation as to why a priori the exogenous world interest rate should equal the SOE's domestic rate of time preference - which is presumably also fixed. The world interest rate restriction imposes potentially terminal limits on studying the dynamic effects of exchange rate policies. However, there is a method whereby to avoid these terminal effects of an exogenous world interest rate. Namely, by modelling the rate of time preference as an endogenous function equal to the inflation-adjusted real interest rate. Obstfeld (1981a, 1981b, 1982) did model an endogenous rate of time preference, but relied on the Uzawa (1968) preference function assuming that time preference is an increasing function of utility (which is itself assumed to be an increasing function of present consumption). Obstfeld avoided the controversy about the modelling of money in the utility function, but his model rests on counterintuitive assumptions about preferences and behaviour.[1]

It is important to position the concept of the nominal exchange rate in its proper macroeconomic context. For the purposes of this discussion, I define the nominal exchange rate as the foreign currency price of a single unit of the domestic currency. If Canada is the home economy, we value our currency against the US dollar per unit of a Canadian dollar.

If the exchange rate increases (decreases), the Canadian dollar depreciates (appreciates) against the US dollar.

In media discussions of exchange rates, it is the *nominal* exchange rate that is most often referenced. However, critical economic decisions must be made using the *real* exchange rate. This is, the nominal exchange rate multiplied by a ratio of domestic to foreign prices. The debate over the appropriate value of the exchange rate and whether the proper mechanism to set exchange rates should be fixed or flexible tends almost exclusively to be centred on the nominal exchange rate *not* the real exchange rate. Smithin (2018, 176) argues that:

> … there seems always to have been an almost total lack of understanding on this point by the supposed experts and policy-makers which has caused countless difficulties in the field of international economic relations, over a period of many centuries.

With a flexible exchange rate the equilibrium value between two currencies is settled by relative demand and supply in the international financial markets. With fixed exchange rates, an international agreement across two nations holds the currencies together in a narrow band. The domestic monetary authority must be willing to use monetary or fiscal policy to hold the nominal value of currency in set boundaries. This explains a proclivity for payment imbalances leading to changes in foreign exchange reserves, as a central authority must be active in the foreign exchange market to buy or sell the volume of required currency. If the domestic currency is undervalued, the authority must purchase domestic currency on the foreign exchange market to raise its value and stop a foreign exchange reserve crisis. Smithin (2018) argues that this foreign exchange crisis is self-imposed and can be avoided by a flexible exchange rate regime.

3 What Does Interest Parity Teach Us?

What can we learn from interest rate parity (IRP) theories? A stringent analysis reveals how these theories are complementary to the terminal assumptions of a fixed natural rate of interest or world interest rate. Purchasing power parity (PPP) is a theory of nominal interest rate determination. The assumption underlying PPP is that the real exchange rate is fixed. It is determined by the non-monetary or barter 'terms of trade' and cannot be altered by monetary or financial factors. This amounts nothing more than imposing a fixed world rate of interest (in the case of an open economy), or a natural rate of interest in an individual economy. These are the sorts of arbitrary assumptions used by neoclassical theorists to predetermine terminal outcomes.[2] The alternative proposed in this paper is to model the real exchange rate as a *monetary* variable which precludes a fixed world interest rate or natural rate of interest.

An IRP condition is a no-arbitrage condition implying equilibrium across investors' interest rates available on deposits in two countries. If parity did not hold, it would create a chance to earn riskless profits from arbitrage. There are three possible IRPs. Each of these parity conditions reveals a unique relationship and different implications for the forecasting of future forward and spot exchange rates. I assume the existence of a forward market for foreign exchange to make the contrast between the forward (future) exchange rate and the spot (present) exchange rate. The former is the foreign currency price of one unit of domestic currency for forward delivery. The economic role of the forward market is to hedge foreign exchange risk, and this generates three distinct potential outcomes:

1. Uncovered interest parity (UIP) where there is no forward contract, and any exposure to foreign exchange risk or unanticipated exchange rate changes is unconstrained.
2. Covered interest parity (CIP) where there is a forward contract to eliminate exchange rate risk. The assumption of perfect capital mobility will imply that the rate of return on financial investments abroad are equal if covered by a forward contract, such that arbitrage can occur where investors transfer funds in search of profits.
3. Real interest parity (RIP) which assumes that world markets for goods, capital, and foreign exchange are integrated, and that real interest rates on perfectly substitutable financial assets are equal across nations. RIP predicts that nominal interest rate differentials adjust to the inflation differential to maintain real interest rate equality.

RIP rests on the existence of a stable 'Fisher condition' where differences in nominal interest rates reflect expected changes in the spot exchange rate across nations. For this condition to hold, the spot exchange rate is expected to change by an equal amount and in the opposite direction to the interest rate differential. The currency of the nation with a higher nominal interest rate is expected to depreciate against the currency of the nation with the lower nominal interest rate, since higher nominal interest rates imply inflationary expectations. Moreover, RIP also rests on assumptions such as efficient markets, the absence of a risk premia, and no change in the expected real exchange rate. Since RIP implies real interest rates are equal across nations and that capital mobility will result in flows that eliminate arbitrage opportunities for RIP to hold, it must be the case that CIP, UIP, and PPP are already in place in domestic markets.

What do these competing theories imply with respect to exchange rate determination? Although it may not be transparent, a closer examination of the parity conditions answers an important question—why *do* many theorists favour a fixed nominal exchange rate? The answer is found in the complexity of the various assumptions. There is no justifiable reason to believe a modern capitalist economy will ever be accompanied by such strict conditions as perfect asset substitutability when there is either a floating exchange rate regime, or a fixed-but-adjustable exchange rate.

To try to mimic or simulate these unattainable assumptions, however, theorists have asked the question—under what conditions *might* such a situation exist? The answer given by most has been precisely that the nominal exchange rate should be permanently fixed. To a large degree, this explains the historical obsession with an irrevocably fixed exchange rate or a hard peg. Perfect asset substitutability for assets with comparable terms to maturity and risk characteristics would also apply in common currency arrangements. With only a single currency, perfect asset substitutability is obtained by assumption. Nominal interest rates must conform to those in the partner nations, thereby rendering it impossible for them to conduct anything resembling an independent monetary policy.

If a fixed nominal exchange rate or hard peg is imposed on the domestic economy we return to the case where the nominal interest rate in the SOE must conform to an arbitrarily fixed world interest rate. The case of a currency union would be analogous. Then there is only one single currency, and a corresponding single monetary policy and nominal interest rate (Marterbauer & Smithin, 2000). Since the nominal policy rate is the main policy instrument, the domestic monetary authorities abandon their ability to pursue an independent policy.

In much of the open-economy literature the notion of RIP seems to be taken for granted. It is treated as merely an extension of the idea of the natural rate of interest to the global economy. This implies that the domestic real interest rate is beyond the influence of the domestic authority. This satisfies the neoclassical desire for fixed exchange rates and non-monetary determined variables, but is not observed in any functioning capitalist economy. There is no real-world evidence of a barter-determined natural interest rate, or of a world interest rate—and therefore no evidence of RIP.

4 What About Economic Stability?

While the various alternatives to a flexible exchange rate may initially appear to be viable, these solutions suffer from the terminal condition of long-run instability. Smithin (2018) argues that the various options for a hard peg for the nominal exchange rate (for example, a metallic standard such as a gold or silver standard, an 'irrevocably fixed' exchange rate, or a currency board with no loopholes) are terminally unstable and ultimately fail. The reason for this is the crucial importance of the domestic government being able to maintain a sovereign monetary and fiscal policy. With an exchange rate peg there is *no* economic policy sovereignty. This cannot therefore be a viable option in the long-run.

A currency union would be analogous. Once again this is an abandonment of policy sovereignty. While the intent is to eliminate exchange rate problems, history reveals that if a hard peg is applied, the currency union actually has similar issues regarding instability as a hard peg. Smithin (2018) notes that:

> ... unless the domestic economy is willing to give up control over economic policy entirely there are only two possible long-run outcomes, either (a) a break-up of the system, which would be the equivalent of an exchange rate crisis in this context, or (b) eventual evolution into a true federal state, with a developed system of fiscal federalism. In the latter case, the different countries literally turn into mere 'Provinces' and no longer have even the semblance of national sovereignty.

Smithin (2022) refers to flexible exchange rates as analogous to maintaining policy sovereignty for the home government, which, he argues:

> … is a logically unassailable proposition of the modern monetary theory (MMT) school, to the effect that the government of an economy with its own sovereign currency and a floating exchange rate faces no binding financial constraints.

Thus, fears about unsustainable budget deficits have no credence because a domestic authority is unconstrained in issuing domestic currency-denominated debt. Therefore, in an economy with a pure floating exchange rate the authorities can conduct the same fiscal and monetary policies as they would be able to do in an individual economy.

For a complete analysis of an open economy, all that would then be necessary is to augment those results with the implications for exchange rate changes and the foreign debt position that are already found in the literature. In the fixed-but-adjustable exchange rate regime, the results will also replicate a single economy with complete control over monetary and fiscal policy. As for a common currency area, this regime is the polar opposite to flexible exchange rates. It tries to do away with the notion of exchange rates entirely. This regime implies a complete abandonment of sovereignty. While the intent is to eliminate potential exchange rate instability currency unions are in fact subject to the identical stability issues that plague the hard peg or irrevocably fixed exchange rate. The equivalent of an exchange rate crisis in this case would be the break-up of the system.

5 The Tobin Effect

The so-called 'Tobin Effect' is often (and mistakenly) ignored because it tends not to appear in monetary models with optimizing underpinnings. With rational agents and perfect competition in production, the return on capital is determined solely by its marginal product. The optimization process implies representative agents have Euler equations that tie down the rate of return on capital and the growth rate of consumption. Assuming no productivity growth and fixed preferences, the capital stock and its rate of return are constant. Fluctuations in the monetary growth rate or inflation rate do not alter steady state real sector variables because savings are endogenous, and depends on investment returns relative to the intertemporal marginal rate of substitution. Euler equations do not depend on inflation and money is super-neutral. Monetary super-neutrality in the optimization framework is most often linked to the work of Sidrauski (1967a, 1967b) who restricted the rate of return on capital to a unique long-run value by assuming the marginal product of capital and real interest rate are 'anchored' or fixed by assuming an exogenous rate of time preference. Steady-state real variables, including consumption and capital, are independent of monetary growth and monetary policy is super-neutral. Super-neutrality is the inevitable result of arbitrarily enforcing equality between an exogenously fixed natural rate of interest and a fixed rate of time preference.

6 The Tobin Effect in an Individual Economy

Consider an economy of infinitely lived, representative agents attempting to maximize lifetime utility by choosing optimal levels of consumption and real money balances. The important variable in this analysis is the rate of time preference, which is modelled as an increasing function of capital plus real balances (Kam, 2005). This breaks Sidrauski's terminal results achieved via the assumption by a fixed rate of time preference. Assuming exogeneity ensures mathematical tractability, but it implies super-neutrality by fixing both the real interest rate and the marginal product of capital thus replicating the idea of a 'natural rate' of interest.

The optimizing agent allocates savings across the two assets. How do we usually interpret the first order conditions for a maximum? These are (i) that the marginal cost of saving an added consumption unit as measured in terms of foregone utility equals the marginal benefit of consumption in terms of the future utility of real wealth, (ii) the marginal benefit of additional real balances as measured in terms of utility equals the value of the opportunity cost of real balances measured by the nominal interest forgone, and (iii) the marginal product of capital equals the real interest rate.

How would this change with an endogenous rate of time preference? The short-run effect of inflation is positive for capital and consumption, but negative for real balances and real wealth. Inflation lowers the initial value of real wealth and raises the opportunity cost of holding real balances. The short run is characterized by a fall in consumption, real wealth, real balances, and the rate of time preference. There is an increase in savings, which creates endogenous time preference wealth effects in the adjustment period which reinforce the substitution effect, and link the real and monetary sectors, converting new savings from real balances into steady state capital and consumption.

Growth-induced substitution effects reduce the initial value of real wealth to raise the opportunity cost of holding real balances. As the demand to hold real balances falls, the rate of time preference falls, and savings rise. Added savings are converted into steady state consumption and the capital stock due to the wealth effect on time preference that endogenize the real interest rate. Non-super-neutrality does not rest on counterintuitive behaviour or *ad-hoc* consumption or saving functions (Begg, 1980).

These results demonstrate the striking difference between the endogenous time preference model and the traditional literature. The motivation does not depend on the counterintuitive behaviour assumptions of Uzawa, or on 'descriptive' consumption and savings functions that lack the required optimizing underpinnings for dynamic analysis. Owing to the reinforcing nature of the substitution and the wealth effect, an interdependence emerges across real wealth, savings, and the rate of time preference. The rise in steady state capital lowers the real interest rate, replicating Tobin's critical inverse relationship between real interest rates and steady state inflation. To break super-neutrality and remain behaviourally consistent with optimal savings and consumption the model transforms the rate of time preference, and hence the discount rate applied to future utility, into an endogenous function.[3]

Kam (2005) paper motivates the Tobin Effect and non-super-neutrality from more primitive assumptions. Owing to the reinforcing nature of the substitution and the wealth effect, an interdependence emerges across real wealth, savings, and the rate of time preference. The rise in steady state capital lowers the real interest rate, which replicates Tobin's critical inverse relationship between real interest rates and steady state inflation.

Unlike most neoclassical analysis of the past century, the domestic real interest rate is neither a given nor beyond the influence of the domestic monetary authority. From the point of view of the SOE, this removes the need to present a case for a fixed exchange rate regime whereby theorists are able to create an illusion of convergence with a non-monetary economy.

7 The Tobin Effect in a SOE with Flexible Exchange Rates

Modelling the rate of time preference as an endogenous function breaks the terminal results of a natural rate of interest and monetary superneutrality. What happens if we apply the same assumption to the SOE with flexible exchange rates?

We begin by assuming our SOE has a single consumption good with a fixed foreign currency price of one. The domestic currency price of the good is therefore simply the nominal exchange rate times the domestic currency price of foreign currency. The inflation rate equals the depreciation rate of the domestic currency. The representative agent is initially endowed with units of a consumption good at any time t and also receives real monetary transfers from the governmental authorities.

The first departure from the lone economy is the assumption of two asset types, (i) real money balances and (ii) internationally traded bonds. These bonds have a fixed price of one in foreign currency terms and each bond pays the holder units of a foreign currency. The real value of assets of the representative agent is the sum of real balance holdings and real bond holdings at time t. The rate of time preference is modelled as an increasing function of real wealth.

The central authority chooses the real money transfers to achieve a desired fixed level rate of devaluation for the domestic economy. Government transfers are financed strictly through an inflation tax. Assume the public sector holds no foreign reserves, bonds, or debt, which implies the exchange rate is perfectly flexible and the central bank controls the rate of currency depreciation by choosing the optimal level of real money transfers. The nominal money stock is solely demand determined. Any level of currency devaluation is accommodated by a central bank by supplying the economy with the appropriate level of real balances, which equals the demand for real balances across the economy.

Representative agents choose consumption and real balance holdings to maximize an intertemporal utility function subject to a standard textbook open-economy budget constraint and intertemporal solvency condition. Note that the maximization problem, the first order conditions, and their interpretations, while not identical, are close enough to the single economy case to not require further derivation and interpretation. However, it is important to note that in the flexible exchange rate model, the determinant of the coefficient matrix is negative so that the dynamic system has one negative eigenvalue. The dynamic model has a single predetermined variable and is saddle-point stable. Smithin (2022) states that:

> The trace is negative but so also is the determinant. It is *not* positive. The upshot is that the system is neither globally stable, nor completely unstable. The equilibrium of the system is actually a *saddle-poin*t. What are the implications of this finding? In the truncated system the only policy option available to the authorities of the domestic economy is to influence the domestic real rate of interest *via* monetary policy. But, in context, this remains a valuable policy tool precisely because the domestic authorities need not be influenced or constrained by whatever is happening in the rest of the world. The key to 'capitalism in one country' is the existence of a separate monetary and financial system with either a floating exchange rate regime or a fixed-but-adjustable regime in which adjustments can be made as required without political or other difficulties. This framework is also capable of explaining the problems experienced by jurisdictions that are *not* in a comparable state of affairs, such as those trapped in the hopeless situations of either an irrevocably fixed exchange rate, or in a currency union with no adequate system of fiscal federalism.

Deriving the steady state effects of depreciating the domestic currency reveals a positive effect on bond holdings and consumption and a negative effect on real balances. Inflation reduces the short-run value of real wealth to raise the opportunity cost of real balances, lowers short-run consumption and real balances, and creates a current account surplus. Along the adjustment path, consumption rises and real balances fall to reach a new steady state equilibrium.

Why does steady state consumption rise along the adjustment path? As the representative agent accumulates assets, their savings rise to place the current account in surplus. Domestic currency depreciation increases the opportunity cost of holding real balances and savings, which are converted into consumption goods, which also raises lifetime utility. The combination of flexible exchange rates and endogenous time preference allows for the emergence of an open-economy Tobin Effect as the representative agent sidesteps the terminal results implied by assuming a fixed world rate of interest.

There is a critical—paradigm shifting—result which may not be initially transparent. Under an irrevocably hard peg for the exchange rate or a currency union, an open-economy Tobin Effect and non-super-neutrality would be impossible. Putting these policy constraints in place in the SOE implies that nominal interest rates are once again 'tied-down' to an imaginary fixed world interest rate. The domestic economy loses the ability to pursue and implement an independent monetary policy. Monetary policy does not, and cannot matter—which precludes the notion of an effective independent monetary policy. Smithin (2022) has argued:

> ... analysts are often content simply to assume that the domestic real interest rate is a given, determined by global market forces and beyond the influence of the domestic policy-makers. But the discussion so far has already provided enough material to show that is not a valid interpretation. There is no natural rate of interest for the world as a whole, any more than there is for a closed economy taken individually. Why then have these sorts of regimes ever been popular? The answer seems to be that many theoreticians and policy makers have traditionally confused the proposition that a fixed rate regime causes nominal interest rates to converge with the (much more contentious) idea of what might be called a global natural (real) rate of interest. Having once made this mistake, 'fixed exchange rates' would seem to be just what is required to make the conditions assumed by classical and neoclassical economics come true. They may come to believe that merely with fixed nominal exchange rates, then real interest rates, economic growth rates, and the unemployment rate would all be at their 'natural levels', and that the real exchange rate would be determined by the barter terms of trade.

On the other hand, in an economy characterized by a pure floating exchange rate, the effects of monetary and fiscal policy will be basically equivalent to those of the case of an individual economy. If there is a Tobin Effect with endogenous time preference in an individual economy so will there also be in an SOE, if that economy maintains a floating exchange rate. Super-neutrality in conventional theory comes about by modelling the rate of time preference as an exogenous variable, which in turn, fixes the interest rate and eliminates the causal link between the monetary and the real sector. To model a truly 'monetary' economy, the rate of time preference must be modelled as an endogenous function, allowing changes in the rate of time preference to generate a Mundell-Tobin Effect, and the exchange rate must be allowed to float. In the open economy context, the supposedly fixed 'world' interest rate plays the same role as the fixed rate of time preference in consumer theory. Binding an economy to a fixed world interest rate, or fixed exchange rate, arbitrarily imposes 'policy irrelevance'—which is antithetical to the study of real-world behaviour in response to actual policy changes If the results are predetermined through a fixed 'natural rate' of interest, a 'world' interest rate, or a fixed rate of time preference, attempting to seriously model real-world economic behaviour is simply a waste of time. Once again, Smithinn (2022) argues that, in these circumstances:

> The dream of 'free markets', 'free trade', balanced budgets, low inflation, and so on and so forth, would be realized, and objective market forces would prevail. [But] [n]one of this is real - it is not how economies work—[nonetheless] these sorts of strongly held beliefs seem to be the only way to explain the passionate advocacy historically of things like metallic standards, fixed exchange rates, currency boards and currency unions. History itself has not been kind to these notions, however. The imposition of policy regimes based on this mindset has very frequently caused severe economic distress, and eventually they seem always to break down in crisis.

In an SOE model combining endogenous time preference and flexible exchange rates provides the necessary theoretical tools to make valid monetary policy predictions. If the domestic economy encounters an unanticipated and permanent depreciation of the domestic currency, the model predicts a long-run current account surplus, a decrease in steady state real balances and a rise in steady state consumption. This framework boldly supports the idea of a flexible exchange rate regime. And, by assuming an endogenous time preference, we completely avoid the terminal pitfalls of a fixed world interest rate/natural rate of interest without relying on the counterintuitive behavioural assumptions that render Uzawa's original time preference specification obsolete.

8 What Does MMT Imply for the SOE with Flexible Exchange Rates?

So-called 'modern monetary theory' (MMT) has two critical elements with respect to monetary policy, (i) currency is a public monopoly and (ii) markets themselves are the mechanism whereby the state's currency is exchanged and circulated.[4] What does this mean in practice? MMT is the notion that there is no binding financial constraint on government spending as long as a nation is a sovereign issuer of currency and does not tie the value of its currency to another nation's currency. As a sovereign issuer of currency, the government is endowed with the ability to borrow money or print money from a country's central bank. The central bank can credit the government's bank account for an unlimited amount of money without charging its government interest or forcing repayment of the government bonds acquired by the central bank. MMT proponents argue it is an efficient way of funding increased government spending by removing the necessity for the government to raise new tax revenues or compete for private sector capital by offering competitive interest rates on government bonds sold to private sector investors.

Markets do not buy or sell goods and services but, instead, buy and sell currency priced in terms of goods and labour. The price of currency, referred to as the 'currency terms of exchange' (CTE), is set by the monetary authority at the required level of public spending. CTE diverges from its structural (equilibrium) level if taxes cause domestic currency to flow from the private to the public sector. Equilibrium CTE is expressed in terms of the foreign exchange rate but with no reference to the trade balance, level of economic openness, or the size of a nation's economy.

What does MMT imply for the monetary base? With a floating exchange rate, base money is the total net financial assets of non-government sectors. Policies like quantitative easing (QE) have no effect on base money since QE reduces interest income. Deficit reduction causes a fall in new base money and directs spending away from debt financing into base money. Government net public sector spending raises the domestic economy's government liability holdings.

What is the MMT position on exchange rate determination? Define the 'marginal terms of exchange (MTE)' as the public sector nominal currency value which makes it difficult for those holding foreign currency to obtain domestic currency. Symmetry implies that the foreign currency has an MTE, and the exchange rate is determined by the interaction of the two currency's supply and demand structure. Unlike neoclassical or (some) heterodox theories of exchange rates, MMT disregards the quantity of the currency. It is concerned instead with the terms of exchange. Any policies reducing domestic prices put downward pressure on the value of the foreign currency. In general, there are three defining features MMT exchange rate policy;

1. Flexible exchange rates allow for a relaxation of the budget constraint in spending for a wide range of open economies.

However, MMT advocates do not claim that the absence of government budget constraints applies to countries with fixed exchange rates or currency unions.
2. A worldwide system of fixed rates would not be desirable because what is good for one country is not likely to work across all nations.
3. Hard pegs and currency unions only enhance the risk of currency crises and banking crises and are not recommended for open economies.

MMT may represent something of a 'counterculture' with respect to the competing mainstream schools of macroeconomic thought. However, it is fascinating to note that this paper's prescription of a flexible exchange rate regime is reinforced by the arguments of MMT.

9 Conclusions

Assuming the real interest rate or the real exchange rate is fixed, or presuming the existence of fictional notions such as a natural interest rate or a world interest rate, amounts simply to embedding the desired answers to economic questions in the premises. Much of the macroeconomic theory of the past decades has concentrated on the false notion of monetary super-neutrality or the supposed inability of monetary policy to affect the real sector. However, this is not a realistic description of capitalism either in one or in several nations. How was this super-neutrality trick performed? Policy irrelevance was imposed by fixing the domestic interest rate, the rate of time preference, and the marginal product of capital and setting them arbitrarily equal to an equally arbitrary fixed world interest rate. An analogous move is to fix the nominal exchange rate to nullify the effect of an independent monetary policy via the same mysterious world interest rate.

The critical mechanism whereby this paper has demonstrated the implications of monetary growth and inflation targeting in open-economy models was by violating the assumption of a natural rate of interest or world interest rate. Alternatively, we have assumed that representative agents are optimizing with respect to an endogenous rate of time preference that is not constrained to equality with any exogenous variables. To be consistent with plausible consumption and savings behaviour the rate of time preference was modelled as an increasing function of real wealth. In an individual economy, inflation yields endogenous wealth effects, which reinforce the substitution effect, link the real and monetary sectors, and endogenize the real interest rate. Added savings are transformed to steady state capital and consumption goods via a Tobin effect. In an SOE, the concepts of endogenous time preference and flexible exchange rates merge—to eliminate the need to assume a fixed world rate of interest.

A flexible exchange rate regime is the strongest of the exchange rate regime options if the criteria for success is any or all of policy relevance, realism, or macroeconomic stability. In open economies, flexible exchange rates completely avoid the terminal pitfalls of a fixed world interest rate or natural rate of interest without relying on the counterintuitive behavioural assumptions which render far too many classical assumptions—including Uzawa's specification of time preference—obsolete, and lacking any resemblance to a functioning capitalist economy. Future research with respect to economic theory and practice would best be served by resisting the temptation to predetermine the results with unrealistic modelling assumptions.

Notes

1. Uzawa's function received significant attention in the open-economy literature regarding the Harberger-Laursen-Metzler (HLM) effect. Obstfeld (1982) showed that with Uzawa preferences, a deterioration in the terms of trade would result in an increase in savings and a current account surplus for an SOE facing a fixed world rate of interest. This result is contrary to the HLM intuition and this created a large literature examining the effect of a terms of trade deterioration in optimizing frameworks (Mansoorian, 1992; Matsuyama, 1987, 1988; Persson & Svensson, 1985; Sen & Turnovsky, 1989; Svensson & Razin, 1983). Persson and Svensson (1985) argue Uzawa preferences are 'arbitrary, and even counterintuitive'. Blanchard and Fischer (1989) suggest that '...the Uzawa function with its assumption that the rate of time preference increases in instantaneous utility is not particularly attractive as a description of preferences and is not recommended for general use'.
2. Smithin (2018) states that

   > ... [the natural interest rate or world interest rate] are classic examples of a naïve naturalist mode of analysis which fails to take into account important results in social ontology, and neglects altogether the significant differences between the ontology of the social world and that of the natural world. Such notions as 'states of nature', and appeals to supposed analogies to the physical and biological

sciences, are beside the point when it comes to discussions of human institutions and social relations, especially of those involved in the construction of composites such as money, contracts, and markets.

3. Kam (2005) derives the steady state and saddle-path stability of this system. The determinant of the coefficient matrix is negative, which implies the dynamic system has two eigenvalues one positive and one negative. The result is a dynamic system exhibiting saddle-path stability.
4. See Kelton (2020) and (Wray, 2012, 2020) for a complete description of MMT.

References

Begg, D. (1980). Rational expectations and the non-neutrality of systematic monetary policy. *Review of Economic Studies, 47*, 293–303.

Blanchard, O., & Fischer, S. (1989). *Lectures on macroeconomics*. MIT Press.

Kam, E. (2005). A note on time preference and the Tobin effect. *Economics Letters, 89*, 127–132.

Kelton, S. (2020). *The deficit myth: Modern monetary theory and the birth of the people's Economy*. Public Affairs.

Laidler, D. (1969). Money, wealth and time preference in a stationary economy. *Canadian Journal of Economics, 4*, 526–535.

Mansoorian, A. (1992). Income effect, wealth effect, and the terms of trade with finite horizons. *Canadian Journal of Economics, 25*, 474–484.

Marterbauer, M., & Smithin, J. (2000). *Fiscal policy in the small open economy within the framework of monetary union* (WIFO Working Paper No. 137/2000) Vienna.

Matsuyama, K. (1987). Current account dynamics in a finite horizon model. *Journal of International Economics, 23*, 299–313.

Matsuyama, K. (1988). Terms-of-trade, factor intensities and the current account in a life-cycle model. *Review of Economic Studies, 55*, 247–252.

Mundell, R. (1963). Inflation and real interest rates. *Journal of Political Economy, 71*, 280–283.

Obstfeld, M. (1981a). Capital mobility and devaluation in an optimizing model with rational expectations. *American Economic Review Papers and Proceedings, 71*, 217–221.

Obstfeld, M. (1981b). Macroeconomic policy, exchange rate dynamics, and optimal asset accumulation. *Journal of Political Economy, 89*, 1142–1161.

Obstfeld, M. (1982). Aggregate spending and the terms of trade: Is there a Laursen-Metzler effect? *Quarterly Journal of Economics, 97*, 251–270.

Persson, T., & Svensson, L. (1985). Current account dynamics and the terms of trade: Harberger-Laursen-Metzler two generations later. *Journal of Political Economy, 93*, 43–65.

Sen, P., & Turnovsky, S. (1989). Deterioration of the terms of trade and capital accumulation: A re-examination of the Laursen-Metzler effect. *Journal of International Economics, 26*, 227–250.

Sidrauski, M. (1967a). Rational choice and patterns of growth in a monetary economy. *American Economic Review Papers and Proceedings, 30*, 534–544.

Sidrauski, M. (1967b). Inflation and economic growth. *Journal of Political Economy, 75*, 796–810.

Smithin, J. (2018). *Rethinking the theory of money, credit and macroeconomics: A New Statement for the twenty-first century*. Lexington Books.

Smithin, J. (2022). *Beyond barter: Lectures in monetary macroeconomics after 'rethinking.'* World Scientific Publishing.

Svensson, L., & Razin, A. (1983). The terms of trade and the current account: The Harberger-Laursen-Metzler effect. *Journal of Political Economy, 91*, 97–125.

Tobin, J. (1965). Money and economic growth. *Econometrica, 33*, 671–684.

Uzawa, H. (1968). Time preference, the consumption function, and optimal asset holdings. In J. Wolfe (Ed.), *Value, capital and growth: Papers in honour of Sir John Hicks* (pp. 485–504). Aldine.

Wray, L. R. (2012). *Modern money theory: A primer on macroeconomics for sovereign monetary systems*. Palgrave Macmillan.

Wray, L. R. (2020). *The 'Kansas City' approach to modern money theory* (Economics Working Paper Archive wp_961, 1–40) Levy Economics Institute.

Index

S. Pressman and J. Smithin (eds.), *Debates in Monetary Macroeconomics*, https://doi.org/10.1007/978-3-031-11240-9

G

H

I

The manufacturer's authorised representative in the EU is Springer Nature Customer Service Centre GmbH, Europaplatz 3, 69115 Heidelberg, Germany. If you have any concerns regarding our products, please contact ProductSafety@springernature.com

Printed and bound by CPI Group (UK) Ltd, Croydon, CR0 4YY
28/09/2026
02224072-0004